MW00627073

A Perfect Gibraltar

CAMPAIGNS & COMMANDERS

GREGORY J. W. URWIN, SERIES EDITOR

CAMPAIGNS AND COMMANDERS

GENERAL EDITOR

Gregory J. W. Urwin, *Temple University, Philadelphia, Pennsylvania*

ADVISORY BOARD

Lawrence E. Babits, *East Carolina University, Greenville*
James C. Bradford, *Texas A&M University, College Station*
Robert M. Epstein, *U.S. Army School of Advanced Military Studies, Fort Leavenworth, Kansas*
David M. Glantz, *Carlisle, Pennsylvania*
Jerome A. Greene, *Denver, Colorado*
Victor Davis Hanson, *California State University, Fresno*
Herman Hattaway, *University of Missouri, Kansas City*
J. A. Houlding, *Rückersdorf, Germany*
Eugenia C. Kiesling, *U.S. Military Academy, West Point, New York*
Timothy K. Nenninger, *National Archives, Washington, D.C.*
Bruce Vandervort, *Virginia Military Institute, Lexington*

A Perfect Gibraltar

The Battle for Monterrey, Mexico, 1846

Christopher D. Dishman

University of Oklahoma Press : Norman

Library of Congress Cataloging-in-Publication Data
Dishman, Christopher D., 1972–
A perfect Gibraltar : the battle for Monterrey,
Mexico, 1846 / Christopher D. Dishman.
p. cm. — (Campaigns and commanders ; v. 26)
Includes bibliographical references and index.
ISBN 978-0-8061-4140-4 (hardcover : alk. paper)
1. Monterrey, Battle of, Monterrey, Mexico, 1846. I. Title.
E406.M7D57   2010
972'.13—dc22
2010015041

A Perfect Gibraltar: The Battle for Monterrey, Mexico, 1846 is
Volume 26 in the Campaigns and Commanders series.

The paper in this book meets the guidelines for permanence and
durability of the Committee on Production Guidelines for Book
Longevity of the Council on Library Resources, Inc. ∞

Copyright © 2010 by the University of Oklahoma Press, Norman,
Publishing Division of the University. Manufactured in the U.S.A.

All rights reserved. No part of this publication may be reproduced,
stored in a retrieval system, or transmitted, in any form or by any
means, electronic, mechanical, photocopying, recording, or
otherwise—except as permitted under Section 107 or 108 of the
United States Copyright Act—without the prior permission of the
University of Oklahoma Press.

1   2   3   4   5   6   7   8   9   10

To the memory of my parents, who taught me

early in life the importance of history

Contents

Illustrations

Maps

Acknowledgments

M any people assisted me in researching and understanding this
battle. First, I would like to thank all of the special-collection
centers listed in the bibliography for their support in providing critical materials for this book. But a few individuals deserve special
thanks. Susan Lintelmann, manuscripts curator at the U.S. Military
Academy, provided documents on West Point officers quickly and
easily; Chris Cottrill at the Smithsonian Institution Libraries provided hard-to-find articles within hours of my requests; Michael Lear
at Franklin and Marshall College located and reviewed important
letters from John Fulton Reynolds; Ben Huseman at the University of
Texas at Arlington assisted in navigating his school's extensive special collections and provided advice on additional useful sources; and
Cathy Spitzenberger, also at the University of Texas at Arlington,
supplied many of the illustrations in this book. My gratitude also
goes to John R. Hébert at the Library of Congress Geography and
Maps Division, who hosted me and walked me through the collection's Mexican War maps. Lacey Imbert of the Amon Carter Museum
also helped locate many of the illustrations used in this book and
provided them quickly to meet my publication deadlines. I am also
grateful to Kathryn Stallard at Southwestern University's Collection
Department. The center provided an electronic version of a Texan
volunteer's unpublished diary that provided terrific material for this

book. Also, the staff at the Rosenberg Library in Galveston diligently searched for another diary of a Texan volunteer until they located the manuscript, which proved to be an important source.

The Fairfax County, Virginia, library system is a treasure. I requested countless interlibrary loans, and the staff was always courteous and friendly when directing me to the right book or article. The staff of the City of Fairfax Regional Library's Virginia Room provided tremendous assistance.

Three individuals gave me great support throughout this project: Doc Stoddard, Tim Denison, and Troy White. Each provided meaningful words of encouragement during the drafting of this book, which meant much more than they probably realized. Doc and Tim were especially supportive to me during the final stage of the book's drafting, when I desperately needed some momentum.

I would also like to thank Kevin Quinlan, who provided terrific hospitality during my time in Monterrey, especially as an escort when viewing various battle sites. Gary Storrs reviewed early versions of the manuscript, and his keen observations and suggestions greatly improved the quality of this book. Chris Logan also edited various chapters of this book. Steve Witek provided much-needed expertise on 1846 weapons technology.

Two groups I have not met aided the development of this manuscript. The first are the historians, past and present, who so diligently transcribed the diaries and letters of soldiers who participated in the battle. The accounts of Napoleon Jackson Tecumseh Dana, Abner Doubleday, and Philip Barbour were particularly valuable. My gratitude also goes to the unnamed workers at Google who digitized many important books published immediately following the Mexican War. These digital versions, offered for free on the Internet, allowed me to quickly locate critical passages through a query function.

The staff of the Monterrey Municipal Archive and the Nuevo Leon State Archive helped me locate important Mexican sources for the book. I am especially indebted to Miguel Ángel González-Quiroga, who upon my inquiries generously introduced me to historians and archivists in Mexico and went far out of his way to help me find materials. I also want to thank J. Jesús Ávila Ávila at the Nuevo Leon State Archive, who patiently answered my questions regarding the Mexican War and provided critical insights on the lead up to the battle. The staff at these two archives went far out of their way to help me find important documents.

I am indebted to Ahmed Valtier and Pablo Ramos, who showed me battle sites, pointed me toward unique source materials, and helped me understand Mexican perspectives on the battle. Ahmed pointed me toward new sources and provided invaluable advice and insights. To these experts I hope I have correctly captured the Mexican perspective of the engagement.

Lastly, I would like to thank my son, Sean, who lost me to my basement for much of his first four years while I drafted this book. And most importantly I would like to thank my wife, editor, friend, and supporter during the drafting of this book, Alison, who patiently supported this multiyear effort.

Introduction

In January 1846 Pres. James Knox Polk ordered Maj. Gen. Zachary Taylor to march his small American army into a disputed strip of territory between the Nueces and Rio Grande rivers in southern Texas. Mexico reacted to this hostile move with force, resulting in pitched battles at Palo Alto and Resaca de la Palma. In both instances Taylor's troops routed larger Mexican armies, forcing their withdrawal south across the Rio Grande. After securing Texas, Polk now hoped to force a negotiated sale of California and New Mexico by seizing control of northern Mexico. Thus the next logical target for Taylor was Monterrey, the capital of Nuevo Leon and the region's commercial and cultural epicenter. The city rested on the north end of the primary thoroughfare from Mexico City to northern Mexico, so its capture would seal off the territory from the rest of the country. If the Americans could take Monterrey, it would be a huge financial, political, and psychological blow to the Mexican government and give the United States an advantage in any negotiations.

Few people have heard of the resulting Battle of Monterrey, yet it is one of the nineteenth century's most interesting engagements. For three days during the fall of 1846, U.S. and Mexican soldiers clashed violently in and around the picturesque city. Best known for its towering mountains and luxurious gardens, Monterrey soon became one of the century's most gruesome battlefields.[1]

For the young U.S. Army, the battle challenged the soldiers unlike any previous action. The fighting contained instances of courage, valor, cowardice, and immense carnage as the two armies dueled on open prairies, on mountaintops, and inside the city. Each day featured combat that required special tactics and generalship for success. For the first time in U.S. history, large numbers of regular troops engaged in house-to-house combat, with enemy soldiers fighting from behind the iron-barred windows of sturdy homes and from above on the town's rooftops. The Americans, lacking training in urban combat, learned the hard way how to fight in a city. Eventually they adopted new tactics that brought some success, though not until after two of the bloodiest days in the army's short history.

The American volunteers enhanced their reputation in the fall of 1846, proving that citizen-soldiers could fight with the same valor, courage, and discipline as regulars. Monterrey was one of the early volunteer army's great successes, though Taylor had taken unique measures to ensure that only the best of them accompanied his army. Col. Jefferson Davis's Mississippians and Col. William Campbell's Tennesseans played pivotal roles in the fighting.

Graduates of the U.S. Military Academy found the battle to be their toughest practical test since the school's founding in 1802. The first two clashes of the Mexican War, Palo Alto and Resaca de la Palma, offered ideal environments for the regulars to showcase their martial skills. The flat plain at Palo Alto allowed the utilization of a new and effective artillery tactic, while the brush-covered ravine at Resaca de la Palma sheltered groups of infantry as they encircled the Mexican lines. Monterrey, however, was different. No amount of academy training could prepare a nineteenth-century soldier for the challenge of staying in formation while being fired on by four different forts or of advancing down an open street blanketed by musket fire. Some old-cadre generals had wondered if the bookish West Pointers had "brawn" as well as "brains"; Monterrey settled the issue once and for all.

The battle included personalities who would later command Confederate and Union armies in the upcoming Civil War: Ulysses S. Grant, Braxton Bragg, George Henry Thomas, Albert Sidney Johnston, Joseph Hooker, George Gordon Meade, and James Longstreet, to name a few. For many of these Civil War greats, Monterrey was the first test of their courage, discipline, and ability under fire. But most

of the West Pointers who fought at Monterrey were not as fortunate. September 21, 1846, the first day of the battle, was one of the
bloodiest for the academy's alumni, as many of the army's best infantry officers fell that day; one can only imagine what their influence
would have been in the Civil War had they survived Mexico.

Although a nineteenth-century battle, Monterrey provided many
stories that relate to modern events. Zachary Taylor planned one of
the first "wars of maneuver," in which soldiers feigned attack in one
direction and then encircled their foe from the rear in a giant hook
motion. Gen. Norman Schwarzkopf would use the same technique
almost 150 years later in the Gulf War, though he relied on tanks and
armored vehicles rather than soldiers marching at "double-time."

The regulars learned new ways of urban warfare from the Texas
volunteers. The Texans had already fought two urban clashes against
Mexican forces—one at San Antonio de Bexar in 1835 and the other at
the Battle of Mier in 1842. From these lessons the Texans showed the
regulars how to clear a room full of the enemy, how to overrun a
rooftop full of soldiers, and how to advance house to house without
entering the street. These nontraditional combat techniques are still
embraced by today's armed forces, though the crowbar and hammer
have been replaced by more modern tools.

The concept of the embedded military reporter, popularized in
Operation Iraqi Freedom in 2003, was first used in Taylor's northern
campaign. A flourishing mid-nineteenth-century newspaper industry spawned a competitive environment in which readers demanded
timely war reporting. Journalists flocked to the frontlines to provide
eyewitness views of the action. Many of these reporters acted as part-
time soldiers, carrying battle orders and conducting camp chores, and
in some cases they even received wounds in battle.

As for the Mexican army, Monterrey was another tragic loss to
the United States, exacerbated by the political nature of its military
leadership. After the battle, as with others during the war, the focus
centered on *who* was at fault for the defeat rather than *why* it had
occurred. Most of the leaders in Mexico's northern army had sought
to use military success for political advantage in Mexico City. The
political infighting was further inflamed by a coup carried out just before the battle that overthrew the Mexican president, which also left
the average Mexican soldier wondering until the last minute whether
he would be ordered to put down the insurrection or to continue

north to confront the Americans. Mexican military technology was not much help to the men either. Their old English smoothbore muskets were notoriously inaccurate, and shoddy gunpowder caused many weapons to misfire. Despite all of these challenges, the Mexican soldiers fought tenaciously, never yielding until their commanders ordered them to withdraw.

General Taylor could attest to their bravery. While the Mexicans did eventually surrender Monterrey, Taylor's army did not look anything like it did prior to the battle. Fourteen percent of his troops became casualties (wounded and killed) in the fighting, an unusually high rate for the Mexican War. More notably, Taylor's officer corps was decimated, with sixteen of his best officers, mostly West Pointers, killed in action. In all, 120 of Taylor's men were killed and 368 others wounded. A song underscored the bittersweet American victory:

> The sweet church bells are pealing out
> A chorus wild and free,
> And everything rejoicing
> For the glorious victory;
> But bitter tears are gushing
> For the gallant and gay,
> Who now in death are sleeping
> On the field of Monterey.[2]

Mexican courage was not the only reason the battle resulted in such high casualties. Monterrey's natural geography made it one of the nineteenth century's most defensible cities. The Sierra Madre Mountains wrap around its southern and eastern sides like a giant, impenetrable wall. The Santa Catarina River runs along the southern side of the town, forming a perfect natural moat. Independence and Federation hills stand like gateposts in western Monterrey, with the only road from Mexico City running between them. Portions of the city's present-day Barrio Antiguo (Old Town), with its narrow streets and solid-walled houses, show how difficult it must have been for the Americans to advance—each house acted as a small fort for its defenders.

Taylor's men were awestruck by Monterrey's strong defensive position. Many soldiers compared the city to the Straits of Gibraltar—the strategic, narrow band of water that connects the Mediterranean

Sea to the North Atlantic. Soldiers often referred to the straits' natural defensive strength, especially its famous Rock of Gibraltar, which towers over the area, in their memoirs or diaries when thinking of Monterrey. Capt. William Seaton Henry wrote following the battle: "After riding over the city and examining minutely its defenses, my only astonishment is how they could yield it. It is a perfect Gibraltar." Lt. Napoleon Jackson Tecumseh Dana of the 7th Infantry similarly wrote to his wife, "The city itself was a perfect Gibraltar."[3]

A Perfect Gibraltar

1

PRELUDE TO BATTLE

"The Plot is thickening."

Lt. George Gordon Meade

In March 1845 Zachary Taylor was sixty-one years old. He stood five feet, eight inches high, with broad shoulders, a full chest, piercing dark eyes, and a thick, muscular frame. His tan, weathered face made him look like "he had been encamping out all of his life." The general was in good physical shape and could outmarch and outride people half his age. Disdaining formal dress, Taylor preferred a blue frock coat, jean pantaloons, and a black neckband. His campsite too was plain, typically consisting of a small tent, a stool, tin cups, and a camp chest that doubled as a locker and dinner table. The general's tent looked no different than the average private's. Despite army custom, Taylor refused to post a personal guard and did not use a protective outer tarp to ward off the elements, as many other officers used. His only vice was brown sugar, which he doled out to visitors on special occasions.[1]

Getting to know Taylor was easy. He assumed no airs and possessed a casual, friendly demeanor. The general could often be found sitting on a ragged stool in front of his tent, laughing and chatting with his staff. Anyone could stop by to speak with him, regardless of rank. And it took a lot to get Taylor agitated, even in the grimmest situations; he rarely raised his voice to his own men.

Hard to discern from this description is that "Old Zack" or "Rough and Ready," as he was better known, was one of the most senior generals in the U.S. Army. By the summer of 1845, he commanded the most powerful army that America had fielded since the Revolutionary War. Taylor, a brigadier with almost four decades in the army, had battled Indians while stationed at some of the most remote outposts in the continent. In the Floridas he led a thousand soldiers against the Seminole Indians in 1837, culminating in a battle at Lake Okeechobee, one of the bloodiest clashes of the early nineteenth century. For the next ten years his duties kept him on the turbulent frontier, including as commander of the Second Military Department in present-day Oklahoma, then the heart of Cherokee Indian country. Taylor, whose real passion was farming, also spent time tending to his Louisiana plantation and selling some of his properties. In June 1844 the general was transferred to Fort Jesup, Louisiana, to command the First Military District, charged with protecting the Republic of Texas, which had petitioned for annexation to the United States, from Mexican invasion.[2]

After Taylor arrived at Fort Jesup, events began to unroll that ensured he would play a leading role in any upcoming hostilities. In 1845 the United States offered annexation to the independent Republic of Texas. Texan leaders warned President Polk that if they joined the United States, Mexico would send troops north to conquer the renegade republic. To protect against invasion, Polk ordered Taylor to advance his troops to the coast near the Sabine River (the border between Texas and Louisiana) once the general learned that Texas had accepted annexation.[3]

Polk had other, more ambitious reasons for moving troops toward Texas. Mexico had broken diplomatic relations with the United States in March 1845 after his predecessor, John Tyler, had signed a joint resolution offering Texas annexation. This ruined Polk's chances of accomplishing through diplomacy one of his most important goals—expanding the United States westward across the continent.

Like many Americans in 1846, Polk was an avowed expansionist. He believed that the United States had a duty to exploit the vast swathes of undeveloped land in Texas, New Mexico, California, and the Pacific Northwest and an obligation to bring republican government to the "backward" people of these territories. The United States, expansionists claimed, had a right and duty to mine, farm, and

Maj. Gen. Zachary Taylor. The American commander rarely wore the formal army attire depicted here and preferred to sit on a stool rather than a chair. After an engraving by Johnson, Fry, and Company from the original painting. From Wilcox, *History of the Mexican War*, 238.

govern this land for the benefit of all mankind. Polk embraced this belief, known as Manifest Destiny, and intended to act on the expansionist promises he had made during his campaign. In his inaugural address he said, "Texas was once a part of our own country—was unwisely ceded away to a foreign power—is now independent, and possesses an undoubted right . . . to merge her sovereignty as a separate and independent state into ours." Thus far the Mexican government had been unwilling to negotiate the sale of their remaining territory, but Polk hoped that a show of force might change their minds.[4]

Under orders to march into Texas, Taylor and his men advanced in July 1845 to Corpus Christi, a small community on the Gulf of Mexico just south of the Nueces River. Three thousand regulars, with many of their officers trained at the U.S. Military Academy at West Point, eventually settled in for a long, sandy stint on the coast.[5]

Despite Polk's anxiety about an invasion, Mexican president José Joaquín de Herrera had no illusions about recovering Texas, which had won its independence almost ten years earlier. Herrera understood that his country did not have the resources or an army strong enough to wage such a campaign and that he had more-pressing issues at home. But he knew that he could not ignore Texas and hoped to prevent annexation by negotiating with the republic. Herrera believed that the best possible outcome was for Texas to remain an independent country with close ties to Mexico.

Unfortunately the Mexican president had little support for his peaceful stance. Most Mexicans believed that Texas was stolen by the United States in an organized plot. Critics wondered how he could negotiate with a country led by "usurpers" and "tyrants." The death knell for Herrera's administration came with the arrival of John Slidell, a U.S. minister appointed to negotiate the purchase from Mexico of California and New Mexico, for which Polk was willing to pay up to $40 million. Herrera thought that Slidell's mission was to make amends for Texas's likely annexation, rather than buy Mexico's territory.[6]

The cauldron boiled over in December 1845, when Texas finally became part of the United States. Herrera's peaceful strategy had failed, and he now lost the favor of even his most ardent supporters. Maj. Gen. Mariano Paredes y Arrillaga, a former ally, overthrew the weak president one month later. In his inaugural address Paredes promised to regain Mexican territory all the way to the Sabine River, thus threatening the new state of Texas. Reports that Herrera had refused to meet with Slidell reached Polk on January 12, 1846. The next day he ordered General Taylor to march his army from Corpus Christi into South Texas and the disputed territory between the Nueces River and the Rio Grande. Polk hoped this confrontational move would force Mexico into negotiations over Texas, New Mexico, and California.[7]

When Texas declared independence in 1836, its leaders claimed a western boundary that ran along the Rio Grande. Mexico in turn argued that the Nueces River was the northern boundary of its state of Tamaulipas. The Rio Grande claim was important to both Polk and Paredes because the western edge of the river runs through the middle of New Mexico. If the Rio Grande was the agreed-upon boundary, the United States could claim Mexican territory west to Santa Fe. A southern boundary on the Nueces River shrank Texas to about a third of that size. Soon after his inauguration, Polk assured Sam Houston, Texas's most influential leader, that the United States would honor the Texans' claim to the Rio Grande. The president also told the U.S. chargé d'affaires to Texas that he would "not permit an invading enemy to occupy a foot of the soil east of the Rio Grande." To Polk this claim was non-negotiable.[8]

But Paredes viewed Taylor's advance as an act of war. This region was Mexican land, as was Texas before it rebelled, and Taylor's presence constituted an invasion. When Texas was a Mexican state, the Constitution of 1824 formalized the Nueces River as the boundary between it and Tamaulipas, so the border was inscribed in Mexican law. Paredes and his allies believed that Texas was the first step by the United States in an unbridled effort to expand across the continent, and that if left unchecked, Polk would soon be seeking to annex more Mexican territory.[9]

When Taylor received Polk's order to march into the disputed region, he had been in Corpus Christi for six months. Because the general knew that war with Mexico was a possibility, he had been drilling his men relentlessly. The nineteenth-century U.S. Army was scattered as company- and battalion-size detachments across hundreds of isolated posts throughout the country. Regiments rarely drilled as complete units (a regiment in 1845 contained around five hundred men), so the army was woefully unprepared to fight set-piece

Maj. Gen. Mariano Arista. Having distinguished himself
in the Mexican wars for Independence, Arista was one of
Mexico's best generals. During the Mexican War, he commanded the Army of the North, which sought to expel Taylor from Mexico. He was from the state of San Luis Potosi in
northern Mexico and was well liked by his men, many of
whom hailed from the same region. After the war Arista
became president of Mexico for a short time. Courtesy of
Special Collections, The University of Texas at Arlington
Library.

battles against opposing forces of thousands of men. Taylor tried to
remedy this deficiency quickly.[10]

After a miserable winter in Corpus Christi, the 3,900 American
soldiers began marching into the disputed territory in March 1846.
Taylor encamped on the north bank of the Rio Grande directly across
from Matamoros, Mexico, and ordered the construction of an earthen

fort that could accommodate 800 men. Named Fort Texas, its presence infuriated the soldiers of the Matamoros garrison, who watched its construction from across the river.

On April 11 Don Pedro de Ampudia, commander of the Army of the North, arrived in Matamoros and demanded that Taylor withdraw his troops to the north side of the Nueces. Taylor's response was to order the U.S. Navy to blockade the Rio Grande to prevent Ampudia from receiving supplies by sea. Tensions ran high as the two armies stood within sight of each other. Taylor insisted that he would not march his men across the Rio Grande and that he hoped the two countries could avoid war. Ampudia, of course, saw the situation differently since from his perspective the Americans had already crossed into Mexican territory when they entered the disputed zone.

To Ampudia's dismay, he would not have a chance to command the army against Taylor. Paredes replaced him with Maj. Gen. Mariano Arista, a well-liked, red-headed officer who had studied for a short time in Cincinnati. Unlike Ampudia, Arista retained the loyalty of many northern soldiers, himself hailing from the region. "It is indispensable," Paredes wrote Arista on April 18, "that hostilities begin, yourself taking the initiative." Arista, like many Mexican generals, yearned for a decisive military victory to bolster his political support. Ampudia was a strong ally of Paredes, and the president only replaced him at the behest of senior northern leaders. Arista knew that repelling Taylor would solidify his position with Paredes and within national politics.[11]

The Mexican troops were confident. They heard rumors that the U.S. cavalry was composed of ill-disciplined foreigners who could not shoot straight or maneuver their horses. One Mexican general summed up the feelings of his men: "Those adventurers cannot withstand the bayonet charge of our foot, nor a cavalry charge with the lance."[12]

In April Arista sent a 1,600-man force of light infantry, cavalry, and sappers under Gen. Anastasio Torrejón across the Rio Grande to cut off Taylor's communications with Point Isabel, the U.S. supply base across from Corpus Christi that supported Taylor's operations near Matamoros. On April 25 Torrejón's force ambushed sixty American dragoons (cavalrymen who traveled by horse but fought like infantry) sent to investigate Mexican activity, capturing fifty and kill-

South Texas, 1846. This map, showing the region in which the battles of Palo Alto and Resaca de la Palma took place, was taken from General Arista's portfolio, which was seized at Resaca de la Palma. Taylor's routes of battle were later overlaid by one of his lieutenants. Map by Luis Berlandier, *Plan of the Ground Situated to the North of Matamoras between the Rio Bravo & the Arroyo Colorado.* Courtesy of the Library of Congress, Geography and Maps Division.

ing fourteen. "Hostilities may now be considered as commenced," Taylor wrote in his official report of the engagement, "and I have this day deemed it necessary to call upon the Governor of Texas for four regiments of volunteers." Taylor, knowing that a large-scale fight was now imminent, left a small garrison of 500 men at Fort Texas and marched toward Point Isabel to ensure that his supply base was secure.[13]

On May 5 General Arista sent Ampudia, who was still commanding a division, to overrun Fort Texas in Taylor's absence. Ampudia bombarded the fort with mortars and cannons day and night. The garrison, under the command of Maj. Jacob Brown, built bombproof shelters out of barrels filled with pork and topped with sticks and earth. A sentry would call out the name of a Mexican battery when it fired—for example, "sand bag fort battery"—and those in its path would take cover or lay flat on the ground.[14]

Taylor could hear Ampudia's bombardment from Point Isabel and knew that the small garrison could hold out for only so long. He quickly accepted the offer of a daring Texas volunteer named Samuel Walker to sneak into the fort to determine the garrison's condition. Walker was already a legend in Texas, where his courageous exploits during battles with Comanche Indians were widely known. Leaving camp at nightfall and dodging Mexican soldiers and bandits for thirty miles, Walker miraculously entered Fort Texas unharmed. Brown reported that his men would hold out as long as necessary. Walker rode back to Point Isabel and gave Taylor the critical information. The general secured his base at Point Isabel, collected supplies, and began the return trip to Fort Texas. With two hundred wagons and two 18-pound cannons in tow, men and oxen trotted down the main road to Matamoros.[15]

On May 8 Arista intercepted Taylor at Palo Alto—a flat, grassy plain in South Texas. The two sides deployed across from each other and prepared for battle. Mexican cavalry charged Taylor's flanks while American and Mexican artillery lobbed shells into each other's lines. U.S. infantry and cannons repulsed the horsemen, and Mexican losses began to mount. As the grass caught fire from hot cannon wads, sending thick smoke across the plain, Arista withdrew.

Palo Alto was a monumental day for the U.S. Army's artillery wing. For the first time in major combat, the army's new light artillery batteries, known as "flying artillery," proved their worth on the battlefield. In the past soldiers or draught animals had dragged the army's field artillery into place on the battlefield, and they rarely moved during the fighting. Their static position meant that the cannons could not respond to changes in battle formations, unexpected charges, or rapid infantry movements. If the enemy attacked the line in an area where artillery was absent, the larger cannons could not change position to assist in the defense. Samuel Ringgold, a major in the U.S. Army, pioneered a new method that relied on smaller, more maneuverable guns. Six horses pulled a light cannon and its ammunition rapidly across the battle zone so the artillery could respond to unpredictable situations and better support maneuvering infantry. The untested idea received little support from army leadership or Congress. Most military leaders believed that the best use of artillerymen was as infantry, believing that cannons rarely decided the outcome of a battle. These traditionalists, including Taylor, did not understand how fast-moving cannons could help win an infantry engagement.[16]

After Palo Alto, however, Taylor was a believer. "Our artillery . . . was the arm chiefly engaged, and to the excellent manner in which it was manoeuvred and served is our success mainly due," he wrote the adjutant general after the battle. Ringgold's men dashed around the battlefield with reckless abandon, running into the middle of fire fights to launch grape and canister shot into enemy formations. They wanted to prove the utility of their new weapon, and indeed they did—their cannons repulsed numerous cavalry charges and helped Taylor's army defeat an adversary almost twice its size. Unfortunately Samuel Ringgold never read that report; he was mortally wounded during the battle and died three days later. In his final hours he spoke with pride about the success of his light artillery, remarking to bedside visitors that his guns were as accurate as a rifle. Ringgold became known throughout the States as one of the first heroes of the Mexican War.[17]

While Palo Alto was taking place, the small garrison of Fort Texas continued to hold out under intense fire. An up-and-coming officer named Braxton Bragg was in this besieged fort with his light artillery battery. He could only watch as the American and Mexican forces dueled with their big cannons and mortars. His small guns could repel soldiers and horses, but they did not have the range for a cross-river artillery exchange.

Braxton Bragg was one of Ringgold's star officers. Like most light artillerymen, Bragg had graduated from West Point. For Bragg and many of his fellow West Pointers, Taylor's campaign was the first army-against-army combat in which they had participated. These graduates filled Taylor's lower-grade officer slots, and they brought an unprecedented level of expertise to the U.S. Army.

When Bragg attended West Point in the 1830s, the institution was a lightning rod for criticism, and its existence was in doubt. The country was reluctant to embrace a standing army, and West Point was a clear step in that direction. State leaders denounced the academy as elitist and undemocratic, believing that it threatened the American tradition of the citizen-soldier. Most West Pointers looked upon the start of the Mexican War with relief, and not just for the chance for promotion. Finally they had an opportunity to prove the worth of their splendid institution. They were proud to attend the school and believed that it gave them the skills to fight intelligently as well as courageously.[18]

West Pointers went into one of five main army branches upon graduation. In the 1830s the school's top graduates went into one of the two engineering arms—the Corps of Engineers or the topographical engineers. The Corps of Engineers was considered the elite branch of the army and received the best graduates. These engineers built fortifications, bridges, dams, and other large-scale infrastructure projects. The topographical engineers, or "topogs," as they were known, were only slightly less prestigious than the Corps of Engineers. They investigated sites for fortifications, explored new territory, and surveyed the routes of rivers and roads among other duties. Taylor had many topographical and regular engineers with his army, and they would prove immensely useful at Monterrey.[19]

Bragg, who graduated fifth in his class, joined the artillery, which was also considered an important arm of the army. Most of West Point's artillery graduates in the 1840s trained under Ringgold and became masters of light tactics. By the time of the Battle of Monterrey, Bragg's company included such future famous West Pointers as George Henry Thomas, Samuel French, and John Reynolds.

The last two components of the army, the infantry and cavalry, were the least prestigious. Many of these graduates went on to attend a special infantry school of practice at Jefferson Barracks outside St. Louis, Missouri, where they developed their skills in drilling, marching, and other areas. The school sought to incite an esprit de corps and instill discipline among the troops. The Third and Fourth Infantry regiments, which would have a big role at Monterrey, trained there just before the war, even though by that time Jefferson Barracks was no longer an official school of practice.[20]

Regardless of their arm of service, all of Taylor's academy graduates would have an opportunity to showcase their talents in combat. At the start of the conflict, the Army of Occupation, as Taylor's army was known, retained a glut of worn-out old officers—mainly regiment and brigade commanders who had no business commanding soldiers in wartime. Taylor needed competent, resourceful officers, and beginning at Fort Texas and Palo Alto, he turned to his West Pointers.[21]

The day after Palo Alto, U.S. infantry got a chance to showcase their skills and bravery. On May 9 Taylor marched his men south down the main road from Point Isabel to the Rio Grande. This road led straight into the center of the Mexican army, entrenched in a formidable position known as Resaca de la Palma. Arista placed his men around a mile-long dry riverbed, known as a "resaca," that curved west to east in a semicircle and was flanked on both sides by swamp and chaparral. He deployed artillery in the middle of the road and also on his flanks. One line of infantry waited at the bottom of the riverbed, while another stood poised on the south side of the ravine. The American light artillery would have a hard time maneuvering through the coarse brush and deep rivulets surrounding this position.[22]

The resulting Battle of Resaca de la Palma deteriorated into a series of small infantry engagements as U.S. soldiers pushed forward in small groups through the dense chaparral. Maj. Philip Norbourne Barbour of the Third Infantry, on the American right flank, could only keep twelve men with him because of the thick undergrowth. The Mexicans launched a cavalry attack against this flank, threatening Taylor's entire line. Barbour placed his men in one of the few areas of the battlefield where they had a clear line of fire and repulsed the attacking lancers. Barbour's actions and those of his fellow soldiers routed the Mexicans and sent Arista fleeing across the Rio Grande.

Like Bragg, Barbour was a West Pointer, though he graduated twenty-three places lower than the artillerist. A smart, brave twelve-year veteran when ordered to join the Army of Occupation, his army career had advanced sluggishly due to the difficulty of promotion during peacetime. Barbour should have moved up the ranks quickly, but old "has-been" officers lingered on rather than retire, occupying many of the precious few command slots that existed. As a result, most officers did not become captain until their mid-thirties and major until their fifties, leaving good-caliber men like Bragg and Barbour in command of smaller units for years.[23]

Nevertheless, stories about Palo Alto and Resaca de la Palma soon filled U.S. newspapers. Readers learned about the death of Samuel Ringgold, the charge of Capt. Charles A. May's dragoons into enemy fire to capture a Mexican battery, and "Old Rough and Ready" casually trotting his horse around the battlefield as if he were overseeing his farm in Louisiana. West Pointers were exultant in the news. "The excitement among the cadets knew no bounds," one cadet wrote, "the rules and regulations of the academy were disregarded, loud and long-continued cheering was heard in the two barracks, boisterous laughing and talking and running about in all directions in defiance of orders." The regulars were proud that they won those battles without the help of any volunteers. "It is to be hoped now," wrote Lt. Jenks Beamen, who fought in both engagements, "that Congress will give us credit of being ready & willing to do our duty at the risk of our lives, and let the Military Academy alone for the present. To that institution the U.S. is indebted for the two signal victories of the 8th & 9th in which the killed and wounded of the enemy was nearly equal to our numbers in the action."[24]

When word of the victories at Palo Alto and Resaca de la Palma reached the United States, adventure-seeking men soon clamored to join the fight against their southern neighbor. They salivated over news of the battles, with headlines like one from the *New Orleans Picayune* that read: "Great Battle! Gen. Taylor Victorious!!! Battle between Gen. Taylor's force and the Mexicans—The American Army victorious—200 Mexicans killed or wounded." Most of these eager citizens would get a chance to serve their country. In April 1846 Taylor asked the governors of Texas and Louisiana to provide eight volunteer regiments—about 5,000 men—to serve for three months. More were called up in May after Congress gave President Polk the authority to muster in 50,000 men to serve for twelve months. Volunteers from Alabama, Tennessee, Kentucky, Mississippi, Ohio, Indiana, Maryland, and elsewhere flocked to recruiting stations to sign up.

The timing of the call was ideal since news of Palo Alto and Resaca de la Palma had reached the nation only weeks earlier. The South's war fervor, in particular, was at an all-time high, and men volunteered in droves. The army eventually enlisted 20,000 of the 50,000 allowed.[25]

Maj. Gen. Edmund Gaines, a bull-headed officer who was second in command of the U.S. Army, initiated his own call up of volunteers. When he heard that the Mexicans had attacked some of Taylor's troops, he raised more than 11,000 men, mostly from Louisiana, to join the Army of Occupation for six months. Unfortunately for those who responded to this call, the law dictated that a volunteer could only serve for three months unless he was granted special permission by the War Department. Gaines did not care that his recruits did not have such a waiver, believing that his actions would save Taylor from annihilation.[26]

Taylor viewed the volunteers' arrival as a mixed blessing. He had only asked for eight regiments, not the 20,000 men that Polk was calling up, nor the men that Gaines sent him. Taylor had commanded volunteers years earlier and had serious doubts about their capabilities: "The more I see of militia, the less confidence I have in their effecting anything of importance," he once said.[27]

Of all of the volunteers called up, those from Texas were the most unique. With their red shirts, slouched hats, blue overalls, and beards and mustaches, they looked nothing like a regular soldier. "A rougher looking set we never saw," remarked one volunteer who served with the Texans. He also observed that their "camp frequently looked more like . . . a group of rude wigwams in an Indian village, than the regular encampment of volunteers in the service of the United States." For a weapon, most Texans carried one or two revolvers, a Bowie knife, and a short-barrel rifle, known as a "plains rifle," that could fire a large-caliber bullet at distant targets. Their "baggage" consisted of a small wallet with salt, ammunition, some tobacco, and parched corn as well as a blanket hung from the saddle.[28]

Many of the Texan volunteers had been Texas Rangers at some point in their lives. Month-long expeditions, during which they slept on the ground and ate from the wild, were the norm for these tough men. Their main enemy was the Comanche Indian, who raided farms and disrupted Texan settlements. The Comanches were expert horsemen who could fire and reload a bow while their horse was at full gallop. They shot smoothbore muskets, carried long lances, and were fearless in battle. For their time, the Comanches were some of the best cavalrymen in the world. The Rangers adapted their fighting style to combat these fearless horsemen, becoming expert marksmen and training rigorously on horseback. Their horse became as indispensable as their weapon. "Centaur-like, they seemed to live upon their horses," wrote one regular who served with the Texans during the Mexican War. When one man wanted to join the famous Company A, First Regiment of the Texas Mounted Rifles, Capt. Ben McCulloch ran his eye over the soldier and said: "Have you a good horse sir! For I have refused a great many because their horses would not do for our service." McCulloch inspected the man's mount, proclaimed it a "good horse," and made the volunteer a part of his company.[29]

The Texans' most revered weapon was the Paterson Colt fiveshot revolver. They used the pistol against the Comanches in close combat. These guns changed the "way of warfare" for the Rangers and allowed them to win important victories against the Indians. The pistols could fire multiple shots at close range, allowing the Texans an important defense against the Comanches in close-combat situations. The Texans brought their Colts to Mexico, and they would provide an important technological edge in the upcoming battle.

Taylor became aware of the Texans' value to his army as the campaign evolved. They were the only men in his force with experience fighting the Mexican army. They were also top-notch scouts who could navigate the dangerous chaparral and chase Mexican irregulars away from U.S. supply lines. The Texans also knew how to collect intelligence in this region and could provide critical information regarding Mexican troop movements.

In contrast, Taylor's regular cavalry troops did not enjoy roaming the prairies in search of Mexican "ghosts," hoping rather to fight a conventional battle against the Mexican army. In its early years the U.S. Army gave little consideration to any kind of irregular fighting. West Point did not even teach cavalry tactics—the key to battling plains Indians—until after the war and had procured horses only in 1839. This absence of training was fine for most of the army's cavalrymen, who believed there was no honor in fighting Indians.[30]

Filling Taylor's need for irregular forces, the Texans were thrilled to be fighting for their new country. Now backed by the U.S. Army, they could fight the Mexicans on their own terms. They even wrote a popular song to celebrate the opportunity:

Mount! Mount! And away o'er the green prairie wide—
The sword is our scepter, the fleet steed our pride;
Up! Up! With our flag—let its bright star gleam out
Mount! Mount! And away on the wild border-scout!

The might of the foe gathers thick on our way—
They hear our wild shouts as we rush to the fray;
What to us is the fear of the death-stricken plain—
We have "braved it before, and will brave it again."

Then mount and away! Give the fleet steed the rein—
The Ranger's at home on the prairies again;
Spur! Spur in the chase, dash on to the fight,
Cry vengeance for Texas! And God speed the right.[31]

The phrase "cry for vengeance" was much more than a lyric for the Texans with Taylor's army. They had a bloody history with Mexico. Just the mention of the Alamo, Santa Fe, Dawson's Massacre, Woll's invasion, Perote, or any number of other events made a nineteenth-century Texan's blood boil. But two more than any emblazoned themselves on the Texas psyche.

During the Texas Revolution, Antonio Lopez de Santa Anna pursued a policy of "no quarter" during the war—he would take no prisoners. His goal was to terrify Texans into leaving the area and to convince the ragtag forces opposing him that it was useless to resist. At a small town called Goliad, he carried out this policy to its fullest by ordering 382 Texans, who had surrendered to the Mexican army, shot or bayoneted. Some of the men escaped the slaughter and spread news of the massacre throughout the region. Texans fumed at his barbarity.

Six years later, in 1842, Texan militia invaded the Mexican border town of Mier in retaliation for an earlier Mexican incursion into Texas. Once at Mier, they clashed with Gen. Pedro de Ampudia and a portion of his northern army. The outnumbered Texans eventually surrendered under what they believed was a promise that the general would keep them prisoners in northern Mexico and parole them soon after. Instead, Ampudia paraded his captives like "dogs" throughout all of the major border towns—Camargo, Reynosa, Matamoros—and then marched them to dungeons in Mexico City.[32]

On the way to the capital, some of the prisoners, including Samuel Walker, tried to escape. They were recaptured after wandering through the northern Mexican desert desperately searching for food and water. As punishment, Santa Anna decreed that every escapee should be executed, though American and British protests persuaded him that only every tenth man should be killed. Col. Domingo Huerta made each Texan blindly pick a bean out of a pitcher in what later became known as the "Lottery of Death." If the bean was white, the man would live; if it was black, he would be shot. Samuel Walker, who later made his daring dash for Taylor into Fort Texas, picked a white bean, as did another famous Texan, William "Bigfoot" Wallace, a 6-foot 2-inch, 240-pound giant who reportedly had monstrous feet. Wallace never forgot the snide remarks that Mexican officers made when seventeen of his friends (the number of black beans in the pitcher) were executed. He and Walker eagerly joined the Texas volunteers in 1846.[33]

The Mexican army, for its part, was eager to settle its accounts with the Texans. It had been fighting the Republic of Texas for over a decade in an effort to subdue the renegade territory's bid for independence, suffering defeat at San Antonio de Bexar in 1835 and at San Jacinto one year later. Mexicans also did not appreciate the Texan strike at Mier, in what amounted to a pillaging expedition. And added to this was Taylor's current invasion of their territory, which had already resulted in two defeats.

Mexico's Army of the North, which had fought at Palo Alto and Resaca de la Palma, was one of six divisions created in 1839 to cover various parts of the country. Officially known as the Fourth Division, it was responsible for the states of Nuevo Leon, Coahuila, and Tamaulipas. Many of its soldiers and officers had participated in prior efforts to keep or reclaim Texas for Mexico.

The two most important components of the nineteenth-century Mexican army were the infantry and cavalry. The infantry was organized into twelve regiments, each with a capacity for about 1,200 men, though their actual strength was usually 50 percent of this. There were also four light infantry regiments created in the 1840s, some of which would see action at Monterrey. Most soldiers were armed with Tower muskets, a smoothbore flintlock musket purchased from British surplus. Typically, infantrymen wore blue

Texians Drawing the Black Beans at Salado. Drawing by Charles M'Laughlin. From Green, *Journal of the Texian Expedition*, 170. Courtesy of Special Collections, The University of Texas at Arlington Library.

trousers and a blue coat except during summer, when they wore white trousers and a white coat.[34]

The pride of the Mexican army was the cavalry, with the lancers considered the elite group. In 1846 there were nine permanent regiments of cavalry. Each regiment contained light, medium, and heavy cavalry units and was supposed to number 780 men during wartime, though actual strength was around 400 men. Most cavalrymen carried carbines, a short-barreled gun suited for carrying on horseback, and swords. Each regiment also had at least one hundred men armed with a lance, an eight- to ten-foot rod tipped with a sharp, steel blade for spearing the enemy; red and green flags, two of the colors of the Mexican flag, usually hung from the rod. Cavalrymen were adorned in the finest dress, including green, blue, yellow, and white coats, depending on the regiment. They also wore tall, cylindrical military caps known as shakos, though some regiments were equipped with tall leather helmets with yellow fittings. Mexican generals used their horsemen to conduct flanking maneuvers, attack enemy infantry from the rear, and chase down routed enemy soldiers. The cavalry was the most respected service in the military, and some of Mexico's best officers led these units.[35]

The mission of the pre-1846 army vacillated between suppressing local rebellions and defending Mexico from invasion. Aside from two pitched battles against Spain and France in 1829 and 1838, respectively, the army was occupied with supporting or quashing rebellions against the presiding authority in Mexico City. Its officers and men could not develop sophisticated military expertise since they usually were marching from state to state, fighting their own countrymen. Such actions taught them little about conventional warfare and the type of battles that they would soon face against the Americans.

General officers in the Mexican military maneuvered their way to the top by allying themselves with successful caudillos—authoritarian leaders who ruled Mexico with an iron fist. Military merit rarely played a role in the decision to make a soldier a general officer. These high-ranking men, who commanded a thousand or more soldiers, had to be counted on to support a caudillo when someone challenged his power. Lower-ranking officers and enlisted men were caught in the middle of these power plays. On some occasions they would be asked to stamp out a rebellion, while at other times they would initiate the revolt; a regiment's actions depended on the often-changing alliances of its general officer.

Enlisted soldiers in the Mexican army were mostly Indian conscripts or Mexican peasants known as campesinos, who suffered physical and verbal abuse once they entered service. Nevertheless, they battled hard when the time came to fight. Mid-ranking officers were usually courageous men who retained the loyalty of their troops. Many lacked military training, but they organized their men well and usually led from the front during battle. These soldiers would need to harness all of their courage and skill, for the Mexican military, which was only twenty-five years old in 1846, was facing its toughest opponent to date.[36]

2

MEXICAN PREPARATIONS

"Victory or Death"

Maj. Gen. Don Pedro de Ampudia

On May 17, 1846, General Arista held a council of war with his senior officers in Matamoros. General Taylor, whose army was encamped across the Rio Grande, threatened to invade the town. Arista's council, or junta, debated whether to abandon or defend Matamoros. After a short discussion, they agreed to evacuate. Their demoralized men were in no position to defend the town against U.S. forces, they argued, especially since the Americans could bombard the city with the 18-pounders at Fort Texas.

Arista ordered the army to withdraw that night, the Second Brigade leading the way. His men hurriedly spiked five pieces of artillery and threw the rest of the cannons into the river, while leaving piles of ammunition, clothes, rifles, and muskets in the town square. The general abandoned three hundred wounded soldiers for lack of transport wagons. Most of the cavalrymen carried their saddles on their backs because their horses had been killed at Palo Alto and Resaca de la Palma. Wounded soldiers, who refused to be left behind, hobbled among the troops. Lacking mules, the Mexicans left most of their personal belongings in the city, carrying only their guns and kettles. It was a humiliating retreat.[1]

U.S. troops entered the undefended city with pride, realizing that Mexico's northern army had left to avoid the American regulars. Taylor's men lowered the Mexican flag at Fort Paredes and raised the Stars and Stripes in its place. The troops gave three cheers to their country's banner, now flying at the top of the thirty-foot flagpole.[2]

Arista did not share the Americans' jovial sentiments, trying as he was to save his army from annihilation. He marched his men to Linares, a strategic point from where he could reach Monterrey or Victoria depending on Taylor's future movements, even though the route lacked food and water. The soldiers marched thirsty, demoralized, and defeated. Many of them died and were left on the side of the road, while some committed suicide. They passed ranchero after ranchero but could find only a few meager supplies. Finally it rained, but the water turned the road into a giant mud track. In their weakened state the soldiers trudged on while watching their wagons mire in the morass. Many of the oxen died on the march, forcing the Mexicans to manhandle the cannons. The wet conditions also fostered disease. Cholera spread throughout the ranks, eventually taking the life of a respected general. "There were so many diseases," another general remarked, "that the whole division suffered, without exception, of all ranks." The soldiers finally arrived at Linares on June 29, forty-five miserable days after leaving Matamoros. The generals pressed the townsmen for money to pay their starving soldiers since the government had not provided any funding.[3]

While there, Arista heard reports that General Taylor's next objective was Monterrey. He probably had deduced this already. Monterrey was Mexico's northern commercial and cultural hub, so its seizure would be a harsh blow to the country's honor and economy. Arista knew the city well because he owned a beautiful house in its northwest suburbs. He also knew what a strong defensive position it could be. So the general sent a section of engineers under Lt. Col. Mariano Reyes Zuloaga and a battalion of sappers under Lt. Col. Don Mariano Reyes to prepare Monterrey for an American attack. This would be Arista's last order as commander of the Army of the North.

President Paredes removed Arista from command and ordered him to appear before a tribunal. Paredes was distraught over the May defeats and the fact that in two days Taylor had cleared all Mexican soldiers from the disputed territory and now occupied Matamoros.

Arista, the once beloved general, became the government's scape-goat. The president believed that Taylor's army had been severely damaged in the May battles and could be defeated if additional troops reinforced those already in northern Mexico. He began to organize and train three brigades of crack troops in Mexico City to bolster the weak and demoralized northern army, intending to take command of those forces personally. In preparation Paredes persuaded the church to donate one million pesos to help raise supplies and men for the campaign.

Meanwhile Brig. Gen. Francisco Mejía, Arista's deputy, assumed command of the northern army, but he fell ill shortly after the change. He therefore ordered his deputy to lead the 1,800 men to Monterrey. The soldiers marched to Cadereyta Jiménez, twenty-five miles from Monterrey, where they encamped for two weeks while their commander recuperated. On July 21 a healthy Mejía ordered his headquarters transferred to Monterrey. At the same time, however, events unfolding in Mexico City would affect the Army of the North and the overall defense of Monterrey. The volatility of Mexican politics was about to assert itself once again.[4]

Unfortunately for Paredes, he had more-serious concerns than thwarting an American invasion: his political enemies were already plotting to overthrow him. The president's support came from the elite of Mexico—the army, the church, and the monarchists. His chief rivals were the Federalists, who wanted to strip the army of its special privileges and empower the states to run their own affairs. They encouraged Paredes to go north with the army so, as he feared, they could take over the government in his absence. Federalists publicly accused him of leaving Mexico's main force in the capital so he could use the troops as a personal bodyguard instead of saving the country from invasion. If Paredes was so interested in defending the nation, they asked, why was he still in Mexico City?[5]

The crisis exploded when a rebellion broke out in Guadalajara against the Paredes government. The president sent a brigade to suppress the belligerents, but it was routed and one of its generals was killed. Paredes had to act decisively if he were to have any chance of saving his presidency. He decided to send his three brigades to Guadalajara to suppress the rebellion, after which they would turn north to fight the Americans.

On July 1 a thousand men of the First Brigade under the command of one of Mexico's most respected generals, Brig. Gen. Don José García Conde, departed Mexico City for Guadalajara. Conde's brigade contained two battalions of infantry, two squadrons of cavalry, and three 8-pound cannons. The next day the Second Brigade, with a thousand more men and seven cannons, left the capital under Lt. Col. Florencio Azpeitia. The Third Brigade got a late start, not leaving the city until almost twenty days later under the command of a respected infantry officer, Brig. Gen. Simeón Ramírez. Overall, roughly three thousand men and sixteen cannons departed Mexico City. Paredes did not accompany the brigades, fearing a coup if he left the capital. But he did pledge to personally lead additional troops north in August, once the political crisis was resolved.

The northern press, believing that the men would eventually challenge Taylor, was thrilled that Paredes was sending reinforcements. The *Tampico Esperanza* reported that a thousand men with cavalry and four pieces of artillery had departed Mexico City. "We pray that they will safely arrive at their destination and that we will not see them again in Mexico until after they have contributed to the salvation of our nationality and independence." News of the troops' departure also arrived in Nuevo Leon. The *Seminario Político del Gobierno de Nuevo León*, Monterrey's local paper, reported that two brigades left Mexico City for San Luis Potosí during the month of July. The paper said that the men were well equipped with 200,000 pesos, horses, munitions, and clothes and hoped that they could stop Taylor's fast-moving army from taking Monterrey and all of northern Mexico.[6]

The Third Brigade left Mexico City on the night of July 26 as a heavy rainstorm descended upon the capital, turning the surrounding marshland into a murky bog. The wheels of artillery caissons sank into the porous earth. Every small creek and dry ravine that crossed the road became a rushing river. Hired mule drivers, who cared little about their jobs, abandoned the guns once they got stuck, forcing the artillery officers to undertake the back-breaking work of pulling the guns out by hand. At the town of Coyotepec, twenty-five miles from Mexico City, Ramírez sent four oxen to the his artillery commander to help pull a howitzer out of an overflowing stream. The oxen failed, and the artillerymen had to leave the valuable weapon in the water. The next day Ramírez sent twenty men and several additional oxen,

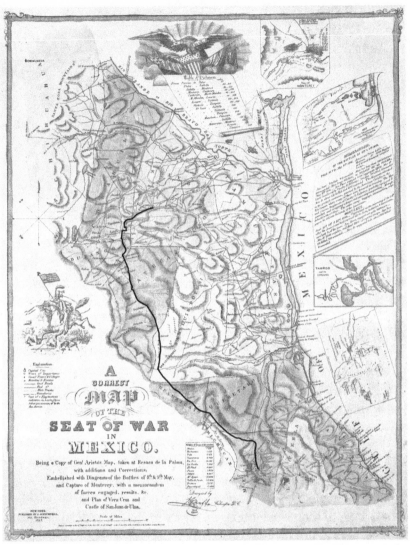

Northern Mexico theater, 1846. In this map of central, northern, and eastern Mexico, one can see the journey that Manuel Balbontin and the other brigades took from Mexico City to Monterrey via San Luis Potosí. Balbontin and later Santa Anna took the treacherous desert road from San Luis Potosí to La Encarnación, then marched north to Saltillo and northeast to Monterrey. Map by Joseph Goldsborough Bruff. Courtesy of the Virginia Garrett Cartographic History Library, Special Collections, The University of Texas at Arlington Library.

which together successfully pulled the gun out of the creek. Throughout this ordeal, the infantrymen, unconcerned about the artillerymen's dilemma, continued marching.

Meanwhile events began to unfold against Paredes, who was still in Mexico City. On August 4 his enemies in Congress pronounced against him for a second time, and on this occasion their decree was supported by a Mexican political giant—Antonio Lopez de Santa Anna, the self-styled "Napoleon of the West." Santa Anna allied himself with the Federalists in order to return from his exile in Cuba. Ever the political opportunist, he saw the war against the United States as the perfect opportunity to return to Mexico and reclaim the presidency. Santa Anna, interestingly enough, had in 1836 been an avowed Centralist who collided with Federalists time and again. He preferred to consolidate power in Mexico City (mainly in his own hands) and force states to bend to the will of the presidency. He had earlier revoked the Constitution of 1824, one of the strongest measures in Mexico's history providing power to the states. Now Santa Anna joined his former enemies, promising his new Federalist friends that he would bring back the very constitution that he had earlier dissolved. But ideology was never Santa Anna's strong suit—obtaining power, especially during times of war, was his real specialty.[7]

The news of the pronunciamento rattled the marching Third Brigade. Should they continue west to Guadalajara to suppress the revolt, or march north to Monterrey? Paredes's power was now clearly in doubt, with Santa Anna involved in the anticipated coup d'état. Paredes ordered General Ramírez to stay in Celaya, a town about 170 miles due east of Guadalajara, where the road to west was intersected by one leading north to Monterrey. The president told the general that he would soon leave Mexico City to catch up with the brigade.

Ramírez held a meeting with his officers to discuss the situation. He told them that he wanted to march west to quash the revolt. Most of his officers disagreed. They thought the brigade should wait in Celaya to see how political events developed. Some of them supported the pronunciamento and were not eager to fight their countrymen. Manuel Balbontin, an artillery officer, believed that about half of the brigade supported the revolution and half did not. This divisiveness did not bode well for a military force about to go into battle against either insurgents or a well-equipped invading force. One of Mexico's finest brigades marching to defend *la patria* now had to worry about who was in power and who they would be fighting first, Mexicans or Americans. "Notwithstanding we lived like good comrades," remembered Balbontin, "the 3d Light still obeying the General's orders; but this state of affairs was liable at any moment to be fatally interrupted."[8]

This turn of events greatly concerned Nuevo Leon's anxious inhabitants. Taylor, by all accounts, was marching from Matamoros to Monterrey, and now the city might not be reinforced by the three brigades that had departed Mexico City. An uneasy Monterrey citizen described the locals' feelings. "A lot of grief has overcome the inhabitants of this department," he wrote. "It is said in this capital [Monterrey] that the First Brigade of the army under the command of Mr. García Conde was directed to go to Guadalajara instead of coming to this department, whose danger [Monterrey's] to be attacked grows closer each day."[9]

Monterrey was the largest city in northern Mexico, with 12,000–15,000 inhabitants. As the capital of one of Mexico's most industrious states, Nuevo Leon, the city served as the region's commercial center. Its proximity to San Antonio de Bexar fostered trade with Texas, the United States, Great Britain, and France. Monterrey's merchants used Tampico, a port to the east, to do business with Europe. A 500-mile-long road ran south from the Rio Grande through Monterrey, Saltillo, San Luis Potosí, and eventually to Mexico City, a vital artery connecting northern Mexico with the country's capital.

Mexicans considered Monterrey to be one of the most beautiful cities in the country. It was surrounded by the Sierra Madre Oriental Mountains, which run diagonally down the eastern side of Mexico. The mountain range bordered the city on three sides, the outskirts of town nearly reaching its spurs. Mitre Mountain stood like a wall to the west, while the Cerro de Silla Mountain ran parallel across the river to the south. On Monterrey's western outskirts, two hills, Independence and Federation, rose like gateposts, with the road from Monterrey to Saltillo running between them. Nothing could move in or out of the city from the south or west without crossing between these two heights. The abandoned Bishop's Palace sat atop Independence, providing a breathtaking view of western Monterrey.

The city lay north of the San Juan River, locally known as the Santa Catarina. As it approached the southeastern corner of Monter-

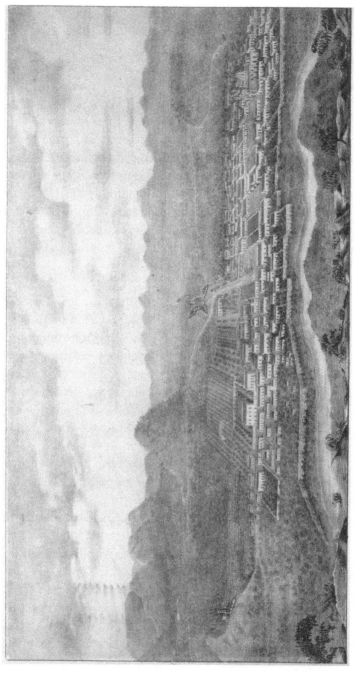

Monterrey from the south. This an accurate illustration of the city shows the Bishop's Palace (to the left), the Citadel (center), and the clump of trees where the Bosque de San Domingo was located (center right). The cathedral and the Grand Plaza are also shown just above the bottom right of the drawing. This is one of a series of illustrations by Stephen G. Hill, an enlisted soldier in the 1st Ohio Volunteers. *View of Monterey—From the Heights South of the City.* Lithograph by Silver and Rowes, after Stephen G. Hill, 1846. Courtesy of the Library of Congress Prints and Photographs Division.

rey, the river made a gradual turn to the northeast to form the rough shape of a hook, with the city located above the flat, east-to-west shank. The main plaza, anchored by a beautiful cathedral, sat in the cradle of this hook, in the southeastern quarter. The center of town was tightly packed with sturdy limestone houses and narrow streets arranged in a grid-like pattern. A narrow, cool stream called the Arroyo Santa Lucia ran west to east in northern Monterrey and separated downtown from the suburbs. El Puente del Purísima, or the Purisima Bridge, crossed the arroyo where the road from Marin entered town. A statue of the Virgin Mary sat prominently on the side of the bridge to greet people as they entered the city. The fringes of the city contained *jacales* (thatched huts), gardens, brush fences, and a few nice homes. General Arista had a palatial estate in the outer edge of northwestern Monterrey containing a beautiful garden, a lovely promenade, and gorgeous interior. A vast plain, filled with rock quarries, corn, and brush fences, occupied the area north of town.[10]

As Americans soldiers would later attest, nature had blessed Monterrey with a defensive position unmatched by any other nineteenth-century city. If a skilled military engineer of the time could move mountains and rivers, he would probably design a city much like Monterrey. One surgeon probably did not exaggerate much when he said, "This town is probably the strongest position to conquer on the continent."[11]

Preparations for Monterrey's defense began in June, when the governor of Nuevo Leon, Juan Nepomuceno de la Garza y Evia, took steps to create a local militia. He called on every Nuevo Leon citizen between the ages of eighteen and fifty, with the exception of priests and servants, to "rise to the defense of the department [Nuevo Leon] and the national territory invaded by the enemy forces." The governor required each town to fill a quota of militia based on its population. His proclamation also requested that the new citizen-soldiers provide their own guns if possible. Neighboring governors published similar proclamations. The governor of Tamaulipas, whose state had already been invaded by Taylor, likewise required citizens between the ages of eighteen and fifty to rise to the defense of the territory. He addressed the city halls, town councils, and mayors in an edict: "since the day of the publication of this decree, in your respective towns, open a registry of all citizens understood in section 1 [males between eighteen and fifty] . . . to be sent to the government of the Department with their own arms and horses."[12]

Although the alcaldes—town mayors—attempted to meet the quotas set by the governors, they had trouble rallying men to join the militia. Many of their townspeople were farmers who depended on their harvests to feed their families. If left untended, their crops would perish and their families would starve. But farmers had other commercial reasons to avoid the call up. General Taylor needed food for his 9,000 troops, and his policy was for his men to pay whatever price local merchants demanded for their fruits, vegetables, and other supplies. One company of American soldiers could purchase a month's production of fruits and vegetables. Local vendors raised their prices to take advantage of this unprecedented commercial opportunity. Other townspeople were reluctant to join the militia because they did not want to leave their families alone to deal with "Los Indios Barbaros," the "Barbaric Indians." Texas was not the only state that suffered from Comanche raids. Tamaulipas, Coahuila, and Nuevo Leon all suffered such attacks too. Newspaper reports are dotted with articles about Indians attacking priests, alcaldes, and ranchers in northern Mexico. The commander of one militia unit in Vallecillo, Nuevo Leon, told the governor that men were deserting from his company because "they did not want to abandon their families at their homes that they inhabit because of the hostility of the barbaric Indians."[13]

Perhaps the biggest challenge the alcaldes faced was that many of the locals were not as devoted to *la patria* as their region's political and military leaders. Most of the north's farmers or townspeople had little interaction with Mexico City, over five hundred miles away. When they did meet with officials from the capital, they were usually forced to donate supplies to the destitute northern army. The underfunded force, which often marched through the region on its way to Texas, took whatever it needed from the farmers and promised to compensate them later. The farmers were rarely repaid.

Francisco Mejía, who took over command in July, set about fortifying Monterrey. He proposed a seven-point plan to ready the city for combat. First he ordered giant blocks of stone, from which to build forts and redoubts, delivered to the city. He sought to remove all the mules and oxen from towns to the north, so the Americans could not confiscate them as pack animals, and asked that all area firearms be collected in the city.[14]

The general also made two demands of his engineers. First, he ordered them to erect stout positions from which to fight a defensive battle within Monterrey. The idea was not bad, considering that Taylor had just handily defeated a strong Mexican army on the open plains of South Texas. Maybe holing up in a city would tip the balance toward the Mexicans this time. U.S. artillery, which ruled the day on the Palo Alto flats, would have difficulty maneuvering in a city's narrow streets. Second, Mejía instructed his engineers to strengthen the northern and eastern parts of the city, anticipating that the Americans would approach from the north. This was a reasonable judgment by any account, for Taylor had to descend on the city from that direction unless he marched hundreds of miles out of his way. Two of Mexico's best engineers, Lieutenant Colonel Zuloaga, assisted by José María Carrasco, implemented Mejía's directions.

Carrasco, who was in charge of fortifying the eastern defenses, centered his efforts on raising a strong redoubt in northeastern Monterrey known as El Fortín del Tenería (the Tannery Fort, referred to hereafter as Fort Teneria). The new stronghold was located just north of where the Arroyo Santa Lucia emptied into the Santa Catarina and had a dominating view of the eastern side of the city's northern plain. The Santa Catarina protected it from attack on its eastern and southern sides, while an old distillery covered the fort's rear. The fully constructed post could hold 150–200 men and three cannon. It was a formidable position. Carrasco also began construction on a second, smaller fort located three hundred yards southwest of Fort Teneria. Known as El Fortin del Rincón del Diablo (the Fort of the Devil's Corner, referred to hereafter as Fort Diablo), it was located on a hill on the south side of the Arroyo Santa Lucia. Although smaller than Fort Teneria, its higher elevation provided the garrison a clear view of northeastern Monterrey. Cannon stationed there would be able to support Fort Teneria and other points in the area with artillery fire. The garrison, once completed, could hold 150–200 men and three cannon.

In north-central Monterrey Mejía's engineers began fortifying the Purisima Bridge, west of Fort Teneria. The bridge was the primary entryway into the city from the north, and the general wanted to ensure that no one could cross it. His men built a masonry-fortified *tête du pont* (a breastwork that guards a bridge) on the south side to control access to the bridge. Two smaller breastworks were erected on the south side of the canal between there and Fort Teneria to prevent Taylor's men from fording the canal in the open space between the two works.

Mejía knew that he would need a strong fort to guard the northern plain. His engineers decided to fortify an old, unfinished church that sat on a small hill in the middle of the plain. The church, which they called the Citadel, was twenty feet high and almost completely black from age and neglect. It was held up by twelve pillars, each of which was twelve feet thick at their base. The garrison, which was two hundred yards from the city, would be on its own once the battle started. Construction soon began on eleven-foot walls to surround the Citadel. Men covered the walls in gray tufa, a soft, rocklike substance, to help absorb artillery shot. They also started building four salients to ensure that their cannons could fire in any direction onto the plain and even into the city. Soldiers began digging a deep moat around the fort and constructing cannon platforms for the guns. A large gateway and drawbridge sat on its southern side, facing toward the city. The Citadel would eventually have embrasures for thirty-two cannon (eight per salient) and could hold four hundred men.

The Mexicans also fortified the western side of the city, especially the two tall hills dominating the western approach. On Independence Hill, engineers erected makeshift walls around a massive stone structure known as the Bishop's Palace and built a priest cap—a V-shaped redan—that faced east into the city. Cannon platforms were mounted in the priest cap because engineers expected Taylor to assault the city first and then move west toward the hill. The palace fort, once completed, could mount four guns and hold two hundred men. On the western end of Independence Hill, opposite the Bishop's Palace, soldiers erected a small sandbag redoubt called Fort Libertad. They did not see the need for a stronger fortification since the terrain below was almost perpendicular; it was unlikely that the Americans would assault the hill from this direction. South across the river, soldiers built two structures on Federation Hill. On its western side they erected a small redoubt, called Fort Federation, that could hold sixty men and mount two guns. East of this and closer to the city, they built a more-solid stone fort called El Soldado, which overlooked almost all of western Monterrey.[15]

Despite the sophisticated plans of the engineers, work on Monterrey's defenses proceeded slowly. Mejía did not have enough laborers to raise the walls, carry the stone, and dig the moats that the elaborate plan required. To remedy the situation, the general demanded that all bricklayers and construction workers report to Engineer Reyes to assist building redoubts and breastworks. Many did turn out to help, but Reyes could not find enough tools to equip them.[16]

While Mejía was preparing Monterrey for attack, Balbontin and the Third Brigade were waiting in Celaya, debating whether to defend the nation from an invader or fight their own rebelling countrymen in Guadalajara. On August 9 the decision was made for them. Paredes, who never left Mexico City as planned, was overthrown. José María Salas, the new Mexican president, ordered the brigade to march north to oppose the Americans. General Ramírez, a Paredes supporter, took stock of the situation and finally declared for the new government on August 11. Many soldiers, however, did not support the new regime and deserted in Celaya or during the ensuing march. But most average soldiers like Balbontin probably were happy just to have orders—any orders. Now they could mentally prepare for fighting Taylor's army instead of putting down an insurrection.

One of Salas's first moves was to place Maj. Gen. Don Pedro de Ampudia in command of the Army of the North. Ampudia was with the First Brigade, which was slightly ahead of the Third Brigade on the road to Monterrey. Once the general entered the city, he would take control of its defenses. Ampudia's appointment spawned controversy throughout Nuevo Leon. Many of the north's political and military leaders did not believe that he could lead the army to victory. In appearance Ampudia looked the part of the successful general. He was tall, with a twirling mustache, a flowing goatee, and broad shoulders. When mounted on his horse, Ampudia's bearing gave the common soldier confidence. In truth, however, his military skills did not match his soldierly visage. Ampudia rose through the ranks by doing the dirty work of some key Mexican caudillos, who overlooked his obvious abuses of power and deficient military skills. In one illustrative case, his men captured a ship containing a rebellious Mexican general and fourteen of his men looking to seize the town of Tabasco. Ampudia ordered the men shot, boiled their heads in oil, and hung them in iron cages throughout Tabasco to discourage any other attempts at rebellion.[17]

Nuevo Leon's governor asked the central government to reconsider this decision. He declared that the northerners blamed Ampudia—not Arista—for the losses at Palo Alto and Resaca de la Palma. The governor pointed out that a good general should have certain attributes, including having "sound judgment, knowledge of [military] instruction and prestige among his subordinates." Ampudia, he noted, possessed none of these traits. But this was not the first time that northern political leaders weighed in on Ampudia's appointment to command. Prior to Palo Alto and Resaca de la Palma, they had asked then-President Paredes to demote the general and replace him with Arista. Most northern leaders supported Arista, who was born in the region and was better acquainted with its people and terrain. He also had the reputation of being one of the best cavalry officers in the world.[18]

Ampudia heard the rumblings about his appointment and felt compelled to "protest before God" those who tarred his character. He wrote a statement that was published in the *Monitor Republicano*, a Mexico City–based newspaper, to set the record straight about his role in the battles of May 8 and 9. The now-humble general discussed how he took quick and energetic measures at those battles while in command of the army. But he noted that he could only do so much once demoted to second in command—it was then up to the new commander to lead the army to victory. He also reminded readers about how he had defeated the Texans at Mier in 1842 and had been with Santa Anna in an earlier campaign against the breakaway region. Wrapping up, Ampudia declared that "[i]mpartiality has guided my pen," leaving it to the reader to judge his character on the basis of the "real" facts.[19]

Yet for the residents of northern Mexico, there was bigger news than Ampudia's appointment. They still were not sure if the three Mexico City brigades were coming to Monterrey or were going to detour toward Guadalajara. On August 8 General Conde relieved their worries in a published letter in which he gave his support to the new government and announced that his troops would be coming to aid Ampudia's defense of Monterrey. Newspapers chronicled every step taken by Conde's brigade. Locals devoured these reports since Taylor was supposedly moving fast and they wondered if the rein-

Maj. Gen. Don Pedro de Ampudia. Displaying a soldierly bearing with a twirling mustache and heavily adorned uniform, Ampudia's military expertise did not live up to his image. The general made critical errors at Monterrey that put his men in a bad position from the start of the battle. Courtesy of Special Collections, The University of Texas at Arlington Library.

forcements would arrive in time. The *Tampico Esperanza*, in one of many stories chronicling the First Brigade's movements, declared that Conde was in La Hacienda del Peñasco, just north of San Luis Potosí, in order to "to save to the Nation from the shameful state in which [it] is found." The people believed that they needed these men if Mexico had any chance of defeating Taylor. They called the brigades the "Redeemers" in hopes that they would redeem the national honor lost at Palo Alto and Resaca de la Palma. They judged—correctly—that the downtrodden Army of the North, short on morale and supplies, could not handle the Americans on its own. Northerners referred to these soldiers as "wooden mouths" because they had been defeated so badly that they had lost their ability to eat.[20]

On August 17 Ramírez's Third Brigade, which was behind Conde's troops by a few days, arrived at San Luis Potosí, about halfway between Mexico City and Monterrey. The brigade included two 12-pound cannons, one 8-pound cannon, and three 7-inch howitzers, which could change the course of battle in the north. This artillery would be vital in protecting Monterrey's buildings, streets, hills, and bridges. Intelligence showed that Taylor was rapidly marching toward Monterrey, so the men dumped or destroyed much of their excess baggage so they could quickly march north. But this was a bad place to dump supplies. Between San Luis Potosí and Saltillo, the brigade's next destination, stretched two hundred miles of arid, unforgiving desert. The barren landscape did not contain well-stocked haciendas from which the soldiers might find food and water. And the brigade had to cross this sandy deathtrap in August, the hottest month of the year. The men marched through the heat to small ranches like Hacienda de Charcos, Hacienda de Solís, and Matchuala. "Today we have marched 16 leagues," Manuel Balbontin wrote, "the brigade arrived late and very tired. On the 29th to Cedral, where we found the water to be extremely bad, and on the 30th to Noria de las Animas, fifteen leagues farther." At the next stop Balbontin scribbled in his diary, "Water scarce and brackish, no rations." On September 3 the soldiers finally found water and shade at Aguanueva ("New Water"), an appropriately named village. "This place, with its deliciously shady grove and its wealth of pure water," Balbontin recorded, "appears beautiful in contrast with the long, arid, and monotonous district we have left behind." The men then marched a short way to Saltillo, where they rested for a day. They had finally arrived in northern Mexico.[21]

Three days later the Third Brigade marched to Monterrey via the Rinconada Pass, a winding, steep-walled valley. On the way into the city, the men encountered some soldiers from the defeated Army of the North. Apparently they avoided talking about the May defeats because the only discussion Balbontin records is one about how the Mexican 7th Cavalry had defeated the Texans four years earlier during Gen. Adrian Woll's "reinvasion" of Texas. Clearly the northerners were trying to think about better times. Both the First and Second Brigades had already arrived in Monterrey by the time the Third arrived. Mejía, at least publicly, welcomed the arrival of the reinforcements, even if it meant that he soon would be replaced as commander. In a public communication he wrote: "Tomorrow arrives from Saltillo the General in Chief don Pedro de Ampudia with the First Brigade that left the capital of the Republic and accelerated its march in order to have the opportunity to be in the theater of operations. . . . [W]e will have in this place more soldiers of the line, abundant artillery, munitions, and all types of necessary elements for war. . . . [T]he Supreme Government [in Mexico City] hurried its resources and marched to this frontier to defend the sacred honor of the Republic."[22]

Ampudia arrived on September 1. The general, eager to revive his waning political reputation, was thrilled that authorities in Mexico City accepted his advice to defend Monterrey. General Mejía agreed with Ampudia. If the Americans controlled Monterrey, he argued, they would also hold the Rinconada Pass, and it would be impossible to drive the invaders out of such a strong position. Mejía also pointed out that it would be "dishonorable" to give up such an important city without a fight. But Santa Anna, who had arrived back in the country from exile in Cuba, argued that the city should not be defended. Instead he thought that a giant army should mass against Taylor for one big, spectacular battle; that army, unsurprisingly, should be led by Santa Anna himself. The government eventually accepted Ampudia and Mejía's rationale. Indeed, the loss of Monterrey would be a severe blow to the national authority, which was trying desperately to prevent all of northern Mexico from falling into Taylor's hands.[23]

When Ampudia arrived at Monterrey, he surveyed the elaborate fortifications that the engineers were busily constructing. He agreed with Mejía's plan to fight a defensive battle and supported the placement of key forts within the city. The general also believed that it was "absolutely indispensable," as he wrote to Mejía, to finish these forts as soon as possible. Ampudia took a more forceful approach than his predecessor to rally the countryside to the city's defense. He declared martial law and demanded that anyone with a shovel, pickaxe, or crowbar assist in building fortifications without compensation. He also prohibited venders from raising the price of corn, meat, and flour. Horses, in particular, were in short supply in Ampudia's army. The Army of the North included large cavalry units, but many of their animals had been killed in South Texas or were lost on the march to Monterrey. The brigades from Mexico City were filled with infantry and artillery but had few horses or cavalry units. Ampudia needed all the horses he could get and forced local ranchers to hand over their horses for ten pesos per animal, which the government would supposedly pay later.[24]

Ampudia's next move was to appoint General Ramírez to oversee the construction of Monterrey's fortifications. This decision was a curious one since Ramírez, an infantry officer, had no engineering experience. Perhaps Ampudia wanted to reward the general, a former Paredes supporter, with an important post in order to win over the Third Brigade. Whatever the rationale, the decision was unpopular with the troops, who knew that Ramírez lacked the skills to construct elaborate fortifications. Balbontin, who respected his brigade commander, wrote that "Ramírez was an officer thoroughly versed in the tactics of light or line infantry, as well as in the maneuvering and fighting of a regiment of cavalry, but not at all acquainted with the science of fortification."[25]

Through the first few weeks of September, it became clear that Ampudia had enemies scattered throughout his officer corps. Cliques developed, with some supporting Arista, others Mejía, and some Ampudia. Many veteran officers in the Army of the North believed that Ampudia should have acted more aggressively against Fort Texas and that he had been slow in coming to Arista's aid at Resaca de la Palma. Others believed that Arista and Mejía were simply better generals than Ampudia. They were probably right.

Even if he did not have his officers' complete support, Ampudia took harsh measures with the local civilian population to prepare for combat. He scribbled decree after decree during September. One of his first measures was to demand that the alcaldes of seven nearby towns evacuate their citizens and remove any cattle, horses, or other supplies that the American army might seize for their own purposes. He also demanded that the mayor of Monterrey order all local plantation and ranch owners to provide corn, meat, beans, and any other items the troops might need. If any refused, the general would consider them disloyal. He also reiterated that anyone caught assisting the American army would be summarily shot.[26]

Ampudia also tried to rally the alcaldes and townspeople in the outlying areas. On September 3 he addressed all of the alcaldes of

Nuevo Leon to ask for their assistance in repulsing Taylor. "In order to have success," Ampudia wrote, "it is necessary that the inhabitants display valor and patriotism. It is important to call the townspeople together so that they can carry out all of the damage possible against an enemy that with so much injustice invades us." The general did not just ask for their assistance, though, he demanded it. During the second week of September, he required Monterrey's locals —mainly the poor who lived in the suburbs—to demolish their jacales and cut down the trees and fences that surrounded the city so that his men in nearby forts would have clear fields of fire. Militarily the measure made sense, but he probably alienated some residents with the move.[27]

On the night of September 15, Ampudia received a hefty boost for his efforts from an unlikely source—Mexico's Independence Day. The country celebrated its *grito*, or independence, from Spain on September 16 (though celebrations began the night before). If there was any holiday that could rile a population against Taylor, this was it. One historian has described the effect the celebration had on Monterrey's population: "[A] night [the 15th] when our most tender recollections of the independence and home were revived. The military bands announced the solemn hour in which our existence, as a nation, was proclaimed. All bowed to the sentiment of patriotism, and in raising their minds to enthusiasm forgot everything around, and desired combat for revenge and for glory."[28]

Gradually the labor force grew, and Ampudia began to make headway building breastworks, redoubts, and forts throughout the city. On September 18 the governor of Nuevo Leon wrote the general that two hundred workmen and prisoners had been provided to help with the fortifications. Another mayor reported that his town's corn could not be picked because all of his farmers were busy constructing forts in Monterrey.[29]

The militia also grew, and by late August Col. Felipe Sepulveda, commanding general of the auxiliaries, had collected 460 men. But Sepulveda lacked equipment, having only 130 rifles for these men. The government in Mexico City had banned the import of firearms because they were concerned about rebellion, so few farmers had any personal rifles to use. Not until August 28 did the government repeal the ban in an attempt to bolster both local and national forces. Along with the lack of arms, Sepulveda also did not have any band equipment, and his men knew nothing about military procedures.[30]

Despite these deficiencies, on Independence Day Ampudia addressed his soldiers in one of his many proclamations. He said that the enemy had only twenty-five hundred cowardly men who had no military discipline. His own troops would fight from strong fortifications and if necessary would charge the Americans with their bayonets. "Soldiers," Ampudia declared, "three large virtues form a worthy soldier: discipline, persevering through fatigue, and courage. The one who in these moments deserts the flag will be a traitor to the country. Our nation and even the foreigners are alert to your behavior. The question right now is whether we will save our independence or lose it forever and this depends on your management." He closed with the words "victory or death."[31]

3

MATAMOROS AND THE ARRIVAL OF THE VOLUNTEERS

"The volunteers are playing the devil and disgracing the country in Matamoros."

Maj. Philip Barbour

While Pedro de Ampudia was fortifying Monterrey, Zachary Taylor was establishing his headquarters in Matamoros. Upon securing the Mexican town, Taylor instructed his regulars to camp beyond its limits. The men grumbled, longing to sleep in Matamoros's houses. A sturdy structure with a floor, walls, and a roof was elegance compared to sleeping in tents in the chaparral. But the general did not want his soldiers bothering the local citizenry. "Instead of taking possession of their houses for our men," one soldier complained, "we remain under miserable canvas, which affords no protection from the storm, and scarcely shade to protect the soldiers from the noonday sun."[1]

Taylor required his men to purchase their supplies from local vendors instead of relying on the age-old wartime habit of seizing local provisions. He even instructed his officers to pay rent if they occupied a house or other building in the city. Local vendors loved Taylor's policy, charging exorbitant prices for their fresh eatables knowing that the Americans were obliged to pay. The high prices prompted one soldier to wonder if Mexico wanted to end a war that was making them so much money. "They say our soldiers treat them much better than their own," wrote Lt. John Sedgwick to his father, "that we pay them for everything, while they [the Mexicans] take everything they want without it. In fact, I think we treat them too well, that they will like us so well, they will petition for annexation."[2]

Indeed, Taylor was a benevolent occupier, as the U.S. government had told him to be. Secretary of War William Marcy instructed him to treat the inhabitants with respect. "The President has seen, with much satisfaction," he informed the general, "the civility and kindness with which you have treated your prisoners, and all the inhabitants with whom you have come in contact." Polk and Marcy believed that befriending the locals might make the national government more likely to negotiate the boundary issue. If Taylor's army wreaked havoc by plundering and marauding, Mexico City would be more reluctant to negotiate an end to a war with "barbarians." U.S. authorities wanted Mexican officials to believe that peace was always within reach.[3]

But the Texans despised these friendly ways. "It was such inhuman brutes," one later wrote, referring to a group of Mexican partisans that had killed some U.S. soldiers, that "General Taylor tried to conciliate and enrich. The Texans did not admire the policy. It cost too many good lives."[4]

Taylor did not disagree with Marcy's directive, though he did not appreciate being micromanaged. He needed good relations with the locals so they would provide food, water, and intelligence to his men. If he seized local supplies, civilians would leave the area and force Taylor's men to forage the countryside for food. The general now had readily at hand all of the supplies his troops needed, though at exorbitant prices. But Taylor did not mind seizing public property, including thousands of cigars owned by the local government, allocating two barrels to each company. "Such a happy set of smoking dogs never were seen, and all at the expense of the enemy," observed one contented soldier. Taylor also distributed four thousand decks of playing cards so his troops could play "monte," a popular Mexican card game.[5]

Despite these indulgences, the reminders of war were present throughout the city. Mexican corpses washed onto the river banks for weeks, and as the Rio Grande fell, some bodies were found entangled in the trees lining the banks. Houses and buildings in Matamoros were also filled with three hundred wounded Mexican soldiers Arista had abandoned during his evacuation. Every street contained a makeshift hospital that housed soldiers recovering from their wounds. Paroled Mexican soldiers walked freely through the town, for it was too much trouble to do anything about them. They drank heavily at the local establishments but posed little threat to the Americans except for the occasional verbal insult.[6]

Matamoros itself disappointed the U.S. soldiers, who expected a more magnificent city. Two-story brick houses lined the streets. "The walls are very massive and their windows barred," observed one soldier, "so that one thinks they were built for defense." Maj. Philip Barbour could not believe how durable the houses were. He saw one that was hit by fourteen cannonballs from Fort Texas but showed few signs of damage. Strong double doors guarded the homes' entrances.[7]

Although some paroled soldiers were probably sending information to Ampudia, a more serious problem were actual spies, who were sent by the Mexican general to ascertain Taylor's troop numbers and report on their movements. These men ambled throughout the city, often disguised as fruit traders, and took diligent notes about what they observed. Taylor never instituted a system to identify and capture them, and when he was lucky enough to arrest one, he usually just paroled him or gave him a short sentence at Fort Brown (as Fort Texas was renamed in honor of Maj. Jacob Brown). One Texan private watched two suspicious vendors peddling cakes and thought that they were probably spies. "The Texans were naturally better aware of the treacherous character of the Mexicans and more suspicious of them," he wrote. He followed the two "vendors" to their horses, and sure enough they began jotting down notes about Taylor's forces. The Texan arrested the men and brought them to Taylor's headquarters, where the adjutant searched them and found a detailed memorandum of the camp and the number of American troops. Taylor ordered them imprisoned at Fort Brown for only a few days. The general's gracious attitude shocked the Texans, who believed that spies should be imprisoned or executed, just like the Mexicans would do to any American spy they might capture. One infamous Mexican spy, Jeronimo Valdez, would be apprehended and released numerous times during the course of the campaign.[8]

When not on duty or interacting with the Mexicans, U.S. soldiers often thought of family back in the States. Major Barbour passed much of his time in Matamoros by writing his wife, Mattie. He hated their separation, though he knew that he had to carry out his duty to his country. While in Matamoros, he told her that he had quit smoking and chewing tobacco: "The commendation I will receive for it [quitting smoking] will amply repay me for the inconvenience I now suffer from my abstinence." Barbour joked that since he did not drink or smoke, he could lead a Sunday school back in the United States. In July Barbour's spirits soared when Taylor gave him a two-week pass to visit his wife in Galveston. "Never in my life have I enjoyed so much happiness as my visit afforded me," he wrote. "The recollection of it will live with me forever." Once the visit was over, Mattie hated to see her husband leave. "Yesterday was, I may say, a day of horror, my dearest husband was obliged from duty to leave me. . . . [T]his last meeting was a pleasure unexpected to us both and will ever remain a bright spot in our existence." Barbour was more fortunate than his comrades, most of whom never saw their loved ones until they returned home from the war.[9]

A few weeks after the regulars entered the city, William Jenkins Worth arrived. Worth, who started the march with Taylor in Corpus Christi, had left the army just prior to Palo Alto and Resaca de la Palma over a seniority dispute. As a brevet brigadier general, Worth believed that he outranked Taylor's other senior commander, Col. David Twiggs. The question was important because whoever was second in command would replace Taylor if he was incapacitated, died, or recalled. Congress had never articulated the authority and privileges of the brevet rank, so each officer weighed in with their own arguments to Taylor, who should have decided the question of seniority. The issue came to a head during a military review in the summer of 1846, and Taylor, unwilling to upset either man, deferred to Washington to take up the matter. At that time regulations stipulated that a brevet could be awarded when an officer performed courageously in battle, but not being a promotion, it did not come with additional pay nor entitle the officer to command at the higher level. Thus, Worth commanded as a colonel, not as a general, and Twiggs had more time in command as a colonel (albeit only one month by commission). President Polk therefore ruled that Twiggs had seniority (meaning that Twiggs would be Taylor's second in command), and Worth resigned in protest.[10]

Brig. Gen. William Jenkins Worth. Soldiers commented that Worth held a commanding presence even though he was not unusually tall or muscular. His actions against western Monterey helped Taylor win the battle and restored to Worth the reputation he had lost when he quit the army months earlier. Courtesy of Special Collections, The University of Texas at Arlington Library.

Worth joined the army as a private during the War of 1812, fighting at the famous battles of Chippewa and Lundy's Lane. He was seriously wounded in the latter action when grapeshot hit him in the thigh, and it took him almost a year to recover. But in that battle he had caught the eye of a senior officer, Winfield Scott, who promoted him quickly up the ranks. Eight years later Worth accepted the prestigious position of commandant of cadets at West Point, where he was responsible for training cadets in infantry tactics. He was perfect for the position because of his vast experience both during peacetime and in combat. One of his first measures at the academy was to teach his students what real marching was like, taking them off the school's grounds and marching them hundreds of miles around New England. He demanded perfection in their cadences and eventually transformed his students into a well-skilled infantry corps. Soldiers like Robert E. Lee learned under Worth at West Point and respected him for his detailed instruction. Years after West Point, Worth was sent to Florida to command a regiment charged with capturing an elusive band of militant Seminole Indians. He quickly changed the lackadaisical approach of his predecessor and put his men into a frenzy of activity. "My headquarters will be in the saddle," he informed his men. Usually the summer heat kept U.S. forces in cool quarters in Florida, but Worth would have none of that. During his first summer, Worth ordered his troops into the heart of Florida to destroy the Seminoles' crops and settlements. Although most of his men thought that he was unreasonable, the campaign succeeded. Most of the Indians surrendered except for a small group, which the Americans defeated in a bloody action at Palatlakaha. President Tyler awarded Worth a brevet to brigadier general for his actions in Florida.[11]

Now Worth, with all of his combat experience, was back with an army in the field, livid with himself that he had missed two major battles. Soldiers were afraid to be put under his command because they believed that he would do anything, including sacrificing his own men, to regain his reputation. Worth realized his mistake and stayed mainly in his tent, sulking, after his arrival at Matamoros. "It is unpleasant to see such a gallant spirit subdued," Barbour observed, "but he only has himself to blame." Zachary Taylor did not need to worry about his own seniority, though, learning on July 15 that President Polk had brevetted him to major general for his performance at Palo Alto and Resaca de la Palma. The troops cheered Old Zack when the news circulated though camp.[12]

As the regulars settled into Matamoros, volunteers poured into recruiting sites in the United States for service with the Army of Occupation. These men had responded to three different calls for volunteers (from Taylor, Polk, and General Gaines) and totaled perhaps more than 35,000 men. So many men responded that it was difficult for Taylor to track their numbers. Eventually 8,000 volunteers arrived in the Rio Grande valley (not all of Gaines's 11,000 volunteers departed Louisiana for the frontlines) and joined Taylor's command. Some of the first volunteers arrived in May 1845, including some Texas infantrymen from Galveston. One month later, in June and July, Gaines's Louisianans began streaming in by the hundreds, ready for a fight. "Point us to your Mexicans," some would say as they disembarked.[13]

From Texas Taylor had requested two cavalry and two infantry regiments. While Gov. J. Pinckney Henderson easily raised the two cavalry units, he could not fill two infantry regiments. He had cautioned Taylor when he made the request that Texans did not like to fight on foot. Even raising a single infantry regiment proved difficult.

Col. Jack Hays and Col. George Wood commanded the two mounted regiments, known as the 1st and 2nd Regiments of Texas Mounted Rifles. Hays's men were a tough breed. They were known as the "Western Texas Rangers" because they hailed from western counties, which in 1846 was rough frontier land. The counties straddled what is now the center of the state, but at that time they were the far western edge of white settlement. The result was that these men battled Indians and bandits on a regular basis just to preserve their way of life. Wood's men were known as the "East Texas Rangers" because the men hailed from the more "civilized" eastern counties. This outfit contained many farmers, doctors, lawyers, and other professionals; the colonel himself was a Texas senator. Most of Wood's men, and some of Hays's, had never been Texas Rangers, but the "Ranger" nicknames stayed with their regiments throughout the campaign. Col. Albert Sidney Johnston commanded the lone Texas infantry regiment. He believed that his men would make the United States proud. His adjutant wrote: "In taking the command Col Johnston again takes occasion to express the high sense of honour conferred upon him.... [E]very exertion he is capable of will be employed to make the regiment what Texas expects it to be, one of the best in the service of the country."[14]

Taylor appointed Henderson as a major general, even though technically the governor should not have commanded at that rank since he only had three regiments (instead of the four required for that position). "I deem it best to retain the governor in the capacity of

major general," Taylor, who probably understood the political importance of coddling Henderson, advised the adjutant general, "and beg
that he may be recognized, with his appropriate staff." Any lower
rank would embarrass the governor, and Taylor needed his support
for the upcoming campaign.[15]

President Polk had also called on states to provide volunteers
under the authority of the May 1846 act. These men, Alabamans,
Tennesseans, Mississippians, and other adventure-seeking citizens,
arrived in South Texas in June and July. Taylor debated what to
do with all of these volunteers. He did not have enough steamboats,
wagons, and rations to sustain them. More problematic were the
thousands of Louisianans illegally called up by Gaines and only
enrolled for three months—Taylor could not count on them being
around when battle commenced. A sympathetic War Department
understood his dilemma and gave the commander the authority either to extend the Louisianans' tours to twelve months or to muster
them out if they refused to lengthen their enlistments. Taylor intended to use this authority as soon as their terms expired.[16]

The volunteers eventually encamped together near Buritta, a
small village fifteen miles upstream from the Rio Grande's mouth.
Taylor situated them on a high ridge along the northern side of the
Rio Grande across from the village. He hoped that the elevated site,
later named Camp Belknap, would spare the newcomers from illness.
Rain poured incessantly on the men, who lacked the proper protective tents. Mosquitoes, thriving in the rain-fed lagoons that formed
near the campsite, attacked them day and night.[17]

The weeks of downtime tested the volunteers' limited patience.
They had not enlisted to camp out for two weeks and live under
extreme hardships, all without ever seeing a Mexican soldier. Lt.
George Gordon Meade observed that the volunteers were "in a state of
mutiny because they are not marched right off to meet the enemy."
One of Taylor's artillerists, Lt. John Reynolds, agreed. He wrote his
sister that the volunteers hated the idleness of camp, the hot weather,
and the marches. "I have no doubt they will fight well enough when it
comes to that but that is not one half of what we have to undergo in
the field." Often they took out their frustrations on their fellow volunteers. A heated argument between two regiments about the proper
owner of a plump catfish prompted those from Ohio and Baltimore
to line up against one another with loaded firearms. Col. Alexander

Mitchell, commander of the Ohio volunteers, cut the Baltimore fisherman with a sword, to which men screamed, "Turn out, Baltimoreans!" Lt. Col. John B. Weller of the Ohio regiment and Capt. John Kenly from the Baltimore volunteers stood between the lines and convinced the men to return to their camp. But bitterness between the two regiments lingered throughout the war. As for the regular soldiers who passed through Buritta, they could not believe the volunteers' lack of discipline. Lt. D. H. Hill observed, "They had driven away the inhabitants, taken possession of their houses, and were emulating each other in making beasts of themselves." For their part the volunteers often shouted obscenities at the regulars passing through.[18]

The volunteers relished their short visits to Matamoros as small vacations from the drudgery of camp life. American privateers filled the plaza with U.S.-style establishments, including theaters, hotels, bars, and billiard rooms. Volunteers and regulars alike guzzled mescal and tequila at the local groggeries. While entertaining for the soldiers, this ready access to liquor fueled depredations against the town's citizens. Most volunteers lacked military discipline when sober, so being drunk only aggravated their freewheeling ways. Reports often surfaced of volunteers murdering, raping, or beating Mexicans. One soldier who was on guard duty regularly believed that there was a murder a day in Matamoros, usually involving the volunteers either killing Mexicans or each other. "The volunteers are playing the devil and disgracing the country in Matamoros," Major Barbour wrote in his journal. A local American newspaper admonished the volunteers to behave themselves: "Have a little patience boys, there will be something for you to do yet. Keep quiet, and for Heaven sake keep out of the filthy Guard House, which you can easily do by keeping sober, observing discipline, and behaving as peaceable and orderly American citizens. The express commands of the General are that the Mexican citizens of Matamoros are in nowise to be molested or insulted. They are in your power now, and it would be unmanly and ungenerous to insult their misfortunes. In one brief word, be Americans."[19]

Most of the U.S. troops, sharing the views of many Americans of the time, looked down on the Mexican people as an inferior, mongrel race. Even educated regulars like Barbour believed that Mexicans were a "half-civilized people" or "semi-savages," as some called them. "Miserable, ignorant, [and] filthy" were the words one volunteer officer used to describe them. Such men believed that the Anglo-Saxon race was culturally, politically, and morally superior to other races, especially the Mexicans. Their negative views of Mexico's people extended to the country's army too, which they believed was weak and would be easily defeated. Lt. Napoleon Jackson Tecumseh Dana, who thought much of himself and Taylor's army, was the most blunt about Mexico's ability to win the war: "If she has not got fighting enough already, we have some of the biggest kinds of whippings in store for her, and if she makes the game last much longer, we will not have the Rio Grande for a boundary but the chain of mountains called the Sierra Madre." Others like Pvt. Barna Upton, an enlisted soldier in the 3rd Infantry, had more sensible views. He knew victory was certain, but he believed, "the disadvantages are on our side: the American Army will be unacquainted with the country and wearied with the march. Besides, you know the wolf fights hardest in his den."[20]

The arrival of the volunteers had pained Taylor. He expected his men to fight and to obey orders, and he knew from past experience that such amateur soldiers often did neither. He was probably also worried about how they would perform in action. At the Battle of Okeechobee in 1837, where Taylor commanded, the Missouri volunteers, who composed 20 percent of his total force, fled at the start of the fighting. Instead of reforming behind the regulars as instructed, the Missourians retreated until they were out of harm's way. Taylor's solution now was to march the volunteers as soon as possible. The quicker he could get them away from Matamoros and toward enemy forces, the better they would behave. He understood that volunteers sought adventure and gallantry and did not want to endure the hardships of camp life.[21]

But Taylor respected some of his volunteers, especially those led by West Pointers. Roughly half of the academy's students who had graduated between 1812 and 1846 had already retired from the army. The mid-1830s transportation boom prompted many academy-educated engineers to pursue more lucrative careers in the private sector. But these men could not resist the call to military service during wartime, and they retained the knowledge and skills necessary to develop their volunteers into a disciplined unit of soldiers. Jefferson Davis and Albert Sidney Johnston, both West Point graduates who had left the army years earlier, trained and drilled their soldiers like regulars.[22]

Academy graduates were not found only within the military

ranks, though. Even some of the newspaper reporters accompanying the army had attended West Point. Christopher Mason Haile, who was reporting on the war for the *New Orleans Picayune*, had spent a year at West Point. Hugh McCleod, who started a U.S. newspaper in Matamoros, had graduated the same year as such standout officers in Taylor's army as Lieutenant Meade and Capt. William Seaton Henry. Attending the academy gave these journalists strong credentials for reporting on the war, for they could better understand and convey military events for their readers than most other writers. They also had greater access to information through their old military friends. In 1846 the U.S. newspaper industry was booming. The *New Orleans Picayune*, the South's most popular newspaper, offered its readers stories about the war daily. To keep ahead of the competition, George Wilkins Kendall, a *Picayune* cofounder, created an elaborate network of horseback riders and steamboats that couriered news to New Orleans in record time.[23]

In June Secretary of War Marcy wrote Taylor: "His [Polk's] determination is to have the war prosecuted with vigor, and to embrace in the objects to be compassed in that campaign such as will dispose the enemy to desire an end of the war. Shall the campaign be conducted with the view of striking at the city of Mexico, or confined, so far as regards the forces under your immediate command, to the northern provinces of Mexico?" Marcy also asked the general if his army could penetrate deep into the Mexican interior, and if it did, would he be able to supply himself from the countryside. Marcy and Polk were thinking three steps ahead of Taylor. The United States had settled the territorial dispute in southern Texas with its victories near the Rio Grande, but the war was now about much more than that. Mexico showed no signs of relinquishing the Southwest. The two politicians were starting to believe that the army would need to advance deep into Mexico to convince its government to cede California and New Mexico to the United States. Polk had believed initially that the Mexican government would cede half of its territory if the army simply overran the desired territories and moved into northern Mexico. But it was not working out that way.[24]

Taylor responded to these questions in a long letter dated July 2. He did not give Polk and Marcy the answers they wanted: "From Camargo to the city of Mexico is a line little, if any, short of 1,000 miles in length. The resources of the country are, to say the best, not superabundant, and over long spaces of the route are known to be deficient. . . . I consider it impracticable to keep open so long a line of communication. It is therefore my opinion that our operations from this frontier should not look to the city of Mexico, but should be confined to cutting off the northern provinces—an undertaking of comparative facility and assurance of success." Taylor did not know it yet, but he had just limited his own involvement in the rest of the war. Months later, when Maj. Gen. Winfield Scott acquired most of Taylor's forces for an assault on Mexico City, Taylor probably reflected on what he had written in July. Perhaps he thought that he could have crossed the desert after all. For now, though, he understood that Washington was getting restless. Polk still had a political goal to achieve that included much more than controlling the disputed territory in Texas.[25]

Once Taylor received Polk's guidance to prosecute the war farther into northern Mexico, Monterrey emerged as the next goal. That city, along with Saltillo to its southwest, was the key to controlling northern Mexico and access to the interior. Taylor also knew that Ampudia was headquartered in Monterrey and was actively fortifying the city. Lt. Ulysses S. Grant, of the 4th Infantry, agreed with Taylor's decision. "Monterrey itself was a good point to hold," the young officer wrote in his memoirs decades later, "even if the line of the Rio Grande covered all the territory we desired to occupy at that time."[26]

Taylor tasked Captain McCulloch's Company A, 1st Texas Mounted Rifles to determine if the road through Linares contained enough water and supplies to sustain the army on the march. The road was the most direct route to Monterrey and the same one Arista had taken when he evacuated Matamoros. McCulloch's men were thrilled to undertake the scout. Not only did it give them something to do, but it also gave them a chance to settle scores with Antonio Canales, a hated Mexican partisan leader known as the "Chaparral Fox," who was reportedly somewhere along the Matamoros–Linares road.

The long history between Canales and Texas began in 1839, when the Texan militia fought with Canales against Santa Anna to reestablish a federalist government in Mexico. In one raid deep into Mexican territory, one of Canales's officers abandoned a group of Texans, who had to fight their way back. Canales eventually gave up the fight against Santa Anna and was appointed as a brigadier general in the dictator's army. Serving under General Ampudia at the Battle of Mier, he also led raids into Texas territory. To Texans, who did not understand the constant alliance shifting of Mexican politics, Canales was a traitor. In addition, Canales had been the officer in charge of the Mier prisoners from Matamoros to Monterrey, treating them very poorly during the long march. Any mission in the field became a chance to capture or kill the Chaparral Fox.[27]

McCulloch's expedition was provided a copy of Arista's map of northern Mexico that was captured at Resaca de la Palma. Like good reconnoiters, the Texans memorized every road and path on the chart. One remarked that "this knowledge [the map] was of much importance to all of us; as frequently during our scout a separation of the command was unavoidable, and often a single man would have to depend upon his own knowledge and skill, to pilot himself through many miles of a wilderness into camp." The Texans eventually went the length of their scout and determined that the route was impractical for artillery and lacked enough water and food for the troops. To their dismay, there was no sign of Canales.[28]

The scout to Linares was quite a feat. McCulloch's Texans traveled 250 miles in ten days deep into enemy's territory without losing a man. They also gathered valuable intelligence by debriefing ranchero owners and intercepting a mail carrier transporting official correspondence. George Wilkins Kendall, a reporter for the *New Orleans Picayune* who accompanied the Texans, was amazed at the tenacity of the small band: "[F]rom the time of our leaving Matamoros, to our reaching [this] place, the men neither took off coats, boots, nor spurs; not an extra or second shirt was carried by one of them; and although the weather was rainy much of the time, and the two heavy northers visited us while encamped, there was not a minute at any time when any man's pistol or rifle would have missed fire, or he would not have been up and ready for an attack. I have seen a goodly number of volunteers in my time, but Capt. Ben McCulloch's men are choice specimens."[29]

The intelligence gleaned from the scout reinforced Taylor's belief that his army should march up the Rio Grande (rather than follow Arista's route) to Camargo. That town was located on the banks of the San Juan River, three miles from its confluence with the Rio Grande. Steamers also could navigate into the San Juan to reach Camargo. From there the Americans could march southwest toward Monterrey.[30]

Capt. Ben McCulloch. McCulloch originally came to Texas to join his friend Davy Crockett but arrived too late to participate in the battle of the Alamo. He went on to fight against the Mexican army elsewhere, including the battles of San Jacinto and Plum Creek, and gained notoriety in a clash against Adrian Woll's troops at the Hondo River south of San Antonio. McCulloch also joined the ill-fated Somervall expedition but turned around before the attack on Mier. From Frost, *Mexican War and Its Warriors*, 292.

On June 5 Taylor set his men in motion by ordering a small advance that included the 1st Infantry, a section of Braxton Bragg's light artillery battery under Lt. George H. Thomas, and a company of Texas volunteers to occupy Reynosa, a small town sixty miles upstream from Matamoros. Lt. Col. Henry Wilson commanded the men. The alcalde of Reynosa made this first leg an easy one because he wanted Taylor's help in protecting his people from Indians and bandits. After Wilson secured Reynosa, Taylor sent the 7th Infantry to capture Camargo. Reports indicated that Canales was in that town with two hundred men and would meet the invaders with force. But the Chaparral Fox disappointed the Americans again. Camargo's alcaldes immediately surrendered to Capt. Dixon Miles, who only had ninety-three men with him.[31]

McCulloch's Company A rendezvoused with Wilson's men in Reynosa following their scout. Wilson instructed the Texans to camp outside of the city because he was worried that they might harm the locals. He probably agreed with Taylor's assessment: "I expect if they [the Rangers] could be made subordinate they would be the best, at any rate as good as any volunteers corps in service; but I fear they are and will continue [to be] too licentious to do much good." But the Texans noted that after he ordered them away from town, the colonel walked into a comfortable stone house, "the best one in the place." The men probably muttered a few choice words for the colonel before moving out to their campsite.[32]

Wilson's actions, though he did not know it, probably did prevent problems between the Texans and Reynosa's inhabitants, who had a rough history with Texas. Bandits from Reynosa were notorious for stealing cattle, horses, and other livestock, from Texas ranches. Rangers often chased the raiders back into the town, where they hid at local rancheros. The residents despised the Texans as well, for many of them had probably felt the heavy hand of a Ranger looking for a bandit. In addition, Texans captured in 1842 at Mier, of whom there were many in McCulloch's company, remembered Reynosa well. Ordered chained together and marched throughout northern Mexico, when the prisoners arrived at Reynosa, the locals threw stones and spat on them when they were displayed in the public square. One volunteer with the mounted rifles, though not a Texan himself, had heard these stories and considered Reynosa's inhabitants "irreclaimable scoundrels" and a "race of brigands."[33]

Despite their hard feelings, the Texans did participate in contests with the townspeople once they arrived. One popular game called the "Correo de Gallinas" involved a horseman carrying a chicken by its feet. He received a hundred-yard head start, after which a large group would chase him on horseback and try to snatch the chicken out of his hand. If the racer kept the chicken until the end, he could keep the bird. The Texans, with their strong horses and great pride, did not want to lose these contests and never declined an invitation to par-

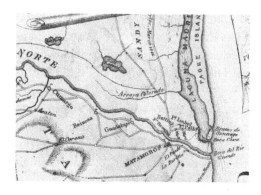

Detail from the Bruff map
(page 27), showing the area
between Matamoros and
Camargo.

ticipate. One game Texan, who owned a particularly ill-tempered horse, described the ferocity of one such event: "Soon the greasers closed in on me, holding my horse back, he [the horse] kicked one [a Mexican] out of the saddle, then commenced the fun, wheeling, 'as quick as lightning,' he let drive at another, caught another with his teeth, then I rode at another and rolled him over, and started for the camp, with the crowd after me." The games continued until the Texans "had chickens galore."[34]

On July 4 the Texans threw a giant party at their camp near a cotton gin to celebrate Independence Day. They procured two large "horse buckets" of whiskey and grated white sugar into it. The men climbed on top of a cotton shed and began dancing, shouting, and hollering. "[T]o describe the scene of feasting, drinking, and revelry which ensued," Samuel Reid declared, "is beyond the power of our pen." Mexicans watched the performance from below the shed. The commotion woke up many of the regulars, including Colonel Wilson. The revelers sent some whiskey to the colonel and asked him to come by for a drink. Wilson came by, but seeing the boisterous Texans, "prudently concluded not to pay us a visit," Reid recalled. That was probably a good decision.[35]

By July 14 Taylor possessed enough steamboats to begin moving his entire army upriver to Reynosa and to Camargo beyond, but he now faced another logistical problem. The enlistments of the Louisiana volunteers had expired, and most of them refused to reenlist for another twelve months. Taylor had to transport these approximately eight thousand men back to the mouth of the Rio Grande so they could embark for New Orleans. The general had no heartache seeing them go, but shipping them downstream to the Gulf coast prevented his army from moving upstream to Camargo. His regulars generally despised the Louisianans for not reenlisting, joking that the volunteers were "falling back on New Orleans." Lieutenant Meade was especially angry with them: "I came down the river on a small steamboat, with 900 men on board—a regiment of volunteers from Louisiana, who had served their three months, and declined remaining for twelve more. . . . [A]s a matter of course they all decline [to extend their service], so that we shall have to transport these eight thousand men out of the country, and they have just been here three months, to eat up two hundred and forty thousand rations; and our means of transportation, so necessary for us to throw our troops and supplies up to Camargo, are taken to carry these people to a point where they can get shipping." Many of them lied about why they were leaving, sheepishly claiming that they had agreed to sign up for additional service, but Taylor did not want them.[36]

One Louisianan, Capt. Albert Sidney Blanchard, did reenlist, and he managed to scrap together enough like-minded men to form a company of volunteers. Taylor gladly mustered them into service, writing the adjutant general, "Of all the Louisiana volunteers, but one company is retained for twelve months—an excellent body of men, under the command of Captain Blanchard." Like some other volunteer officers, Blanchard had attended West Point, serving in the army long enough to be promoted to first lieutenant. The regular officers who knew him vouched for the captain and his men. Blanchard recorded in his diary: "Assumed the name of Phoenix Comp.— as being the only one raised from the Louisiana Brigade of the Fourth Regt [regiment]—commanded by Gen. Smith—High position, hope to be worthy of it."[37]

Taylor began sending his army upriver to Camargo, which soon became a U.S. supply base. Some soldiers traveled by river aboard the steamers while others traveled by land. Upon learning that he would be marching, Lieutenant Meade wrote, "I should have preferred myself going by water, as I would avoid riding in the hot sun, but in other respects the land journey will be the most pleasant, as the boats are dirty and uncomfortable and are filled with troops." Camargo was still 128 miles away when he wrote these lines.[38]

4

MATAMOROS TO MONTERREY

"It was like marching in an oven."

Lt. Napoleon Jackson Tecumseh Dana

Z achary Taylor could not have picked a worse time to march his men. The heaviest rainfall in the area's history was turning the Rio Grande valley into a swamp. Toward the end of June 1846, rain fell almost daily, raising the river to unprecedented heights and flooding the plain surrounding Matamoros. The road to Camargo rapidly filled with mud and sludge. Deep, lake-sized lagoons formed throughout the area.

Lieutenant Meade could not believe the bad luck. He soon was fed up with the rain, the Quartermaster Department, the steamers, and anything else that delayed the army's progress: "Obstacle after obstacle presents itself to us. . . . At first we had not boats or provisions to throw forward. Now, when the boats have come, the river rises to its maximum height, overflows the whole country above and below, [and] cuts off all communication by land. . . . [I]t rains as if heaven and earth were coming together, and renders the road from here to that point [Camargo] impassable, forcing us to send the troops by water, which will be the work of months, as one boat can only take half a regiment at a time." Ankle-deep mud sapped the men's energy as they slogged through the mire. Artillery and wagons crept along at a snail's pace, occasionally getting stuck in the mud and compelling the tired men to pull them out by hand. Some troops detoured off the main road to avoid the lagoons that submerged it for long stretches. One unit became lost in doing so, adding at least thirty miles to its march.[1]

When it was not raining, the sun cooked the countryside. As July and August approached, hot, dry days became the standard. Temperatures soared to over 100 degrees during the day. The hot ground burned the soldiers' feet and further sapped their strength. In just four days the battalion of Maryland and District of Columbia volunteers, known as the Baltimore Battalion, marched seventy-eight miles, a tremendous feat for any troops. The baking sun soon dried up the lagoons that had earlier overflowed the area, leaving inches of dust covering the road. The marching soldiers and horses along with the turning wheels of wagons, cannons, and caissons kicked up the dust while a midday sun bore down on the tired men. "Those who have never tried marching under a blazing sun," Lt. Napoleon Jackson Tecumseh Dana, a tough-minded regular, wrote his wife, "have yet to learn the real suffering consequent upon excess of heat. It was like marching in an oven." The commanding officers realized that they would ruin their men if they continued to walk during the day, so they instead began marching at night. The men awoke at midnight, packed their goods, and hiked by moonlight, stopping at around 9–10 A.M. to rest for the day. The transition to night marching was tough, but as Capt. William Henry of the 3rd Infantry reasoned, "this 'turning night into day' causes nature to *rebel*, yet it was much better than to cause it to be *roasted*."[2]

Despite the rain, the route had little potable water. Rain-filled lagoons transformed into stagnant, polluted ponds after cows and other animals bathed in them. Many of the volunteers, new to marching long distances, gulped down all of the water in their canteen early on. John Kenly observed crazed soldiers digging frantically in a dry bed, hoping in vain to discover fresh water. He also saw men drink from a pond that had cattle standing in it. Few of them kept their nourishment down. Men who could not find water began to straggle or drop out of the march. An emotional Kenly described what he observed of this: "I saw men fall down in convulsions on this march, frothing at their mouths, clutching the sand with their hands." Many of these same men (and others) became prey for the hundreds of Mexican irregulars roaming the army's flanks. When halted for the day, exhausted soldiers fell down in the road until nightfall, after which they had regained some strength to continue moving forward.[3]

The tired and thirsty volunteers were in no mood to haggle for food and water at the few rancheros they approached. One Galveston volunteer noted the dilemma from his point of view: "We were Texans and would help ourselves occasionally to the beef, poultry, and other eatables for which we always paid what we considered a fair price—and no more. This fair price for anything is all an American wants, or all that he is willing to give, but it will not satisfy a Mexican. They sometimes tried to prevent us from taking what we wanted, or tried to compel us to pay more than it was worth, and this usually created a row. We lost in all, three men on the route [from Matamoros to Camargo] by the Mexicans, and for our part, we killed about fifteen of the rancheros and twenty-five beefs [cattle]." The Americans pressed on in the heat, with or without such supplies. Kenly described the mindset of the weather-beaten, thirsty soldier. Only one thing could keep them going: "No word of encouragement, none of command, was heard. . . . [T]o reach the river was the leading, the only, object of that brigade on its memorable march to Camargo."[4]

Some men considered themselves fortunate, at least before they started the journey, to be among the select few chosen to take steamboats to Camargo. They would avoid the hard marching, the muddy or dusty roads, and the heat and would arrive in Camargo ten days before their walking comrades. But those expecting a nice river cruise were sorely disappointed. The steamers varied in length, but few of them had enough room on their decks to handle the dozens of military passengers they were expected to convey. The men were forced to lie side by side on the deck without any covering to protect them from the sun. Mosquitoes had filled the river since the June deluge, and they ferociously attacked the boat riders. The men placed haversacks over their faces so they could protect at least one part of their bodies from insect bites. Illness spread like wildfire on the steamers. Those who had camped at the mouth of the Rio Grande had contracted fevers, measles, and dysentery. Eager for battle, these sickly men jumped on the steamers for Camargo, where they figured they could recuperate. Unfortunately for the healthy passengers, one sick soldier could infect a whole boat. Often up to half of the travelers became sick with dysentery.

The steamer's captains struggled to control their vessels in the swift and overflowing river. When a boat rounded a bend, a strong current would sometimes shove it downstream, and it would take the boat thirty minutes to make up the loss. The fast current also caused the boilers to overheat, since the engines had to work double time to keep the steamer moving forward. Because of this, boilers sometimes exploded, causing severe damage to the vessel and injuring the crew and passengers. But the journey could have been worse. The meandering course of the Rio Grande was a blessing to the captains, who otherwise could not have driven their steamers upriver at all. Its many bends tempered the swift current, which gave the skippers a fighting chance. "It was mighty well that it [the Rio Grande] ran so crooked," captains would remark, "for if it did not, a streak of lightning could not go up it."[5]

Whether by steamer or by foot, U.S. soldiers eventually arrived at Camargo. The dusty town's normal population was 4,000 people, and like Matamoros its center contained a plaza with a worn-down church, well-paved streets, and sturdy flat-roofed homes. But when the 7th Infantry entered Camargo, they found it deserted and wrecked. The San Juan, a narrow but deep river, had flooded its streets only weeks earlier. Four to five feet of water had covered the town during the flood, melting away most of its sun-dried brick houses and leaving piles of clay and straw in their place. Six inches of sand covered the plaza when Miles arrived, and all the town's stores, except a druggist shop, were closed. "Camargo is a miserable little place, and abominably filthy," thought one surgeon upon entering the city. About half of the population left after the flood.[6]

Steamers arrived daily with men and supplies. The activity surprised the few remaining Mexicans, who had never before seen such commotion. Once all of Taylor's men had arrived, they more than doubled Camargo's normal population. A newspaper reporter for the *New Orleans Picayune* described the scene to his readers: "Steamboat after steamboat is arriving and departing, barrels, boxes and bales are seen rolling in all directions, drumming and fifing is heard in all quarters, soldiers are marching and countermarching." Barrels of pork and of beans as well as sacks of corn covered the city's streets.[7]

In late July General Worth arrived and took control the town. He kept the 7th Infantry in the plaza, while the rest of the troops camped about two miles outside of town along the banks of the river. Once again the men would face the discomforts of sleeping in cleared chaparral, with its ants, thorns, and mosquitoes. "All bushes have thorns, all insects have horns," the soldiers repeated throughout the campaign. In addition, the heat that August turned Camargo into an inferno since it was built on limestone rock which reflected the sun's rays. A reporter for the *Picayune* wrote: "Yesterday and today . . . were the hottest days I ever heard of. The atmosphere, the earth, and the limestone walls of Camargo seemed to be on fire." He noted that no one had a thermometer to measure the temperature, "but nothing is lost by the deficiency, as I am satisfied that no instrument of the kind has ever been manufactured of sufficient length to reach the height of the temperature at this place." In fact there was a thermometer in camp, and it often reached 112 degrees.[8]

The heat wore down the men, making their bodies susceptible to a vast array of illnesses. The *New Orleans Daily Tropic* reported that six hundred sick soldiers were in Camargo's hospitals and "dying fast." Many of the men had already contracted disease by the time they arrived in town. The grueling march further broke down their immune systems and exposed the weakened men to local diseases. "[M]y Regt. of one thousand is fast wasting away in this tropical climate," the commander of the 1st Tennessee wrote. To make matters worse, the volunteers knew little about sanitized camp practices, which made them more vulnerable to disease. They rarely bathed or changed clothes, and when they did bathe, they drank from the same river. Malaria, yellow fever, diarrhea, pneumonia, and measles spread throughout their ranks. Northern and western volunteers, unaccustomed to the southern climate, were hit the hardest. One observer estimated that half of the men from those states were incapacitated by disease at any given time. Zenith Matthews, a Texas volunteer, noted in his diary, "The northern volunteers are dying fast." Almost every hour funeral escorts brought corpses into the chaparral for burial. "The dead march was ever wailing in our ears," said one soldier. Camargo became known as a "graveyard."[9]

Locals knew how "sickly" the area was, but Taylor wanted to camp there anyway. The general then blamed the rampant illnesses on the lack of medical officers. But the surgeon general pointed out that the law allowed two surgeons for every 750 men, and Taylor enjoyed a greater ratio than that in his army. No one, including the surgeon general, expected that American forces would lose 1,500 men to disease in two months. As for the men, they yearned to leave the "graveyard" as soon as possible. The *New Orleans Picayune's* George Wilkins Kendall, who had been in many miserable places in his lifetime, told his readers: "Everyone is anxious to get away from this place, to move anywhere. You may think you know something about hot weather and mosquitoes. You don't know nothing."[10]

General Worth tried to maintain some normalcy amid this small crisis. He drilled his healthy men in the morning and evening. The entire army desperately needed large-unit drilling practice since many of the officers were unfamiliar with commanding regimental or brigade-size formations. Taylor had been slowly organizing brigades over the previous few months, and by the time the troops reached Camargo, almost every regiment and company was incorporated into a brigade. Mexican spies, disguised as vendors, meandered throughout Worth's camp, taking detailed notes about the army. Samuel Walker told the general that he could keep the camp clear of spies if he would give him permission, but Worth refused to do so.[11]

On July 21 Richard Addison Gillespie, a famed Texas Ranger, and his company of Texas volunteer cavalry made their appearance at Camargo. Gillespie took a steamer to Matamoros, where Taylor remained headquartered, to report that his company had arrived. Once in the town the Texan got drunk in a local tavern and threatened to shoot an American soldier whom he said "had made some remarks in favor of the Regular army, in answer to some made against it." Gillespie's victim narrowly escaped. When five soldiers came to subdue Gillespie, he cocked his pistol and threatened to shoot all of them. Once imprisoned, he shouted insults to the senior guard. "You have treated me damned badly," Gillespie screamed at Lt. Robert Hazlitt, a soldier of the 4th Infantry, "and I am not accustomed to being ordered around by a Lieutenant and pushed and knocked about by a damned set of Corporals." According to Gillespie, the guards' rough treatment meant that one of them would have to fight him in the morning. Hazlitt observed in a letter afterward that Gillespie was "much under the influence of liquor." He eventually released Gillespie to Taylor, after which the Texan, who did not recognize the general, continued his tirade. Taylor, probably as punishment, ordered his company to stay encamped in Camargo with the 7th Infantry. Gillespie was not off to a good start with the U.S. Army.[12]

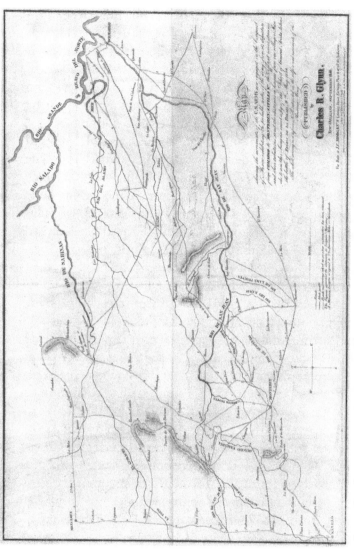

The region between Camargo and Monterrey. General Taylor considered two lines of approach to Monterrey. An eastern or southerly route ran directly south out of Camargo, through the town of China, and into Monterrey. A more westerly route ran west out of the city, southwest through Cerralvo and Ramos, and turned south at Agua Fria toward San Francisco and eventually Monterrey. Texan volunteers scouted both approaches and found that only the western one could handle the American artillery. Map by Charles R. Glynn. Courtesy of the Library of Congress, Geography and Maps Division.

On August 7 the commanding general arrived in Camargo and ordered another Texas volunteer, Ben McCulloch, to take his Company A and scout the two main roads that led from Camargo to Monterrey. The eastern (and most direct) route toward the city ran through the town of China, about seventy miles south of Camargo. The second, a longer, more westerly route, traveled through the towns of Mier, Cerralvo, and Marin. Taylor wanted his Texans to tell him which would be better for approaching Monterrey.[13]

McCulloch's men rode out of Camargo to scout the eastern road to Monterrey (through China) to determine if it was practical for artillery. Juan Seguin, a former ally to the Texan cause, was reportedly in China with one hundred men. McCulloch longed to capture Seguin, who had supported the Texan bid for independence by fighting at the Battle of San Jacinto but later returned to Mexico and participated in General Woll's invasion of San Antonio in September 1842. When the Texans arrived in China, Seguin was not there. McCulloch was not pleased with this result and rode into the town with the brim of his hat up, "a sign for all of us not to be familiar [with him]." The company returned to Camargo on August 9 and told Taylor that the eastern road was impractical for artillery because of narrow gorges and ravines. "This expedition had given valuable information," Taylor later informed the adjutant general, "touching one of the routes to Monterrey"[14]

The Texans remained in camp for three days before Taylor ordered them to evaluate the western road to Monterrey past Mier and through Cerralvo. McCulloch's men already knew the route to Mier well, for they had just returned from that village, but Taylor wanted them to scout farther down the road to Cerralvo, a town seventy-five miles south of Camargo. This time the general allowed Gillespie's company to go with McCulloch and enjoy a good scout. He probably figured that by placing him under McCulloch, someone the general respected, Gillespie would exercise good behavior. What Taylor did not realize was that while Gillespie was a loudmouth, disrespectful drunk, he was also one of the toughest fighters among the Texas volunteers. The captain had fought in almost all of the major battles in the young state's history. He had clashed with Indians, outlaws, and Mexican soldiers. His men knew Gillespie's reputation, and they would follow him and his popular lieutenant, William "Bigfoot" Wallace, anywhere the two led—and for now that was toward Cerralvo.

At dawn Gillespie's and McCulloch's companies, along with Capt. James Duncan and Lt. Thomas Wood of the topographic engineers, rode out of town headed west.

For the Texans, the scout also offered another opportunity to capture Antonio Canales, who hovered between Taylor's army and Monterrey. Not long after leaving Camargo, they learned that the Chaparral Fox was reportedly going to attend a fandango in the town of Punta Aguda, only fifteen miles away. Excited at the prospect of catching Canales, the men spurred their horses to Punta Aguda, arriving there about 10 P.M. They established a perimeter around the town, blocked all avenues of escape, and descended on a lighted outdoor square where two hundred men and women were dancing. They searched the revelers but discovered no sign of Canales.

An odd scene ensued. The Americans shot two Mexicans who tried to escape. One died, while the other suffered a broken arm.[15] Both were brought to the square. As the American surgeon tried to set the survivor's arm, the Texans demanded that the party's hosts start the music again. The band struck up the "Old Virginia Reel"—an American fiddle classic—and young Mexican girls began to dance. One of Duncan's men, allegedly a tall handsome fellow, jumped onto the dance floor and began to dance with the women. The Texans, who loved waltzes, clamored out too once the waltzing began. The Mexican women seemed to truly enjoy themselves. For all of the widely reported acts of cruelty against Mexicans, strange occasions like this one repeated themselves throughout the campaign. Women held a special protected status even for volunteers, who treated them with respect and reverence. Men took their hats off to Mexican women and typically offered a pleasant smile. That night in Punta Aguda, like many others elsewhere, Mexican men and U.S. soldiers amicably discussed politics, government, books, and other subjects at length.

The surgeon eventually finished setting the Mexican's broken bone, and the Texans departed for Cerralvo. They left at midnight, full of stories, food, and liquor, and rode for three hours before going to sleep. Some were still woozy from the mescal, so laying down on their blankets in the dirt probably never felt more welcome. The next day the men entered Cerralvo unmolested, and the alcalde surrendered the town to Captain Duncan.

On their return trip to Camargo, the men made a side trip to Mier, only three miles off the main road. McCulloch's company had visited the town previously looking for Indians, but this time they stopped for a different reason. A veteran of the 1842 action in Company A offered to give a tour to everyone in the group. The soldiers jumped at the chance to explore the battlefield about which they had heard so many stories. The veteran pointed out all of the important sites in town. He showed his comrades a famous house where a group of Texans, including the guide, held out for much of the battle. The group found bullet holes still in the home's walls and iron bars that were bent from grapeshot. They also discovered an oven in which the Texans had found loaves of fresh-baked bread during the fighting. From there they had picked off Mexican artillerymen who tried to load and fire a cannon from the city's main plaza. And this was not the only tour given to soldiers in Taylor's army. Many other soldiers wanted to visit the battlefield too, and there was no shortage of potential guides among the men of the 1st Regiment of Texas Mounted Volunteers. But these history enthusiasts could not have known that these Mier tours would prove to be much more important than they ever anticipated.

After the scout Captain Duncan reported to Taylor that the Mier–Cerralvo road was in adequate condition for artillery and wagons. He also informed the general that the Mexicans were conscripting militia and fortifying Monterrey. Messages regarding the fortification of the city deluged the American commander throughout the next few weeks.

Taylor collected around 10,000 men at Camargo, 3,000 of whom were regulars. The volunteers stayed busy drilling, unloading supplies, and carrying out other camp chores. Rumors abounded among the men about the Mexican army making a stand in Monterrey. The locals seemed to know: "mucho fandango at Monterrey," they would tell the Americans. Francis Schaeffer, adjutant general of the Baltimore volunteers, nevertheless worried that there would not be a battle. "I am really beginning to be fearful myself that we shall have no fight," he wrote from Camargo. "I would like to have one chance on the battlefield, if it were only just to see how I should feel . . . but I am almost certain we shall have no fighting to do." Pvt. Barna Upton, a soldier in the 3rd Infantry, wrote a more reflective letter to his friends. "We shall no doubt have some hard fighting," he wrote from Camargo. "All the troops here seem anxious to be led on to the fray. Is it not sad to think how many, either in battle or by disease, will lay their eye in the sand (as the soldiers say) before the close of this exten-sive campaign? I realize that my own chance is with the rest in the lottery of life and death, yet let what will happen, I trust I shall always be found doing my duty."[16]

Most of the regulars were excited about the prospect of combat at Monterrey. Many believed that a fight would not happen, but if it did, the Americans believed that they would once again triumph. Just before the regulars departed Camargo, Ephraim Kirby Smith de-scribed the feelings of many: "We are all busily engaged in making our preparations for crossing the mountains—and in fine health and ex-cellent spirits the camp, resounds with the merry hum of our voices—jokes and hilarity circle round." But Major Barbour did not think much about Monterrey; his mind was on his wife and his home. He longed to be back in the arms of his dear Mattie, but he knew that he had to finish the campaign first. Barbour cherished his wife's letters, and after reading one he exclaimed in his journal, "How blest am I in the possession of such a jewel!" He spent the rest of his spare time reading Shakespeare's *King Henry the Fifth*.[17]

In mid-August Taylor cleared up the rumors by informing his troops that they would depart Camargo in eight days. He decided that Cerralvo, the town that had already surrendered to McCulloch, would be his forward supply depot. Volunteers and regulars alike cheered the news. At last they would be leaving the "graveyard" for better ground. But then the general made an unusual move that disappointed hun-dreds of men eager for combat. "The limited means of transportation, and the uncertainty in regard to the supplies that may be drawn from the theatre of operations," Taylor wrote in Order 108, "imposes upon the commanding general the necessity of taking into the field, in the first instance, only a moderate portion of the volunteer force now under his orders." In other words, he would only take about a third of the total number of volunteers at his command. Taylor named the regiments that would march to Monterrey: the 1st Kentucky, the 1st Ohio, the 1st Tennessee, and another to be designated later. All of the volunteers had assumed that they would be marching to Monterrey, so those to be left behind were crushed. Curiously, Taylor did not mention his former son-in-law's regiment, the 1st Mississippi, but it would eventually fill the coveted "regiment to be designated" slot. Perhaps the general did not want to appear partial to his former rela-tion, Col. Jefferson Davis.[18]

Davis had met Taylor's daughter, Sarah Knox Taylor, in 1832 while posted at Fort Crawford, Wisconsin. Davis was still in the army, and his new commander, then-Colonel Taylor, had three lovely daughters who were the talk of the post. Eighteen-year-old Sarah was her father's favorite, interesting, curious, and attractive. Davis fell in love and pursued her relentlessly. The two became engaged, but the colonel refused to allow her to marry Davis because he did not want his daughters marrying into the army. "I know enough of the family life of officers," he told a friend who tried to persuade him to relent. "I scarcely know my own children or they me." Taylor eventually transferred Davis to Fort Gibson, a remote outpost far away from his daughter. He also recommended him for a promotion, knowing that Davis was a good officer and not wanting to hurt his career. Nevertheless, Sarah moved in with her aunt to be closer to Davis.[19]

Desiring to marry his love and to leave the isolated army life, Davis resigned his commission and married Sarah in 1835. But tragedy soon befell the couple. A few months after their wedding, the couple went to visit his sister in Louisiana, where they contracted malaria. Sarah died, while Davis barely clung on to life. Zachary Taylor was grief stricken. His favorite daughter had died running off with Davis, whom he now blamed for her death. Davis recovered and became a recluse, studying law and working a plantation for eight years until he ran for Congress and won in 1844. Shortly before the election he met his future wife, Varina Howell, an aristocratic daughter of the governor of New Jersey. In 1846 Davis resigned his congressional seat and raised a regiment of volunteers for service in Mexico, the Mississippi Rifles. Taylor and Davis reconciled at some point prior to the Monterrey campaign, but neither recorded how or when they repaired such emotional damage. Just before Davis's second marriage, the two men encountered each other while Taylor was on leave. Taylor wished him well and showed no animosity toward his former son-in-law.[20]

Now in Mexico, Davis and his regiment, as well as the other volunteers chosen to march to Monterrey, were inspected by Taylor before they departed. The general ordered that the Monterrey-bound volunteer regiments be reduced by two hundred men. Maj. Gen. William Butler, commander of the volunteer division and a medical board decided who would remain in Camargo. Men who were sick, weak, or "not deemed capable of undergoing the fatigues and privations of the campaign," as Major Giddings put it, remained at the Rio

Grande. The order also gave Butler the loose authority to cull anyone who did not seem likely to hold up under fire. Taylor wanted only his best volunteers heading south. Those cleared for action were ecstatic. The men of the 1st Mississippi, the 1st Ohio, the 1st Kentucky, and the 1st Tennessee would all be marching to Monterrey for glory. But the approximately 3,500 volunteers ordered to guard Camargo and other points along the Rio Grande were distraught. They despairingly wondered if they had come all this way just for guard duty. Most wanted the opportunity to fight the Mexican army. A volunteer would hardly have exciting stories to tell if all he did was patrol a dust-ridden, blistering hot city. An anonymous soldier wrote a letter to the *Niles Register* expressing his frustration: "The idea of keeping 12 or 15,000 volunteers in the hot sun, cutting chaparral, meets the disapprobation of every individual in the army."[21]

Taylor also made another unusual move: incorporating a few elite volunteer companies into regular outfits. Captain Kenly's Baltimore Battalion was attached to the 1st Infantry under Col. Henry Wilson. Captain Blanchard's Louisiana Volunteers also had the honor of being attached to a regular unit, Blanchard's men even donning regular uniforms. Lt. Napoleon Jackson Tecumseh Dana, who was no admirer of the volunteers, agreed with the general's decision to incorporate Blanchard's company into his brigade, noting that they behaved as "precise" and "well disciplined" as the regulars.[22]

The terms of service for one volunteer regiment scheduled to go to Monterrey, Colonel Albert Sidney Johnston's Texas infantry, expired in early September just before the army departed Camargo. Johnston, with Taylor's approval, set about to reenlist the men for another three-month term of service so they could continue the campaign. He believed that his men's reenlistment was a formality. When the Texans lined up for the ceremony, Johnston ordered those willing to reenlist to step forward two paces. When he shouted "March," only 80 of the 550 men advanced. Johnston was dumbstruck. Recovering, he put the men back in line and shouted "march" again. The same 80 soldiers stepped forward. Johnston glared at the regiment with scorn. Finally, he spoke. "Are these my brave men, upon whom I have placed so much reliance? Are these they, deserting the field in the time of need? Alas! All the valiant deeds of the Texan soldiers for the last ten years are buried forever—buried by this one day's action." One soldier claimed he saw tears coming down the colonel's cheeks.[23]

Texas Rangers and Mississippi Rifles, 1846. Mississippi riflemen were notable for their trademark attire of red shirt and white tweed pants throughout Taylor's campaign. This Mississippian is depicted wearing a bowie knife, which proved critical for hand-to-hand combat because their long rifles did not have a bayonet. The Texas Rangers did not wear uniforms, though they were distinguishable by their slouched hats, long beards, and rifles.

A distraught Johnston walked to the general's tent to give him the news. Since the Texan had no soldiers to command, he believed that Taylor no longer required his services. But being a good judge of character, the general never let a good man leave the army who wanted to stay. "I fully appreciate the value of his services," Taylor wrote the adjutant general, "and the disappointment which the disinclination of his regiment to continue in service has occasioned him." Taylor asked Johnston if he would serve as inspector general, without rank or pay, to General Butler. Johnston readily agreed. He wanted only to serve his new country.[24]

One company did rise from the ruins of Johnston's regiment. Capt. William Shivers's Mississippians, who had rounded out Johnston's Texas regiment, still wanted to reenlist. Taylor was fond of Shivers because he knew that his men had paid their own way from Mississippi to Texas to participate in the campaign. They also did not mind serving under the Texas banner, giving that state any potential glory so long as they could join the army. "Captain Shivers expressed a great desire to remain," Taylor reported, "and entered the service under such peculiar circumstances—having come from Mississippi to Galveston in order to find an opening—that I have accepted it for three months, and attached it to the third brigade of regular infantry."[25]

For the march, Taylor divided his regulars into two divisions under the commands of newly brevetted brigadier generals David Twiggs and William Worth. The 1st, 2nd, 3rd, and 4th Infantry regiments were assigned to Twiggs, along with the light artillery companies commanded by Braxton Bragg and Randolph Ridgley. Although he did not record it, Worth was probably worried that his poorly timed resignation had hurt his chances to be assigned a quality division of regulars. Surely Taylor held a grudge against him since he had abandoned his commander when he needed him the most. Plus most regulars ridiculed Worth for his childlike behavior when he resigned, jeopardizing his ability to command a division with any authority. But Taylor entrusted Worth with command of a fine set of regulars: Thomas Childs's artillery battalion; the 5th, 7th and 8th Infantry regiments; James Duncan's and William Mackall's light artillery batteries, and Captain Blanchard's Louisiana volunteers.[26]

Taylor's magnanimous behavior is remarkable. Few generals would have been as compassionate as he was in this situation. Part of his reasoning probably stemmed from his own experiences in 1814, when he resigned from the army because he believed that he merited a promotion, but the War Department thought otherwise. (His resignation did not last long, for a year later he was offered the rank that he desired and returned to the army to lead a fruitful career). Taylor probably also wanted his best general at Monterrey. Worth had the most combat experience of any of his officers, including Taylor, and he could be counted on to run independent operations without Taylor's oversight. The same could not be said for his other generals. Taylor also created a third division, under General William Butler, that contained the volunteer regiments from Ohio, Tennessee, Mississippi, and Kentucky.[27]

The American army of 3,000 regulars and 3,200 volunteers would begin marching to Cerralvo in mid-August. Taylor designated Worth's Second Division to lead the advance on the nineteenth and establish a supply depot at the town. The First and Third Divisions would follow soon afterward. Taylor also ordered General Henderson to take some of his Texans down the eastern road through China (where he would find the remainder of his men) and rejoin the army at Marin. Almost two weeks earlier Taylor had ordered Jack Hays to ride with his regiment of mounted Texans on a long "hook" from Matamoros, through San Fernando, to China, bypassing Camargo altogether. They were to remain in China until the rest of Henderson's command arrived, then push on to Marin.[28]

Taylor's lack of transport wagons forced him to purchase mules to carry his baggage. Mules were the traditional means by which armies transported supplies in Mexico, and Taylor would have to make do with the stubborn creatures. He allocated one pack mule for every three officers and one for every eight noncommissioned officers. Many of the officers, lacking their own army-issued mule, purchased one to carry personal items. Only three wagons were assigned to each regiment. As instructed, his quartermasters procured 1,000 mules from *arrieros*, or muleteers. Col. John Garland needed someone from his regiment to purchase and organize his regiment's share and chose a young, popular officer whom he believed could finagle it using his refined social skills. The officer was also one of the best horse and mule wranglers in Taylor's army. Ulysses S Grant, to his horror, was the man for the job. "I respectfully protest against being assigned to a duty," Grant wrote Garland, "which removes me from sharing in the dangers and honors of service with my company at the front and respectfully ask to be permitted to resume my place in line." Garland denied Grant's request.[29]

Worth's division left Camargo with 1,000 pack mules. The first day with these old-fashioned cargo carriers did not go well. The muleteers had loosely packed the camp kettles on the animals, so they rattled loudly as the mules trotted ahead. This noise scared the creatures, who began to kick and buck, prompting laughter from all of the soldiers watching the spectacle. The laughter further frightened the mules, so hundreds of them "bolted in a regular stampede style, bounding over musquit shrubs, in every direction, throwing their burdens of flour and pork high into the air." Baggage was strung out for miles in the chaparral. Camp kettles hung from mesquite trees, while bags of flour lodged in the forks of limbs, looking like "large birds' nests." It took the men hours to collect the goods and repack the mules. "I am not aware of ever having used a profane expletive in my life," Grant later wrote, "but I would have the charity to excuse those who may have done so, if they were in charge of a train of Mexican pack mules at the time." The time wasted repacking was precious because any delay meant a marked increase in temperature during the march. The men would again be under a scorching August sun, on dusty roads, and with little water. Each of the soldiers carried heavy personal loads of forty one-ounce ball cartridges, a bayonet scabbard and belts, a haversack of provisions, a canteen, a musket, blankets, and a knapsack.[30]

Reveille began before dawn in an effort to save the men from the sun, but they usually did not start moving until 8–10 A.M. It took hours to load the mules in the predawn darkness, and by the time the men and mules began moving, the temperature was over 90 degrees. The chaparral was thicker on the Cerralvo road than it was along the Rio Grande. Cactus, mesquite, and other thorny shrubs dotted the landscape. The commander of the 1st Tennessee, William Campbell, wrote a relative, "This whole country is covered by a dense growth of small timber and shrubbery of the most cragged and thorny I ever beheld—every bush, tree, plant and every insect and serpent here, has a sting or a thorn." The dense growth also prevented any breeze from getting to the men. Ankle-deep dust kicked up from the tramping soldiers choked the men's lungs. Some fainted and were placed in the few wagons accompanying the column. Numerous white crosses lined the road, signifying where locals had died of sunstroke or had been murdered—an ominous sign to the worn-out men. Indeed, the narrow route enclosed by dense chaparral forced Worth to stretch out his columns, making them more vulnerable to enemy harassment.[31]

Most commanders realized that they could not continue this routine without exhausting or killing their soldiers. They decided to march before dawn without the mules and allow the train to depart whenever it was ready. This new schedule was good for those who could avoid a late departure, but some troops had to stay behind to guard the valuable supplies. Since most of Taylor's mounted men, who were ideal for guarding a mule train, were on a different road, foot soldiers had to march with the animals. The poor souls chosen for this duty found themselves walking in blazing heat alongside fast-moving mules that kicked up dust and occasionally dashed into the chaparral. Worth tasked D. H. Hill's artillery company with guarding a mule train for a portion of the march. The lieutenant was near his breaking point. "We had to march on a parched desert for 15 miles," Hill recorded. "The great heat, the dust raised by the mules and their brisk gait made this march horrible beyond conception." He estimated that thirty to forty men fainted during the day. Captain Henry, who was chosen to command the rear guard one afternoon, said that for dinner that night, "I might have been served as a *rare dish*."[32]

The volunteers, accompanied by General Taylor, departed for Cerralvo after the regulars. Once again they downed their valuable canteen water in the early stages of the march. The men peeled off into the chaparral hoping to find water or to lie down and rest their weakening bodies. Some tried to squeeze water out of the thorny shrubs lining the road, ending up with only bloody hands as a result. Others brushed the green scum off the top of nearby ponds and gulped down the water underneath. "Then, when we were not more than a mile or two from water occurred some touching scenes of human misery," Luther Giddings remembered. "Here and there, the weakest men began to reel from the ranks. Sinking upon the road-side, they declared that their strength was spent, and that they could go no further." Once Giddings's healthy men reached the first watering hole, they ran back to their stranded comrades with full canteens. After a few days of marching, the men saw a glimmer of relief in the distance. The towering Sierra Madres loomed on the horizon, offering the possibility that cool air and cold water were nearby. "And like the visions of hope," a Tennessee volunteer wrote, "they [the mountains] seemed constantly to recede as we advanced."[33]

General Worth's advance, which had left two weeks earlier, was then already enjoying the benefits of higher altitude. The soldiers arrived in Cerralvo, a town of about 2,000 people, on August 25. They marched into the city with drums and fifes playing and stacked their firearms in the plaza. Twiggs's First Division arrived another two weeks later, and the volunteers shortly thereafter. The town was an idyllic resting spot for the sun-baked, thirsty men. After days of marching in the heat and dust, Cerralvo offered cool, bubbling streams and clean well water. The townspeople ran irrigation ditches from the streams to their gardens, resulting in the most abundant supply of fruit that the men had yet seen in Mexico. Fig, pecan, and lemon trees lined the banks of the main stream in town. Colorful flowers covered most of the landscape. Soldiers gulped down limeade and vino de Parras, a local wine. They also found their first apple trees since entering Mexico. "It is decidedly the neatest and most pictur-esque town I have noted," Captain Henry wrote about Cerralvo. "It is impossible to feel the heat; for, if the house is disagreeable, take a water-melon, go under that huge pecan, rest thyself beside that rush-ing, bubbling stream, and you'll all but freeze."[34]

General Ampudia and his forces ensured that the Americans re-membered that they were at war in this heavenly environment. He had his men circulate a proclamation stating that anyone caught aid-ing the Americans would be killed. Taylor's men noticed an immedi-ate effect from the decree, because the townspeople suddenly became less helpful. Worth prohibited anyone from leaving the city after he read the notice. A spy also informed him that Ampudia was in Mon-terrey with three brigades and provided a description of the city's fortifications. Worth forwarded the information to Taylor. Even after reports filtered in of fresh brigades and new fortifications, Taylor was not convinced that the Mexican army would offer opposition. On September 10 he wrote a friend: "whether the enemy will fight for Monterrey is quite uncertain. . . . [M]y impressions are we shall meet no resistance out of the city." The enemy had fortified a city before, he probably reasoned, only to retreat as the American army approached. Maybe the same would happen now.[35]

Fifty miles to the south, General Ampudia had quite different thoughts on his mind than retreating from Monterrey. He had received his government's backing to fight the Americans and intended to do so with the 3,000 fresh troops and sixteen new guns from Mexico City. He also had 2,000 men from Arista's old Army of the North and around 1,000 militiamen at hand. Since Ampudia's arrival on September 1, the Mexicans had been erecting walls, digging moats, stacking stone and sandbags, and punching out holes in the soft limestone walls of Monterrey's houses.

When Ampudia learned that Taylor's army had departed Camargo, he sent General Torrejón and his cavalry north along the Marin road to harass the American army as it approached. He instructed Torrejón to evacuate, by force if necessary, all civilians living between Camargo and Monterrey. Torrejón's men ordered the people out and to take any possessions with them that would be useful for Taylor's army. The cavalrymen undertook their mission with ferocity, forcing villagers to flee into the chaparral with their pigs, goats, and cows in tow. Local priests assisted by spreading rumors that the Americans were ruthless killers who would slay anyone in their path. Men and women fled their homes when U.S. troops were rumored to be nearby. Ampudia also had Torrejón's men spread pamphlets throughout the villages urging Taylor's men to desert from the army and join the Mexican cause.

In mid-September the Mexican commander decided that he did not want to fight a completely defensive battle after all. He dispatched Torrejón's cavalry, along with some light infantry, to confront the Americans at Marin, twenty-five miles north of Monterrey. He did not record his rationale but probably wanted to bruise Taylor's army before it reached the city. Ampudia held a meeting with his senior officers to discuss the plan. Surprisingly, the only general who supported the move was the man whom Ampudia had replaced—Francisco Mejía—while the others thought it was bad idea and refused to send their men to Marin. No account of the meeting was recorded, but the generals probably disagreed with the plan more for political than military reasons. Many of them despised Ampudia and likely did not want to support any decision he made apart from defending the city proper, which the government had already authorized. On September 11 Ampudia rode to Marin himself to see if any kind of defense was possible. He spent one night there and returned to Monterrey the following day, realizing that he needed to cancel his plans for Marin's defense.

General Worth's men of the Second Division enjoyed Cerralvo for almost three weeks. The First and Third Divisions, which arrived later, stayed in the mountain paradise for only a few days. After the last troops arrived from Camargo on September 10, Taylor prepared to move his army to Marin. First he formed an advance party, which contained a group of pioneers, McCulloch's Company A, three topographic engineers (including George Gordon Meade), and some dragoons, all under the command of Capt. Lewis Craig. The advance departed Cerralvo on September 12 and worked diligently to make the road practical for artillery by bridging ravines and removing boulders.[36]

Craig's party marched for two days before reaching Ramos, a small town six miles east of Marin. There McCulloch observed two hundred Mexican cavalry poised for battle. These horsemen, part of Lt. Col. José María Carrasco's cavalry regiment, had been scouting up and down the Marin road for weeks to monitor Taylor's movements. The Americans expected the cavalry to retreat, as other Mexican horseman had before on this road. But Carrasco's men stood their ground. The two sides exchanged fire at about one hundred yards, the Texans shooting their accurate long rifles, while the Mexicans discharged muskets and carbines. The clash only lasted a minute or so before Carrasco retreated from Ramos. McCulloch's men rushed after them but soon retired in case the Mexicans had more men in reserve. The Texans killed one horseman and wounded two in this skirmish. One of the wounded prisoners revealed that Torrejón had 1,500 cavalry at Marin and was prepared to defend that town.

With the way cleared for the advance, Taylor's army began departing Cerralvo for Marin. The Americans left the town with regret, but they were rejuvenated and in better spirits than they had been for months. The men marched with more enthusiasm, discipline, and energy, especially because of news that they would meet the enemy at Marin. For the volunteers, who had signed up to fight the enemy, the thought of combat excited each and every one of them. All of those days marching in the desert with little water while carrying heavy packs would finally pay off. They felt confident because the regulars told them stories about how easily they had defeated the

Mexicans in the opening battles of the war. "The victories at Palo
Alto and Resaca [de la Palma] had given a confidence to these men
[the regulars] which was communicated to the volunteers," Captain
Kenly wrote. His Baltimore volunteers were also in the envious position of being attached to a regular unit, the First Division. The captain thought this was a smart move by Taylor because the regular's
confidence rubbed off on Kenly's amateur soldiers.[37]

The First Division moved out on September 13, with the Second
and Third Divisions leaving on the fourteenth and fifteenth. The road
to Marin ran through a gorgeous valley with towering mountains on
each side. Beautiful, clear streams crossed the road, and cool mountain air soothed their skin. "I cannot attempt a description of the
scenery of this country, it is beyond my powers," Captain Henry remarked. For Captain Kenly, September 14 was the first day that he did
not suffer from the sun's heat. "The cool air from the slopes of the
adjacent mountains, and the elevation we are attaining, have ren-
dered the temperature so pleasant that we feel as if we could march
thirty miles a day with more ease than twenty lower down the country." For hundreds of miles the Americans had traversed desert, chaparral, and bogs, all under a punishing August heat. Dust had filled
their mouths and noses. Their feet had ached. Now the men could
finally enjoy some cool water and air, and their spirits were better
for it.[38]

As the advance approached Marin, the Americans observed Mexican cavalry dashing across the town's principal street. The horsemen
wore bright red uniforms and lavish hats and brandished sparkling
carbines and lances. Kenly, who was near the advance, watched the
lancers too, appearing to him as if they were trying to figure out what
to do. General Taylor soon approached, extending his hand and telling Kenly that he remembered the meeting they had had in Matamoros. The captain was probably a little nervous that the general might
remind him that the discussion concerned a potential riot that his
Marylanders nearly caused over a plump catfish in Buritta. But instead the general remarked: "Captain, move forward cautiously, and
if you can, continue your march through that town [pointing to it as
he spoke] and halt on the other side until the column gets up." Although the men expected a fight, the Mexicans retreated and the
Americans entered Marin without firing a shot. Ampudia had sent
Torrejón north only to harass Taylor, not to lose any cavalrymen. But

the Mexicans did make some last-minute evictions from the town's households.[39]

As they approached Marin, some Texans discovered a group of Mexican families hiding in the chaparral with their livestock. These locals told them that Torrejón had threatened to burn the town if they did not leave and had robbed most of the residents of their livestock and crops. They urged the Americans to move in quickly to save their property. "Rather a strange request to make of an enemy," a Texan at the scene later wrote. "They were more afraid of the injury their countrymen would do than they were of us." The town was empty when the Americans entered, but after a few days the townspeople began to trickle in from the chaparral, livestock in hand. They stood around in small groups, "probably discussing their misfortunes," but eventually became friendly to the Americans and offered to sell them corn and meat. One little girl brought in a pet goat, and upon seeing a Texan, declared, "Why you ain't the devil, the priest told us you were all devils." The little girl sat in the Texan's lap as he told her stories about his own little sisters.[40]

Marin proved to be another idyllic spot for the soldiers, situated on a plateau with a commanding view of the valley toward Monterrey. From there the men could see the Mitre and Saddle mountains encircling the distant city. From atop of the town's beautiful cathedral, they could see the Bishop's Palace west of Monterrey. Bountiful homes and delicious well water invigorated the troops. Samuel Reid wrote that the troops in Marin "almost imagined we were in some little New England village."[41]

New intelligence arrived that the Mexican army in Monterrey numbered 9,000 men—6,000 rancheros and 3,000 regulars. A Mexican prisoner described the city's forts in detail, having worked on them only two days earlier. He told Taylor that Ampudia intended to defend the town at all costs. The U.S. commander was slowly becoming convinced that Ampudia might make a stand at Monterrey. "Whether we shall meet with any opposition on our arrival at Monterrey or between here and that place is quite uncertain," Taylor wrote a friend on September 16, "but it would appear somewhat strange if they do not risk a battle for so important a place as Monterrey." Other soldiers did not think that the Mexicans would fight until they could gather enough men to build a colossal army. Lt. Robert Hazlitt said as much in a letter to his sister: "Well I suppose you want to know what the prospects are for a battle. I, in truth, do not see any yet. . . . We will go to Monterrey in two days. They say that Santa Ana is coming up to give us a turn but I do not believe it. He got beaten badly enough at San Jacinto without trying it again. . . . The truth is we might have a little fight but that is doubtful for the Mexicans will not stand unless they can get twelve to fifteen thousand men and I think that is almost impossible. . . . This army is not to be easily beaten. We are fighting characters." Hazlitt closed by asking her a favor. Concerned about his mother's impression of him, the young officer asked his sister to "[t]ell Mother I am no chicken."[42]

At this point in the campaign, Taylor probably understood that General Ampudia had two options for making a defensive stand north of Saltillo. He could not defend Saltillo, which stood on a small plain with few defensive positions, but he could post his men in the Rinconada Pass, which some of his generals had recommended. The pass was a natural choke point between Monterrey and Saltillo and would give a decisive geographic advantage to Ampudia. The other option was to defend Monterrey itself, and as General Mejía informed his government, losing the city would be a tremendous blow to the country's honor.

None of Ampudia's considerations influenced Taylor's preparations. The Mexican army was at Monterrey, so that was where he was going. The American troops, however, cared a great deal about whether Ampudia defended Monterrey or retreated into the pass. They knew that the infantry would bear the brunt of the fighting if the Mexicans defended the city. Taylor did not bring his heavy artillery to Monterrey, so any battle in that city would be an up-close, personal engagement. "If we do fight," Captain Henry reasoned, "the Infantry will have to do the work, as our deficiency in heavy guns will render our field batteries useless." Why Taylor did not bring his big guns and left them at Camargo is not clear. The two 18-pounders could have battered the city's defenses from afar. Maybe he believed that the heavy guns, which were so slow to move, would hurt his ability to press forward quickly and arrive at Monterrey before it became too well fortified. He also may have doubted that they could be safely transported down the mountainous road to Monterrey.[43]

Whatever his reason for leaving behind the heavy artillery, Old Zack was a hardened frontier general who believed that losing men in battle was a simple fact of warfare. At the Battle of Okeechobee in

1837, he led 1,000 men—a combination of regulars and volunteers—deep into Florida to chase after an elusive Seminole commander. Taylor abandoned his supply lines, left his artillery at a distant fort, and marched his men through swamps and bayous. When his troops located the Seminoles, they had fortified themselves in a swamp hammock. A half mile of marshland filled with sawgrass five feet high occupied the front of their position. The defenders had cut lanes through the vegetation so they could see their enemy approaching, and had notched trees into which they could lay their rifles to steady their aim. Any commander besides Taylor probably would have rethought attacking the Indians. He was miles from the nearest military fort, he had no artillery, and the Indians held a dominant position. But in minutes he had decided what to do: attack the Indians head on directly through the swamp and the well-established corridors of fire. The result was one of the bloodiest American battles of the nineteenth century. The 6th Infantry lost almost every commissioned and noncommissioned officer in the assault, but his men eventually beat the Seminoles. Taylor's mindset had not changed ten years later, when he found himself marching toward Monterrey. The general knew that the big guns might allow him to batter the city from afar, but he also knew that Ampudia would not surrender Monterrey to two 18-pounders. Eventually he would need to send his men into the streets to wrest control of the city from the Mexicans.[44]

The men were dismayed by their commander's decision. "The city *has to be carried*," Barbour wrote on September 19, "as there are no guns in our train of sufficient caliber to batter, the bayonet will probably have to do the work." D. H. Hill was more incisive: "We occupy the anomalous position of an army marching to the attack of a fortified City without a single siege piece. The blunders, follies, and mistakes already made are unprecedented in the annals of warfare."[45]

But Taylor was not the only commander being criticized by his men. In Monterrey, on the eve of battle, Ampudia began making a series of poor decisions that proved to many why he should not be commanding an army. General Simeón Ramírez, an infantry officer with no engineering experience, recommended that the army destroy all the fortifications between the Citadel and the Obispado, leaving only Fort Teneria and a few other works. Ampudia agreed. The decision stunned the soldiers and their senior officers, who had labored for weeks at constructing the defenses. Taylor was only twenty-five miles from Monterrey, and now was not the time to be making major decisions about the city's defense. Soldiers were going through the last-minute preparations of readying their arms, putting shoes on their horses, and finishing up the fortifications. And now, so close to battle, Ampudia ordered them to destroy many of the forts they had worked so hard to build.

But Ramírez was not done making bad recommendations. On September 15, when Taylor's army was spotted at Marin, he told Ampudia that they should destroy Fort Teneria, a bastion pivotal for the city's defense. The fort sat on top of a small hill, with its east face protected by a river and its rear guarded by a fortified building. It offered clear fields of fire onto the northern plain, while two nearby forts protected its flanks with artillery fire and infantry support. Tear it down was Ramírez's suggestion, which Ampudia obliged. "As was to be expected he [Ramírez] made several blunders," Balbontin recalled, "the greatest of which was his ordering the demolition of Fort Teneria." Morale plummeted. Ampudia's constant wavering about how to defend the city proved to most that he was unfit for command. And as all of this was happening, Taylor's army was on the march.[46]

On September 18 the Army of Occupation departed Marin for San Francisco, located about halfway between Marin and Monterrey. Captains Gillespie and McCulloch led the First Division's advance, which was followed by the Second Division one hour later. Taylor dictated a battle formation should a clash arise: the First Division would be on the right, the Second Division on the left, and the Third Division (the volunteers) in the center. Putting the volunteers in the center should steady their nerves since the regulars would be supporting their flanks.

Just prior to reaching San Francisco, the troops saw dust rising on the road toward China. Someone screamed, "Canales! Canales!" The muleteers scrambled every which way; Canales, like Torrejón, showed no mercy to Mexicans who helped the invading army. In fact the horses belonged to General Henderson's Texans, who were arriving from their long ride down the eastern road through China, collecting Hays's men there before riding on to Marin. For the first time since the start of the campaign, all of the Texans were together, and they presented an interesting sight. These rough-looking men with slouched hats and beards rode on hundreds of horses, carried Colt pistols, and screamed the Texas yell. Surprisingly, some regulars

Monterrey's Grand Plaza and cathedral. This drawing depicts the city's main plaza after it was occupied by American troops. General Ampudia stored his ammunition and gunpowder in the cathedral and collected Monterrey's noncombatants in this square. *A Front View of the Cathedral, from the Main Plaza, Monterey.* Lithograph artist after Stephen G. Hill, 1847. Lithograph, 8 1/4 × 13 1/8 in. Courtesy of the Amon Carter Museum, Fort Worth, Tex.

seemed impressed. "They are a fine body of men," Henry said upon their arrival.[47]

San Francisco was deserted when the men arrived. The soldiers could feel that they were entering a more hostile region. Two Mexicans tried to shut off water courses that ran through the town but were captured by the Americans. San Francisco's priest told Taylor that Ampudia would defend Monterrey and that the city was heavily fortified. "Mucho fandango at Monterrey," the few remaining townspeople told the men. Nevertheless, the night spent in San Francisco was a beautiful one. Bright stars and a light cool breeze comforted the men as they chatted and laughed until twilight. "All were in fine spirits," Samuel Reid recalled, "young hearts beat high with the assurance of victory." The men cleaned their pistols, practiced artillery drills, and shined their muskets. "The general impression is that the struggle will be fierce, but soon over," Henry wrote.[48]

The First Division departed San Francisco at 8 A.M. on September 19 for the seven-mile march to Monterrey. Taylor's pioneers repaired a few bridges destroyed by Torrejón's men. But the men had to wade across the San Juan River and through another cool stream called the Agua Frio. Afterward, for the first time in the campaign, the soldiers felt cold.

In Monterrey, tensions ran high as the Americans approached. Ampudia allowed husbands to evacuate their families from the city but warned them that they would be "severely punished if they are not present immediately" to fight. Many did not return. But Mexican soldiers did receive some welcome news on August 18 in the form of 28,000 pesos from Mexico City to pay the men, who had not received a salary in months. At least they could enter the coming battle with full wallets. Ampudia made final preparations, positioning his men and horses throughout the city. He kept the militia in the Grand Plaza along with most of the army's excess rifles, food, and other supplies. The general established his headquarters in the sacristy of the cathedral and placed 17,000 pounds of gunpowder and munitions in its nave. Afterward he climbed to the top of the cathedral to watch the American army approach.[49]

As the Americans crested a hill overlooking Monterrey, General Taylor dashed to the front of the column. He saluted the men and cheered them as he galloped by. "Boys, the general himself is going to lead us forth to battle," someone shouted. Captain Gillespie's

American army approaches Monterrey. This is one of a dozen lithographs published jointly by Carl Nebel and George Wilkins Kendall. These illustrations are the most accurate and popular of the Mexican War. Kendall and Nebel usually sketched following, not during, the battles, taking great pains to ensure that the buildings, terrain, and other features were correct. Nebel was probably at some of the battles he sketched, but it is not clear if he was at Monterey. If not, he probably sketched the battle soon after it took place. This particular scene attempts to depict the first two days of fighting at Monterrey, showing the regulars and volunteers marching across the plain on the 21st and Worth taking the Bishop's Palace on the twenty-second (right center). Opposite the Bishop's Palace is Federation Hill (center). The illustration shows the correct location of the Citadel, which stood roughly halfway between El Bosque de San Domingo and the Bishop's Palace. *Capture of Monterrey.* Lithograph by Carl Nebel. Courtesy of Kendall company had the honor of being the van of Taylor's entire army, quite a compliment considering Gillespie's earlier encounters with the general. Behind Gillespie was McCulloch's company, the rest of the Texans under General Henderson, and the First, Second, and Third Divisions, in that order.[50]

From the top of the hill the men gazed into the valley below. Thick, morning fog covered the area. They could make out the turrets of a large cathedral jutting out from the mist on the northern plain. A giant Mexican flag poked through the fog west of the city. Soon the morning sun burned the fog away, revealing the city of Monterrey. "In the beautiful valley below us," Major Giddings wrote, "lay the beautiful capital of New Leon [Nuevo Leon], sparkling like a gem in the bright beams of the beaming sun." The towering Sierra Madre Mountains loomed just to the south, with the Mitre Mountain to the west. The men had longed to see these mountains since Camargo, and now they stared in awe of their magnificence. But more somber sights quickly attracted their attention. A giant fort surrounded an old church on Monterrey's northern plain. Its twenty-foot walls, blackened with age, prompted the soldiers to call it the "Black Fort." The Bishop's Palace came into full view to the west, with its heavy cannons and high-flying Mexican flag. The men could also see where the Marin Road, which they were presently occupying, entered what appeared to be a heavily fortified city. Taylor and his staff veered to the right to examine the enemy's works. Suddenly, smoke belched from the Black Fort as Mexican gunners launched the battle's first salvo at the mounted officers. At first the cannoneers' range was off, but soon they found the distance, and a cannonball landed within ten feet of General Taylor and bounced through his party. The Black Fort's gunners quickly earned the respect of the Americans for their accuracy.[51]

Mexican trumpets sounded, the noise echoing across the plain. Cavalry emerged from the fort and formed for battle on the plain. Their red and green pennons, hanging from the shafts of their lances, fluttered in the breeze. The Texans prepared to charge but soon realized that the challenge was a ruse to get them within firing distance of the Black Fort. Nevertheless, they could not stand still and galloped toward the fort, dodging the cannonballs shot at them. Major Giddings described the scene: "Like boys at play on the first frail ice with which winter has commenced to bridge their favorite stream, those fearless horsemen, in a spirit of boastful rivalry, vied with each other in approaching the very edge of danger. Riding singly and rapidly, they swept around the plain under the walls, each one in a wider and more perilous circle than his predecessor. Their proximity occasionally provoked the enemy's fire, but the Mexicans might as well have attempted to bring down skimming swallows as those racing dare-devils."[52]

The men in the rear of Taylor's mile-long column yearned to see what was happening. How frustrating it must have been to be miles back in a column when a battle was beginning. The men were quiet, listening to the sounds of the cannon, until their commanders shouted, "Column forward! Quick march!" Captain Kenly recalled that at this command: "Every pulse fluttered, and many a long breath drawn; we still hurried on: a halt was ordered, and our astonishment was great when we saw General Taylor and staff slowly countermarching, and Paymaster Major Kirby, of Taylor's staff, carrying in his hands a twelve-pound ball which had been fired at the party and fallen near the feet of the general." Taylor was his casual self, calm as ever on his horse, Old Whitey. Just another day in the army for the general. He moved his men out of range of the fort's fire to a fine-looking campsite three miles northeast of Monterrey called Walnut Springs, or Bosque de San Domingo. Here his soldiers prepared for battle.[53]

Ampudia, even with Taylor's army camped only yards from the city's outskirts, was not done making changes to his plan. Don Luis Robles, his best engineer and a true military professional, recommended to the general that they rebuild Fort Teneria. Robles, who understood the importance of the fort, had probably been suggesting this ever since the general ordered it torn down. Only now did Ampudia heed the advice. What a shock the decision must have been to the men. They had wasted precious days destroying the fort, and now it was to be rebuilt. The general put Robles in charge of the reconstruction. A light drizzle and cool breeze swept upon the engineer and his men as they dug out the moat, established cannon platforms, and refortified the walls. Robles lined the parapet with cotton sacks, the only material he could find, in order to give the soldiers something from which to fire. The cannon platforms were nothing more than bare, muddy ground since he could not find any wood to construct a solid base.

As dawn broke the next day, the Mexicans continued working. From Teneria's parapets they could probably see Taylor's men setting up camp at Santo Domingo. The cool drizzle continued, and some of them perhaps reflected on the significance of the date, September 20, 1846—it was Monterrey's 250th anniversary.

5

TAYLOR'S DIVERSION

"Our little band was fast melting away like frost before the sun"
Soldier, 1st Tennessee

Walnut Springs was a delightful military campsite. The grove contained towering pecan and oak trees and well-groomed grass. Clear, bubbling springs quenched the Americans' thirst and gave them a cool place to bathe. Pvt. Zenith Matthews scribbled in his diary that it had "large live oaks . . . [and] the finest springs I ever have seen." In peacetime the Bosque San Domingo served as a picnic area for Monterrey's inhabitants. There was not a bad spot in the whole area to sit or pitch a tent. The American soldiers erected their shelters, organized their supplies, and prepared dinner. Thoughts of war faded from their minds as they drank cool water and relaxed under the shade of the trees. General Taylor picked one of the nicer spots in the grove for his tent: good shade, flat ground, and clean water from a nearby stream. One soldier joked that the Walnut Springs was better suited to a caballero strumming a guitar for his sweetheart than it was for an invading army.[1]

But Zachary Taylor had more-pressing concerns than his campsite's location. He wanted to learn more about Monterrey's fortifications so he could develop a plan to assault the city. Taylor knew that Pedro de Ampudia had spent months constructing fortifications, but he wanted to know exactly what his army was up against. He sent engineers Joseph Mansfield, John Sanders, and Jeremiah Scarritt, escorted by Captain Gillespie's Texans, to reconnoiter the city's western approaches. Taylor also sent Capt. William G. Williams of the topographical engineers, protected by Randolph Ridgley's light artillery battery, to observe the eastern part of the city. The two groups departed on the afternoon of September 19.

Taylor's engineers, especially his topographers (or topogs), were ideal candidates to help the general learn more about the composition of Monterrey and its fortifications. The peacetime duties of topographical engineers included surveying new territories, scouting the area ahead of advancing military columns, and mapping new land. Taylor at first did not use his engineers effectively but soon learned that they were among his most valuable staff officers. The topogs with the Army of Occupation included Lieutenant Meade, Captain Williams, and Lt. John Pope. Early in the campaign, Meade was frustrated with Taylor because the general had not taken any of the engineers' recommendations, and the lieutenant felt like he was not helping the army at all. He believed that he could be better utilized in southern Florida, where the army was surveying new islands. "General Taylor has his own views and plans," Meade wrote his wife, "and does not intend to trouble himself, with those of other peoples so that there was no use in my coming."[2]

Although he did not keep a journal, Captain Williams probably did not complain about how Taylor employed his engineers. He was known as a likeable and reliable soldier who completed his missions diligently with little complaint. Williams had been in the army for twenty-two years prior to Monterrey, and like most topogs he had never seen combat. But he did not take his success in the army for granted. Williams had a rough childhood, losing his mother at an early age, while his father spent most of his time traveling on business. He applied for West Point on his own initiative, convincing some influential persons of his ambition and succeeding in obtaining an appointment. Williams performed well at the academy, graduating fifteenth in his class, and was assigned to the topogs, an elite service in the army. Like most topogs, Williams spent much of his career surveying railroads, supervising harbor construction, and exploring new terrain. He supervised the construction of new harbors at Lake Erie and surveyed the boundary between Wisconsin and Michigan. Williams loved painting and produced some outstanding sketches of

Gen. Zachary Taylor at Walnut Springs. **This depicts a typical scene at General Taylor's tent, where his key officers often congregated to discuss events. The illustration shows a fly over the tent, though most accounts say that Taylor usually did not erect one. Courtesy of Special Collections, The University of Texas at Arlington Library.**

his adventures. He was even an honorary member of the National Academy of Design. When the war broke out, Williams asked to join Taylor's army. His request was approved by his superiors, and he arrived at Matamoros in the summer of 1846. The captain would soon see how different his new duties were from those he had known.[3]

Taylor now tasked his engineers, including Maj. Joseph Mansfield, to reconnoiter the strength and locations of Monterrey's defenses in mid-September. Thick fields of corn and sugarcane covered its northern plain, which forced the men to creep dangerously close the city to observe its works. Mexican cannoneers, upon spotting the unwelcome observers, launched grape and canister at them. Mansfield, while observing one battery, told his mounted escort to remain hidden in a hollow while he moved closer to observe the cannon. He dismounted his horse and peered through his spyglass to observe the enemy position. The artillerists fired on him, so he dropped flat to the ground. After the ball passed over his head, he stood up again to look through his glass. He continued this "up and down" routine until he had observed the whole area, then mounted his horse and rode off.[4]

While the engineers were conducting reconnaissance, large parties of Texas volunteers ventured out of camp to capture prisoners and conduct their own observations. One unlucky Mexican, Jeronimo Valdez, who the Texans started calling their "old acquaintance," was captured in Camargo, released, and then recaptured for spying a second time during one such scout. He had followed Taylor's army since Matamoros, often disguised as a fruit trader. But this would be his last time spying. The Texans shot him as he sprinted into the chaparral attempting to escape. On his person they found a notebook with an accurate count of Taylor's men and artillery.[5]

On the Texas plains, life or death depended on good information. Knowing the size, strength, and location of an enemy was critical there because the Texans, whether as private citizens or as Rangers, usually traveled in small groups and rode hundreds of miles from civilization. No reinforcement or additional supplies were available, so the men had to choose their battles wisely, and this depended on knowing as much as possible about their enemy.

The volunteers now brought these intelligence skills to Monterrey. After killing Valdez, they caught another previously captured spy gathering information on the army. The Texans decided to use harsher measures on this repeat offender. They looped a rope around his neck and threw the other end over the limb of the tree, then pulled hard on the rope until it tightened and the spy begged for his life. "We haven't had time to bother with you," a Texan told him, "the first lie, up you will go to remain." The Texan described what happened next: "We had with us an intelligence officer who gave me questions to ask; occasionally the rope was taughtened by way of a reminder, and we forced him to designate the position of the batteries and the number of guns and troops in them and in the city. We also got a careful plot of the position of the artillery and troops on the farther side of the city." The information turned out to be accurate.[6]

The engineers returned unharmed at dark. Even though Meade did not accompany Mansfield, he now realized that he would soon be much busier than he would have been in south Florida. He wrote his wife that conducting the reconnaissance was "a duty, I assure you, sufficiently hazardous, as they [the engineers] were obliged to go with

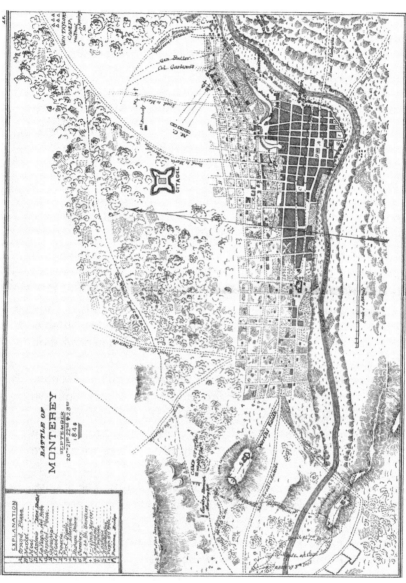

Battle of Monterrey. Many maps were produced on the battle, but this is probably the most accurate and detailed. The key landmarks are the Citadel in the top center, the Bishop's Palace located to the left of the city (north of the river), and the Grand Plaza (A) shown in the bottom right. Map by J. M. Stewart. From Wilcox, *History of the Mexican War*, 92.

small parties and far from the camp, giving an enterprising enemy ample opportunity to cut them off." Major Mansfield, who brought five prisoners back with him, told Taylor that western Monterrey could be turned by a flanking movement, despite the Mexicans having some formidable positions prepared. There is no record of Captain Williams's report, probably because it did not contain much information. Reconnoitering the eastern part of the city was even more hazardous than scouting the western approaches. Williams had to crawl through tall stalks of corn and sugar to view the city while constantly hoping that no cavalry surprised his group. The thick fields of corn and sugarcane obstructed his view, and he probably could not see very far into the city.[7]

Taylor still wanted more information, so that night he sent James Duncan of the light artillery to confirm Mansfield's assessment. Duncan was an odd choice to reconnoiter territory since he was an artillerist, but Taylor had come to trust his judgment about whether a road or path was practical for artillery. Like Braxton Bragg, Duncan was a proud West Point graduate who commanded one of the army's new light artillery companies. Unlike Bragg, Duncan had fought at Palo Alto, where the flying artillery proved its worth to the army and the nation. His company had been prominent on the field, and he was brevetted to major for his actions there. Many of his peers believed that the brevet was well deserved—an unusual tribute in an era when soldiers often put down the courageous actions of others in order to self-aggrandize their own battlefield actions. Duncan, like Captain Williams, had a tough upbringing. He was orphaned at an early age but managed to secure a West Point appointment from some friends. He excelled at the academy, graduating sixth in his class, and was assigned to the prestigious artillery. Duncan served in Florida under General Gaines and was wounded in a vicious fight with the Seminole Indians. Now Taylor asked his accomplished artillery officer to carry out a harrowing night reconnaissance, a hazardous duty by any account. The Americans could bump into a large group of Mexican cavalry that could cut them down easily with carbines and lances. But Duncan and his men survived, scouting for five miles before returning to camp. He reported to Taylor at 11 P.M. that the western fortifications could be carried.[8]

The Texans also kept busy that night. They patrolled the area in small groups and captured thirty more prisoners. Although no record exists of what the prisoners said, they probably revealed some helpful information about Ampudia's strength and fortifications. Meanwhile in camp the soldiers sharpened their sabers, nailed shoes onto their horses, and organized their supplies. A light drizzle began to fall toward morning, and the men huddled around campfires, wrapped in blankets, guarding the prisoners. They speculated about how events would transpire the following day.

Taylor held a council of war on September 19 to discuss possible courses of action. His staff agreed that Monterrey should be assaulted from the west in a giant hook movement. If their army controlled the Saltillo road, they could prevent reinforcements or supplies from reaching Ampudia. Also, with Taylor in control of that thoroughfare, he could cut off the Mexicans' only avenue of retreat and capture their entire army. Taylor knew that this maneuver could win him the battle, so he assigned his best general to the job. "Deeming this to be an operation of essential importance," he wrote in his official report, "orders were given to Brevet Brig. Gen. Worth." Taylor added Colonel Hays's regiment of mounted Texans to the Second Division, giving Worth a total of 2,000 men.[9]

Jack Hays was already a legend in Texas by the time of the war. He had moved to the state in 1837, when he was nineteen years old, to be a surveyor. As a young man he ventured alone into remote areas to scout locales for new settlements or businesses, sometimes encountering Indians or bandits bent on killing or robbing him. Young Hays thrived in this dangerous environment, so when a Texas militia was formed to fend off Indians and banditti, he was selected to lead the outfit. A natural leader, Hays never panicked during a fight, no matter how bad things got. He calmly issued smart commands that his men usually obeyed. There was no real chain of command in Ranger groups, but the men always executed Hays's instructions, because if they wanted to get out of a scrape alive, they did what Jack told them. An Indian who had fought Hays before said of him, " 'Blue Wing' and I, no 'fraid to go to *hell* together—'Capitan Jack,' great brave—no 'fraid to go to *hell* by himself."[10]

In addition to the Texans, Worth also had two "embedded" reporters with his division. Christopher Mason Haile and George Wilkins Kendall, both from the *New Orleans Picayune,* joined the Second Division and provided their readers with daily updates on its movements and activities. No other part of the forthcoming battle would be chronicled as well as those involving Worth's command. Haile had attended West Point, knew many of the men, and was eminently qualified to write about military matters. Kendall was a celebrity in his own right. In May 1841 he had accompanied some Texans on an ill-fated expedition to wrestle New Mexico away from Mexico. The group, including Kendall, was captured, and 180 prisoners were marched to Mexico City. The men were released almost a year later, after which Kendall wrote a book about their journey. Perhaps no journalist understood the Texan and Mexican mindset better than he did, and he always was willing to put himself in danger to get the best story.

Kendall and Haile, along with the rest of Worth's men, prepared to march on September 20, though the general did not inform the Texans of the division's objective. Samuel Reid, who was in Hays's regiment, thought that he would be returning to camp the same day, so he and his fellow Texans did not bring their blankets, jackets, or any food with them. The regulars, however, prepared four days of rations. The men departed camp at noon, moving west through corn, sugarcane, irrigation ditches, and chaparral. Pioneers, under the command of Capt. John Sanders, carved a path for Worth's artillery, cutting through chaparral fences and bridging small ravines so Duncan and Mackall's cannons could keep up with the men.[11]

Worth tried to hide his advance by moving along the far north side of the plain, but not long into his march, Mexican soldiers on Independence Hill (where the Bishop's Palace was located) spotted the Americans. When Taylor noted the Mexicans running to the western peak of the hill for a better look, he ordered the First and Third Divisions onto the plain, out of range of the Black Fort, to distract the observant enemy.

Worth soon reached the Pescaria Grande Road, the last major route to enter Monterrey from the north. His men then turned south down a smaller road lined with jacales that led toward the Saltillo road. Worth intended to advance down this path all the way to the Saltillo road that day. The general and his staff stayed in front of the main body, escorted by some Texas horseman, to reconnoiter ahead. Kendall joined the group as they climbed a rise so they could better observe Independence Hill's defenses. Meanwhile, Mexican soldiers crept down the south side of Independence Hill, concealed from the Americans' view, and snaked around its base to hide in some cornfields next to the Saltillo road. Maj. Edward Burleson, a senior aide de camp to Worth, saw the men and rode to warn him. Instead he found Kendall, who offered to carry the message for him and galloped off to find the general. Worth received the message but wanted to continue reconnoitering. The division had moved a thousand yards south when cannons on Independence Hill erupted, pouring shot all around the Texans. Their horses, unaccustomed to exploding shells, bucked violently. The riders held on the best they could and tried to regain control of the scared animals. Meanwhile, Mexican infantry and cavalry moved forward, attempting to separate the advance from the main body. The two sides exchanged fire, but the Americans managed to safely return to the column.

One young Texan did not retreat because an artillery shell had killed his horse. The animal had been with him for the duration of the campaign, and he cherished it above all else. Anger boiled inside of him. He stood alone, clearly visible on the road, ready to take down as many Mexicans as possible before he was killed. "I'll own up," he later wrote, "if the old Nick ever did possess me, he did then. Heretofore my duty had been done as a soldier, with no hard feelings against the Mexicans. . . . [N]ow, I wanted to avenge the death of my noble friend, and stood there alone, loading my rifle, and taking deliberate aim." Lucky for the soldier, a lieutenant in his company swooped him up from the field and hauled him back to camp. The horse was later recovered and buried with full honors. All of the Texans turned out to pay their respects at its funeral.[12]

After returning to the column, Worth ordered his men to establish camp near some jacales, far away from Independence Hill. The hungry soldiers, who had not eaten since breakfast, found chickens roosting in trees near their campsite. Some Texans climbed the trees with swords and "commenced an assault upon the chickens" in order to obtain their first meal of the day. Others wildly chased pigs around their pens but were unable to catch the wily creatures. "Many a laugh was had at the unsuccessful racing that was going on." The earlier exchange of fire apparently did not affect the Texans' spirit. During the pig chase, though, some Mexican cavalrymen climbed a nearby hill and fired their muskets on the playful soldiers. "The tables were now turned," wrote Samuel Reid, "to the evident delight of the pigs and chickens." The men slid or jumped out of the trees to avoid fire. Colonel Hays posted some men by a nearby chaparral fence, and they repulsed the offending cavalry with no loss of life. The Mexicans gave way easily since nightfall was near and they did want to instigate a major engagement. The Americans stayed in their positions for an hour. A cold, drizzling rain descended on the soldiers, but they kept lookout for an attack. The hungry men could not light any fires to cook their meals because Worth feared the light would give away their location. "Cold, cheerless, and hungry, the men lay sleeping on their arms, while all around prevailed a gloomy quiet." The jittery men awoke at the slightest noise, ready for a fight.[13]

That night, using a flaming corn shuck as a light, General Worth wrote Taylor asking him to make a diversion the next day (September 21). He hoped that a feint in the northeast would draw some enemy forces away from the daunting western defenses. Worth knew that once he controlled Independence Hill and the Saltillo road, the Mexicans would have to sacrifice scores of men to regain them. He only needed a one-day diversion.

That same night at Walnut Springs, soldiers in the First and Third Divisions prepared for battle. Rumors circulated that Taylor was going to attack the city the next day. They sat around campfires in small groups, chatting quietly, sharpening their swords, or polishing their muskets. Some wrote letters to their friends and relatives in case they did not live through the day, while others drafted wills that they left in their trunks. Many of the volunteers, who had never been in combat, probably wondered how they would hold up under fire. Lt. Rankin Dilworth of the 1st Infantry did not have time to write in his journal that night as he usually did, busy perhaps with preparations for the coming fight. But he did pen an entry on September 19. Dilworth wrote of having climbed to the top of a tree in Walnut Springs, spotting a Mexican flag waving in the city (probably flying from the Bishop's Palace), and being asked by a dragoon if he had heard the "elephant roar" (a metaphor for having seen combat). "At one-half past four I saw the smoke curl up from a gun," the last sentence in Dilworth's journal reads, "and in short time the report came to me. They were firing at Captain Williams' party [on reconnaissance]. Returning to camp, I met Generals Taylor, Twiggs, and Worth going out to reconnoiter."[14]

Unlike Dilworth, Philip Barbour did have time to write in his journal that night. He noted that Major Mansfield should receive another brevet for his brave reconnaissance in western Monterrey and also described a drunk soldier who had deserted from the Mexican army and offered to help General Taylor. Barbour closed by reflecting on the coming battle and on his duty to his country: "I feel as calm and collected as if I were in the Astor House, having long since made up my mind that, during a time of war, my life is the rightful property of my country, and cannot be taken from me, or preserved, except by the fiat of the great God who gave it. And to His will, whatever it be, I am perfectly resigned." The major had a lot to live up to in order to honor his family's heritage. His father had fought in the War of 1812, participating in the Battle of the Thames, where William Henry Harrison defeated Tecumseh and his British allies. Barbour's grandfather had risen to the rank of major general, fighting first in the American Revolution and later during the War of 1812. Having graduated only twenty-eighth in his West Point class, Barbour was assigned to infantry—the least coveted army branch. Although he might not have realized it at the time, the infantry was a perfect fit for him. In his younger days Barbour was known for "steadiness, patience, and perseverance, . . . and the amiability of his bearing made him a general favorite of his young companions." These qualities made him a natural leader on the battlefield. He was composed and courageous under fire and could organize men in unpredictable situations, like he did at Resaca de la Palma. Barbour was brevetted to major for his "gallant and distinguished services" at Palo Alto and Resaca de la Palma. He already had been brevetted twice before that, including once in 1842 for his courageous service in Florida against the Seminoles. Barbour knew that with the morning, he would probably get another chance to lead men in battle.[15]

That night Taylor instructed two of his officers to place a 10-inch mortar and two 24-pound howitzers about 1,400 yards from the Black Fort. The artillery deployed in a small depression in the plain where the guns were partially sheltered from the fire from the Citadel. Because they did not have the materials necessary to build a platform, they placed the mortar directly on the ground. Maj. George Ramsey, an ordnance officer in charge of the mortar, remembered later that it was as "efficiently secured as it could have been without a platform." Ramsey probably harbored private doubts whether his artillery pieces would do much against the massive Black Fort, but he and his men followed orders anyway. At dawn Ramsey opened up with the mortar on the Citadel, over a mile away. He fired at such a distance that he had time to run to a nearby hill to observe where the bomb landed. But it fell short of the fort like most of the shots from this battery, which caused little or no damage throughout the day. Taylor's regulars probably shrugged at the spectacle. They knew that a mortar and some howitzers did not constitute heavy artillery. Without the 18-pounders, the only way to force the Mexicans from the city was at the point of the bayonet.[16]

At 8 A.M. on the 21st, Taylor formed elements of the First Division on the plain, consisting of the 1st and 3rd Infantry regiments, and the Battalion of Maryland and District of Columbia Volunteers. He planned to march his regulars into northeast Monterrey to divert Ampudia's attention from the west, where Worth's division was advancing. Taylor did not receive Worth's request for a diversion until 9 A.M.—an hour after the U.S. commander began moving men onto the plain. The two generals were thinking alike.

Notably absent from the deployment was General Twiggs, commander of the First Division. Twiggs took some medicine that morning to loosen his bowels, believing that if a musket ball hit him, it would do less damage if he had empty intestines. The medicine apparently knocked him out and made him unfit for duty. "Old Davy" Twiggs, who also was known as the "Bengal Tiger" by his men, stood six feet, two inches tall with ghost white hair and a matching mustache. He had served in the War of 1812 and the Seminole Wars. Despite his service, Twiggs was known to always be "thirsty for a fight" and was not viewed as one of the army's intellectuals. He was probably better known in the army for his clash with General Worth over brevet rank than for any of his military exploits. Taylor did not think twice about placing John Garland, a colonel, in command, telling him to "make a strong demonstration toward the lower part of the town, and carry one of the enemy's batteries if it can be done without too heavy a loss. Consult with Major Mansfield, you will find him down there." But it was difficult for any of the engineers to get close enough to the city to ascertain fort and troop locations; the Americans would have to rely on the intelligence collected from prisoners and defectors for information about the city's defenses.[17]

The Mexican garrison inside Fort Teneria watched the formations develop on the plain and believed that a vicious battle was about to begin. The exhausted soldiers, who had worked all night to reconstruct the fort, sipped mescal to regain their energy and strength. And now, after such exertions, they were about to meet the best army the United States had ever fielded. General Mejía warned Colonel Carrasco, who commanded Fort Teneria, that the Americans would feign an attack on the Citadel but then proceed with a real attack against his garrison. Carrasco urged his 200 men of the 2nd Light Infantry and the Querétaro Battalion to be ready. Their artillery consisted of 4- and 8-pound cannon and a small howitzer.

On this drizzly, gloomy morning, there was an unlikely source of inspiration for the Mexican soldiers in Fort Teneria and throughout the city. María de Jesús Dosamantes, a respected Monterrey dame, dressed herself in a Mexican lancer uniform, mounted a horse, and rode back and forth along the lines, rallying the men to fight. She swore that she would never leave the field until the "northern barbarians" were driven from her land. Her example encouraged the men as they watched her ride.[18]

Colonel Garland sent one company of the 3rd Infantry to protect the engineers making yet another reconnaissance of the city. Soon Mansfield, who also was having a difficult time trying to reconnoiter eastern Monterrey, requested two more companies to support him. Garland's division formed into columns and began marching across the plain. After a hundred steps the Citadel's artillery erupted on them. Cannonballs rolled through the tightly packed columns, knocking down soldiers and opening large holes in their formation. One shot removed Lieutenant Dilworth's leg. Mortally wounded, Dilworth suffered until he died eight days later.[19]

Although Garland and his men did not know it, they were probably being fired on by American deserters. John Riley and some other foreign-born U.S. soldiers had deserted to the Mexican army earlier in the year. Riley had been a private in the 5th Infantry and had served under Capt. Moses Merrill. Perhaps he was one of the Irish Catholic immigrants in Taylor's army who felt mistreated by Protestant officers. Other deserters left out of frustration after being passed over for promotions. The Mexicans seized on this dissatisfaction, spreading pamphlets calling for American Catholics to join their army and promising large tracts of land and a pension following the war for any who changed sides. Those who decided to take the Mexican offer later formed what became known as the San Patricio Battalion, and their first major battle occurred at Monterrey. Although no evidence firmly places Riley and his men at the Citadel during the battle, its location made the most sense since the Mexicans employed the deserters as artillerists throughout the war.[20]

Garland's men quickened their pace to continue through the torrent of shot and shell coming from the Citadel. They scampered into and out of a limestone-ridged ravine into a mature cornfield. Once the Americans cleared the corn, Fort Teneria's gunners had a clear view of the columns and opened fire. The Citadel also fired on the men as did the cannons at the Purisima Bridge, 300 yards west of the fort. Garland's men also received artillery fire from an unknown battery, Fort Diablo (or the Devil's Corner), located 300 yards to the southwest of Fort Teneria with 200 men and two cannons. Despite all of Taylor's reconnaissance and prisoner debriefings, this was the first time that Garland had learned about its existence.[21]

The disciplined men stayed in their lines, but they needed to find cover. Garland looked for Major Mansfield. He needed that officer to direct him into the city. The colonel finally saw him in the distance and, as Garland noted, Mansfield "then indicated a movement to the right, which would enable us to gain a position in the town and in rear of the first redoubt [Fort Teneria]." He wanted Garland to enter Monterrey on a road about 200 yards west of Teneria. "I there saw the practicability of covers among the stone buildings," Mansfield reported, "and of attaining the gorge of the redoubt." The engineer acknowledged that he could not get close enough to the street to see if Garland's men would meet stiff resistance but concluded, "if our troops were there it [Teneria] must of necessity fall, and, I presumed, without serious loss."[22]

Mansfield's guidance meant that Garland's men had to change direction under heavy fire. To conduct such a maneuver greatly tested the regulars' discipline, and for the Baltimore volunteers, it was more than they could handle. Col. William Watson, commander of the battalion, screamed to his men, "Shelter yourselves, men, the best way you can." Many of them broke formation and dove into quarries or small ditches. "At this time the battalion was scattered over a space of about an acre," a Baltimore soldier recalled, "and the men were lying down, the shot in most instances flying over our heads, but the guns were soon depressed, and the shot began to take effect." Meanwhile the remaining troops followed Mansfield until they approached a major north–south road that ran from the plain, across the Arroyo Santa Lucia, and into the city. Mexican soldiers had fortified

Garland's advance against eastern Monterrey, September 21. This illustration depicts Mexican gunners at the Citadel firing into U.S. troops as they cross the plain. The scale of the drawing is incorrect, but unlike others, it correctly shows Fort Teneria and Fort Diablo sitting prominently on hills to the left of the Americans' line of approach. The size of each hill is probably exaggerated for effect, but the Mexican army did place the forts on the highest points in the eastern part of the city, which greatly aided the garrisons in their defense of the strongholds. From Thorpe, *Our Army at Monterey*, 71. Courtesy of Special Collections, The University of Texas at Arlington Library.

themselves behind the canal, capitalizing on the arroyo as a natural barrier between the plain and the city.[23]

As the Americans approached, Lt. Col. Joaquín Castro of the 3rd Light Infantry reinforced Fort Teneria with 150 men and an 8-pound cannon. The garrison then unloaded their muskets and cannons against Garland's men. At the same time, hundreds of Mexican soldiers, perched on flat rooftops near the street, discharged their muskets into the columns. Gunners at Fort Diablo, the Citadel, and three other nearby works also fired cannons at advancing column. It was a murderous crossfire that put Garland's men in serious trouble. As Captain Henry described: "From all its embrasures, from every house, from every yard, showers of balls were hurled upon us. Being in utter ignorance of our locality, we had to stand and take it; our men, covering themselves as well as they could, dealt death and destruction on every side; there was no resisting the deadly, concealed fire, which appeared to come from every direction. On every side we were cut down."[24]

The Americans, in shock from the horrific fire and completely ignorant of their surroundings, stood around in confusion. The men could barely hear each other through the roar of cannon and musket fire. Thick smoke settled into the narrow streets, virtually blinding the soldiers. Their officers tried to keep them organized, but it was an impossible task. "Upon entering the town," Colonel Wilson remembered, "the obstruction of stone walls, houses, water courses, and shrubbery intersecting the streets, precluded all possibility of maintaining the order of the respective lines." Major Barbour, standing before the 3rd Infantry, cheered his troops and encouraged them to press forward. Most of the regiment followed him across the canal on a narrow bridge leading into the city. As soon as Barbour made it to the other side, a musket ball pierced his heart, and he dropped dead. The 1834 West Point graduate would never again see his dearest Mattie.[25]

The 1st Infantry largely remained on the north side of the arroyo (possibly witnessing the carnage among those who crossed the bridge) and jumped over a thorn-covered wall. They sheltered themselves in a courtyard long enough to organize some of their companies. An officer with the unusual name of Capt. Electus Backus collected two companies and proceeded east toward Fort Teneria. His men crossed the canal on a log about a hundred yards east of the 3rd Infantry's crossing, then grouped together on a road running along the south side of the canal. But this street was a deathtrap for U.S. soldiers attempting to enter the city. Ampudia established a string of redoubts to reinforce each other along this line. Five Mexican batteries—six counting the Citadel—covered the road and arroyo.

Backus's men were fortunate, though. They crossed the canal on a small, makeshift span rather than on one of three major entryways into the city, and the Mexicans did not notice them collecting in the road. Soon after Backus began marching his two companies, numbering forty-four men, east toward Fort Teneria, some Mexican soldiers spotted them and fired a volley from a tall building. The captain figured that the building must be important given how furiously the Mexicans were guarding it. His men entered the structure and successfully routed its defenders.

Backus now took a page from the Mexicans' notebook. He climbed to the roof to observe the area and immediately understood why Ampudia had posted so many soldiers in the building. Backus could make out all of the fortifications in northeast Monterrey. He saw Fort Diablo, perched on top of a hill, its cannons blazing on the 3rd Infantry, and noticed hundreds of Mexican soldiers on rooftops throughout the area. The captain also observed a building, later identified as a distillery, thirty yards behind Fort Teneria, its rooftop covered with troops who guarded the throat of the fort. Backus ordered his men to join him on the roof, where they dropped to their bellies behind a two-foot wall and fired at the enemy on the distillery's rooftop. The Americans had a clear line of fire against the Mexicans, who not anticipating being fired on from the west, had stacked sandbags only on the distillery's north side. The Mexicans were surprised by the fire, and some jumped off the roof while others slid down ladders to the ground. Infantry poured out of the building's main door, but Backus ordered his men to hold their fire because the soldiers trailed some women and children, and he did not want to risk shooting noncombatants. Some infantrymen became separated from the women, and the Americans quickly shot at them. The flustered Mexicans sprinted back into the group of women and children, apparently realizing the Americans' rules of engagement.

Another 1st Infantry officer, Capt. Joseph Lamotte, sought to dislodge some Mexicans firing from a line of houses running from Backus's building to the distillery. His small group moved from house to house, clearing them of Mexican soldiers, until a musket ball hit him. Four of his men bent down to pick up the fallen officer, and a cannon ball hit the whole group, instantly killing two and tearing the leg off the third. Backus did not try to approach the distillery again. He could not assault the fort with only forty men.

While Backus defended his toehold in eastern Monterrey, farther west the soldiers of the 3rd Infantry were fighting for their lives. The 3rd, unlike most of Taylor's other infantry regiments, had undergone a rare year of regimental training at Jefferson Barracks. There, the men had learned about marching cadences, battle-line formations, and firing in volleys. Now on the streets of Monterrey, that training provided little help or guidance for how to react to Mexican snipers concealed on rooftops and inside houses. The men could not form battle lines or fire volleys because of the city's narrow cobblestone lanes. Instead, the regiment's organization fractured, and men split into small groups as they tried to cross the canal and enter the city. Monterrey was turning out to be a different type of battlefield than the men had been trained for.

Engineer Williams pressed across the canal and urged others to follow. He was instantly hit by a musket ball and crumpled to the street. His friend and fellow topog Lieutenant Pope carried him to the safety of a house but was forced to leave him behind due to the intense fire. As Pope was leaving the house, Williams asked him to make sure that everyone knew that "he fell while leading the advance and in the discharge of his duty." His request was unnecessary since everyone knew that the captain was wounded leading his men from the front, but Pope reassured him that he would. The Mexicans would later recover the wounded Williams and reportedly treated him well, but he eventually succumbed to his injuries. Writing about his death, General Taylor said, "Capt. Williams, Topographical Engineers, to my great regret and the loss of his service, was mortally wounded while fearlessly exposing himself in the attack on the 21st." Williams was forty-five years old.[26]

Once most of the men had made it to the south side of the canal, Mexican fire began to take serious effect. The 3rd Infantry's commander, W. W. Lear, was shot through the nose and mortally wounded, the bullet exiting out the back of his ear and ripping apart his jaw. Major Mansfield, who was next to Lear when he was shot, believed the colonel was dead. When he saw him moving, the engineer took a

Combat in the streets of Monterrey. This lithograph, though it depicts action on September 23, more accurately portrays the fighting on September 21. The U.S. soldiers are advancing down the middle of the street, with Mexican snipers firing upon them from nearby rooftops. *Third Day of the Siege of Monterey, Sept. 23rd 1846.* Lithograph by Sarony & Major. Toned lithograph (hand-colored), 8 1/4 × 12 7/8 in. Courtesy of the Amon Carter Museum, Fort Worth, Tex.

blanket from three Mexican prisoners and ordered his men to carry their commander back to camp and out of harm's way. Lear suffered in agony until his death one month later. Meanwhile, another bullet pierced the neck of the 3rd Infantry's adjutant, Lt. D. S. Irwin, an 1840 West Point graduate, killing him instantly. The Mexicans also captured Lt. J. C. Terrett, who was injured by a musket ball and eventually succumbed to his injuries. The tattered remnants of the regiment rushed to a side street for protection. "The troops availed themselves of the building walls," Colonel Wilson recalled, "so to avoid the fire and return their own to the best advantage." They carried as many dead and wounded with them as they could. The Mexicans now enclosed them on three sides. Perhaps one journalist put it best when he wrote, "Had the enemy selected it for the special purpose of decoying our men into a slaughtering pen, it could not have been more fatally contrived."[27]

Major Mansfield nevertheless cheered the men and pointed out places to attack. His behavior would have been considered crazy if he were not such a well-respected soldier. He proceeded alone down Monterrey's streets, looking for a way to enter Fort Teneria from the rear. At one point he walked the 100 yards east to Backus's position. From the roof the captain watched him strolling down the street. "His efforts to obtain a closer observation," he wrote, "were frustrated, for as often as he raised his spyglass, just so often were Mexican muskets presented toward him." Mansfield spoke with Backus briefly, then went to look for Colonel Garland. A musket ball hit the major in the leg, but he tied a handkerchief around it and continued on. Mansfield was not just full of physical courage and fortitude, though, he was also an intelligent soldier who graduated second in West Point's class of 1822. He was one of Taylor's more experienced officers, having been in the army for more than twenty-four years when the war began. But the brave and smart Mansfield could only do so much to help the besieged men of the 3rd Infantry.[28]

Lieutenant Colonel Watson, commander of the Baltimore Battalion, could attest to that. He rallied his frightened volunteers, who were hiding behind hedges and in ditches on the plain, telling them, "Now's the time, boys, follow me." The men stood up and sprinted into the city to link up with the regulars. They rounded a corner when a shower of grape shot and musket fire rained down on the battalion. Five officers and many privates fell to the ground wounded or killed.

Lt. Col. William H. Watson. A lawyer by trade, Watson bravely acquitted himself in Monterrey and tried to rally his rattled volunteers, who scattered under intense artillery and small-arms fire. His death not only affected his men but also his hometown of Baltimore, which lowered flags to half mast in his honor. Watson died on the same day that his daughter was born in Maryland, and she was appropriately named "Monterey." He is remembered by a statue in Baltimore established in 1903 and the fourth stanza of Maryland's state song, "With Watson's blood at Monterey." (Thorpe, *Our Army at Monterey*, 127–29.) From Brooks, *Complete History of the Mexican War*, 178.

All of the survivors sought shelter. One Baltimorean hid from the fire by sitting with his back to the wall of a house. When two wounded men, who had been hit by grapeshot, also sought shelter in the house, he tried to tend to their wounds the best that he could. Suddenly, Mexican artillery fired another round of grapeshot at the house, hitting one of the wounded men and tearing off his leg. He died instantly. Watson was determined to honor his Maryland. Some of his men encouraged him to retire. "Never, boys! Never will I yield an inch! I have too much Irish blood in me to give up!" The color sergeant responded and, with his right arm shattered, carried the battalion flag into the city to rally the men. Watson found Colonel Wilson, asked for orders, and was told to attack Fort Teneria. Watson galloped off to collect his few remaining men. A Mexican soldier shot the colonel's horse out from under him, throwing him to the ground. He rose and continued on foot, collecting some men and proceeding toward the fort. As Watson approached the redoubt, a musket ball hit him in the neck, killing him instantly. The rest of his company halted and sought shelter.[29]

Watson's death greatly affected the men. He was immensely respected, and his soldiers could not believe that he had been killed. When the news reached his native Baltimore, the city went into mourning. They lowered the shipping flags to half mast, and civic and military societies throughout the city gathered to grieve the loss of a leading citizen—the second such loss incurred by Baltimore in the campaign (the first being Samuel Ringgold, also a native of the city). The legal bar to which Watson belonged passed resolutions to honor his name and gallantry.

More corpses piled up in Monterrey's narrow streets. Five officers, including four West Pointers, had been killed or captured in the hour that the Americans had been in the town. Things clearly were not going as planned. Intense fire around Watson's body prevented the men from retrieving it for two days. He was eventually buried in a small stone house about 400 yards from where he made his charge.[30]

Around this time, Taylor ordered Braxton Bragg's crack 3rd Artillery company to support the struggling regulars. The battery with its twenty-four horses and four gun caissons began a dangerous sprint across Monterrey's northern plain. This perilous gallop was Bragg's first real battlefield test, and he probably relished it. Four forts opened fire on his men and horses as they dashed across the open plain.

Captain Bragg had graduated with honors from West Point in 1837, and he saw little fighting early in his career. He was stationed in Florida during the Second Seminole War but was absent from the Battle of Lake Okeechobee, where Taylor fought a pitched battle with two Indian chiefs. Bragg was later transferred to Charleston, South Carolina, where he spent three uneventful years. He now commanded Company E, 3rd Artillery, staffed by Lts. George H. Thomas, John F. Reynolds, and Samuel G. French. These officers, themselves West Point graduates, despised Bragg's gruff demeanor and painful attention to detail. But they could not argue with his success. Bragg had made his unit into one of the best light artillery companies in Taylor's army. Earlier in August, volunteers and regulars alike gazed wide eyed at Bragg's skilled men as they drilled on Camargo's parade ground, guiding and unlimbering their caissons in expert fashion. In May the company had been hemmed in at Fort Texas while under bombardment from the Mexicans. Bragg's light guns could not participate in the fort's heavy cannon duel, though, because they lacked sufficient range. Although missing out on Palo Alto, Captain Bragg and his men now had an opportunity to prove their mettle.

Cannonballs landed all around the artillerymen during their frantic mile-long gallop across the open plain to the suburbs of Monterrey. Their two dozen horses dashed with all their might to cross the treacherous expanse. They safely reached the outskirts and darted into the middle of the fighting. Garland pointed Bragg toward a narrow street filled with Mexican soldiers and one cannon, which was well concealed behind a masonry barricade. Bragg unlimbered his guns under withering fire and moved them into position. "When we got there, in the narrow streets with four guns, four caissons, and six horses to a carriage," Lieutenant Reynolds wrote after the battle, "it was discovered that only *one* gun could be brought into action." Mexican soldiers unloaded their muskets on the exposed Americans from nearby rooftops and windows. The lone cannon also lobbed shells at Bragg's company from behind the safety of its breastwork. Bragg returned fire. Cannon shells from both sides plunged into the soft-clay adobe houses, causing giant clouds of white dust to settle throughout the street. Bragg could scarcely see to aim. His men and horses began to drop.[31]

Garland, realizing that Bragg's cannon was useless, ordered him to retire. The light artillery that had proved so successful on the plains of South Texas could not maneuver Monterrey's constricted roads. The street was so narrow that the Americans had to pull the cannon out of danger by hand rather than reattaching the gun to its horses. Bragg retreated to the suburbs to reorganize his unit. Fourteen of his company's horses, and many of his men, were either dead or wounded. Throughout the affair, the meticulous captain ordered his men to salvage every strap or buckle from the wounded animals, regardless of the fire that rained down around them.

As the company retreated back across the plain, cannon fire killed four more horses managed by Lieutenants Reynolds and French. Two died instantly, and the officers dumped their carcasses and saddles into a ditch. Two others survived, if briefly. "These horses were loosed," French later wrote, "and with their entrails dragging, in agony of pain, I suppose, commenced eating grass." French and Reynolds made it safely out of harm's way. Then came an order from the martinet Bragg directing French to recover the harnesses he had thrown into the ditch. This seemed suicidal, for it meant that the lieutenant would need to cross the plain for a third time, alone, and enter the dangerous suburbs to recover a few replaceable harnesses. French successfully rode close to the outskirts, where he ran into General Taylor, who had come up briefly for a closer look at the situation. The general asked the lieutenant, "Where are you going?" French told him about Bragg's order. "That is nonsense," Taylor said and ordered him back to camp. Now French was in for the ride of his life. The Citadel's garrison, noting the officer's return, decided to direct their guns on him. "The gunners must have become quite vindictive," he recalled, "for they opened fire on me, a lone horseman." French watched the cannons closely as he galloped: When smoke poured out from a cannon's barrel, he would hold back his horse and allow the ball to fly ahead of him, executing this maneuver multiple times. French finally made it safely to camp. "I never forgave Bragg for that picayune order," he declared.[32]

Back in the city, Major Mansfield recommended to Colonel Garland that the First Division withdraw. Too much blood had been shed, and the division had made no headway in locating the rear of Fort Teneria. Many promising, young officers had been killed, wounded, or captured in the fighting. The Americans' retreat came just in time for

General Taylor at Monterrey. Taylor is depicted here on his horse, Old Whitey, watching the battle of the 21st unfold. Courtesy of Special Collections, The University of Texas at Arlington Library.

Teneria's defenders. Despite the one-sided affair, the garrison's soldiers were worn down from the exchange. From their perspective, the
Americans were close to overrunning the fort, and they were surprised to see them withdraw. As Manuel Balbontin recalled: "The
fight was terrible. The Americans in full possession of the ground
around the work, and covering themselves wherever cover could be
found, kneeling, lying prone, and in every possible position, at pistol
shot . . . kept up a heavy fire on the parapets." Nevertheless, at the
sight of the retreating First Division, the Mexican victory reveille
sounded throughout the city, and the tired soldiers in Fort Teneria
cheered wildly. They had much to be proud of, having just repulsed
one of the best infantry divisions in the world.[33]

At Walnut Springs Taylor sat atop Old Whitey and peered through
his spyglass. He knew his regulars were having a tough time of it
and appeared to be trapped in the city, unable to make any progress
against Fort Teneria. Taylor decided to reinforce Garland with three
regiments of volunteers and the 4th Infantry, ordering Brig. Gen.
John A. Quitman to take the 1st Mississippi and the 1st Tennessee
and assault Fort Teneria.

Quitman, commander of the Second Brigade of the Third Division, was the model politician-soldier. For most of his career, Quitman had practiced law, sought political office, and lived the life of
Mississippi's elite. He married into a wealthy family early and ran a
sugar and coffee plantation. A fervent expansionist, he never missed
an opportunity to lead his local militia in wartime. Polk appointed
Quitman, a Democrat, to Taylor's army because the president was
concerned about the lack of his political party's representation among
the army's generals. Many army regulars wondered how Polk's political generals would hold up under fire. They would soon find out about
Quitman.

By late morning Taylor's diversion was turning into a larger affair.
In addition to Quitman's men, he ordered the 1st Ohio Volunteers,
under Brig. Gen. Thomas L. Hamer, to take his men and enter the city
at a more central location. Although he did not record his reasoning, Taylor probably hoped the Ohioans would find an unguarded
pathway into Monterrey and flank the Mexican troops currently engaged with the regulars. The diversion had now become a full-scale
assault against multiple points of the city. Two-thirds of his army
soon would be committed to "diverting" Ampudia's attention from

Brig. Gen. John A. Quitman. A lawyer by profession, Quitman
was appointed by Polk largely to put more Democrats in command positions in the army. Many questioned his abilities, but
Quitman proved to be an asset to Taylor, helping overrun one of
the Mexican army's most formidable positions. Courtesy of Special Collections, The University of Texas at Arlington Library.

Worth's movements in western Monterrey. No wonder the Mexicans thought that the diversion was actually the main attack.

The tired and thirsty soldiers in Fort Teneria desperately needed reinforcements. They hoped that after repelling the regulars General Ampudia would relieve them with fresh soldiers. But the defenders soon observed 2,000 U.S. volunteers forming up on the plain. The tired soldiers needed help—and fast. Ampudia disagreed, though, retaining his reserve in the city's plaza. The eastern garrisons were on their own.

On the plain Major General Butler, commander of the volunteer division, formed his men in a slight depression offering shelter from the Citadel's artillery. A lot depended on his leadership now. Taylor was counting on him and his men to rescue the regulars still ensnared in a vicious fight for Fort Teneria and overrun that well-defended stronghold. Like Quitman, Butler was another of Polk's hand-selected political generals, a Democrat who had been elected twice to Congress and barely lost a bid to be governor of Kentucky. Prior to Congress, he had been a lawyer for twenty-five years. Despite his legal-political career, Butler had seen probably more fighting than most of Taylor's young regulars. When the War or 1812 began, he had joined the army and fought in a vicious battle on the Raisin River in present-day Michigan. At that action a joint British-Indian force defeated the Americans and massacred the survivors. Somehow Butler had survived this horrific slaughter and was taken captive by the British, who marched him hundreds of miles through the frigid Canadian wilderness to be imprisoned. He survived that ordeal too and was later paroled. Instead of convalescing, though, Butler rejoined the army and fought with Andrew Jackson at the Battle of New Orleans. Armed with this combat experience, the general hopefully could provide the command guidance that his volunteers would so desperately need.[34]

As Butler's men began forming on the plain, three companies of the 4th Infantry, under the command of Maj. William Graham, began marching toward Fort Teneria. They had become separated from the initial assault by the First Division (of which they were part) and were eager to enter the fight. Before the volunteers began moving, Graham's men began to march across the plain alone. Disgusted by their earlier absence, they probably wanted to make amends to their regular brethren. The three companies, totaling 90 men, lacked the individual cover that a 700-man regiment would have provided. Emerg-

Maj. Gen. William O. Butler, U.S. Volunteers. Like Quitman, Butler was one of Polk's handpicked generals, but he had more battle experience that many of Taylor's other officers. From Frost, *Mexican War and Its Warriors*, 166. Courtesy of Special Collections, The University of Texas at Arlington Library.

ing from the cornfields directly in front of Fort Teneria, their small group proved an enticing target for the skilled artillerists of Fort Diablo, Fort Teneria, and the Citadel as well as for hundreds of infantrymen. The Mexicans showered the Americans with bullets and cannon shot as the exposed regulars double-timed across the plain. Man after man fell dead or wounded.

Earlier that morning, Ulysses Grant, 4th Infantry, had heard the awful fire from Garland's engagement. In his role as regimental quartermaster, Grant was tasked with safeguarding the regiment's public property. Yet his "curiosity got the better of his judgment," as he put it, and he mounted a horse and rode to the plain to see what was happening. Soon after he met up with his regiment, the 4th Infantry was ordered to march. "Lacking the moral courage to return to camp," as he later wrote, Grant charged on horse with his men. Despite the obvious target he presented, the lieutenant remained mounted. Grant eventually lent his animal to Lt. Charles Hoskins, who was "not in robust health" and was fatigued from the charge across the plain. He soon saw another mounted U.S. soldier in the distance. Unconcerned with the fire around him, Grant sprinted to him, requested his horse, and returned to his regiment mounted. He was lucky that he did not stay on his original horse. A bullet pierced Hoskins's heart, and the 1836 West Point graduate died without saying a word. Grant took his place as adjutant of the regiment.[35]

Other West Pointers tried to encourage the men by leading from the front. Like Hoskins they faced the grim consequences of charging a strong position with only ninety men. Lt. James Woods, an 1844 West Point graduate, was shot dead soon after Hoskins. Lt. Richard Graham, who graduated from West Point in 1838, waved his sword over his head to cheer the men until he too was mortally wounded.[36]

The 4th Infantry came within thirty feet of the fort before being forced to move east into a cornfield, away from Fort Teneria and the Citadel, by the terrible fire. The regiment, or "what was left of it," as Grant later wrote, found a safe place to regroup. Grant had been the only mounted horseman among the original ninety regulars (except for Hoskins, who was dead) and miraculously was not hit. About one-third of the men in the charge were either killed or wounded.

Meanwhile, the 1st Mississippi, the 1st Tennessee, and the 1st Ohio formed into columns to march across the plain. Col. William Campbell, commanding the 1st Tennessee, ordered his men to load their rifles once the march became imminent: "Load in double quick time" ran down the Tennessee line. Jefferson Davis, not wanting to be outdone by the Tennesseans, fumed at their premature loading. "They are getting the start of us," he complained to one of his officers. Quitman had ordered the Tennesseans to march first because they were armed with bayonets, which would be useful in fighting the fort's garrison. Tennessee officers shouted, "Left face, double quick time, forward march!" Their column filed past the Mississippians, and loud huzzas emanated from their line. Davis's men followed Campbell's regiment in column, with the Ohioans—who would be attacking a different part of the city—trailing behind. A few regulars

Citadel

The Teneria

1st Tenn.
Rgt.

1st Miss.
Rgt.

North
Face

East
Face

Northwest
Flank

Southeast
Flank

to Martin

to Saltillo

to Cadereyta

Eastern Monterrey
September 21–23, 1846

N
E
S
W

1. The Teneria
2. Fortified stone building (tannery)
3. Building occupied by Backus
4. Street or lane bordered by irrigation ditch
5. Point of Davis' farthest advance, Sept. 21
6. The du-pont
7. Purisima bridge
8. El Diablo
9. Breastworks
10. Tenaille
11. Barricade where Davis is first fired upon, Sept. 23
12. Stone hospital
13. Point of Davis' farthest advance, Sept. 23
14. Cathedral

— Route of Quitman's brigade, Sept. 21
——— Masonry wall
········· Chaparral fence
ᴠᴠᴠᴠᴠ Brushwood abattis

0 100 200 300 400 500
yards

Eastern Monterrey, September 21–23. The bulk of fighting on the 21st occurred in eastern Monterrey, where the Mexican army repelled Taylor's best division and was only overrun after the U.S. commander committed a second division. Taylor lost some of his best men in this assault, which even after the battle he referred to as a "diversion." The diagram of Fort Teneria was drawn by Manuel Balbontin; other artists then overlaid the positions of the Mississippians and Tennesseans during their assault of the 21st. From Davis, *Papers,* vol. 3.

intermixed with the volunteers. Pvt. Barna Upton of the 3rd Infantry marched with the First Division but had been ordered to veer hard left to search for some lancers supposedly hiding in a ditch. Upton went so far left that eventually he came upon the Tennessee regiment as it was forming and joined their charge.[37]

The Citadel's artillerists lobbed 18-pound shells at the head of the Tennessee regiment, perhaps reasoning that soldiers who walked over their dead comrades might be less inclined to continue. One shell raked the front of the column, killing four men and badly wounding three others. Campbell shouted to his men to walk over the fallen bodies: "March on! March on! No time to stop! To the Fort! To the Fort!" The cannonading added to the dozens of American bodies strewn on the plain, men who never made it to the city. Surgeons rushed onto the battlefield to aid the wounded men, most of whom were grievously injured by artillery. They performed quick amputations and extracted bullets while under fire from the Citadel and Fort Teneria. "I was operating upon a poor fellow, whose foot was shot off by a cannon-ball," Dr. E. K. Chamberlain recalled, "and in a place where twelve and eighteen-pounders were tearing the ground, and the chaparral all about us." Wagons ferried the mangled men from the plain to the camp at San Domingo. The Citadel's gunners trained their cannons on these wagons, firing shells into the ambulances and killing many of the wounded.[38]

After the Tennesseans crossed the plain, they came within range of Fort Teneria and Fort Diablo. The eager volunteers, who so badly wanted the opportunity to fight the Mexicans, were cut down in droves by cannon and musket fire. Like the 4th Infantry, the Tennesseans approached Fort Teneria from its front and came face to face with its cannons. Fort Diablo and a redoubt at the Purisima Bridge (farther west) also fired on the group. One poetic volunteer described the harrowing assault:

> Two hundred yards brought the head of our column upon the open plain, and in a moment the "Black Fort," shrouded in smoke, was blazing like a volcano, and its angry missiles came whizzing and whirling about our ranks and tearing up the earth, ricocheted over our heads and rolled along the plain. Quickening our already rapid pace, we dashed on through the thorny shurbs [sic], while the new forts on our front and flank

[Teneria, Diablo, and Purisima Bridge] poured on our column a perfect hurricane of balls, that howled and hissed around in fearful dissonance. Shot after shot crashing through our ranks or enfilading our line, strewed its pathway with mangled bodies, shattered limbs, and headless trunks; but unheeding all, on we rushed over the dead and wounded, and with reckless impetuosity continued with unslackened speed toward the enemy.[39]

Both regiments formed from columns into battle lines once they were within 300 yards of the fort. The Tennesseans fronted the fort's north face, while the Mississippians deployed opposite its northwest side. Cannon fire poured into the American lines. "Our little band was fast melting away like frost before the sun," wrote a Tennessee soldier. Capt. William Allen, who swore to his father that he would not disgrace his sword (which he carried), died with it in his hands when a musket ball entered his breast. This destructive fire caused Campbell's entire regiment to recoil and fall back fifteen or twenty paces. General Quitman and the adjutants of both regiments rode up and down the lines issuing commands in an effort to organize the companies into their correct order from left to right.[40]

Colonel Davis ordered his Mississippians to advance and fire as Campbell's Tennesseans did the same. "Boys take good aim," one of Campbell's officers instructed, "don't let them fire that cannon again." Some shot from the cover of grass or chaparral, while others slowly walked toward the fort. "We commenced firing, advancing; the men were directed to select their objects and aim as sharpshooters," a Mississippian recalled. Davis, a West Pointer, ordered his men to fire in volleys, though to no avail. "The attempt was made to make the firing regular," noted one Mississippi officer, "but it was futile for every man, [who] loaded & fired with the utmost rapidity." The thundering noise from the blazing cannons and muskets made it almost impossible for officers to issue orders. "All words and orders were lost and drowned in the roar of battle and the shrieks of the dying," recalled the soldier.[41]

Quitman ordered two companies of the Mississippi Regiment's right wing to advance within sixty yards of Teneria so they could deliver a more accurate fire into the fort. The remainder of the regiment aligned themselves with these lead companies, forming a giant

U.S. soldiers form to attack Monterrey, September 21. This illustration, which greatly condenses the size of the plain, shows the regulars and volunteers marching in column toward eastern Monterrey on the 21st. The formation is accurate, though the two groups did not march simultaneously. Notice the direction of the columns—the volunteers (left) are marching straight toward Fort Teneria, whereas the regulars (right) are marching toward a more central part of the city in their attempt to locate the rear of the fort. Note also the mortar in the forefront of the picture. *A View of the Battle of Monterey, Sept. 21, 1846*. Lithograph after Stephen G. Hill. Lithograph, 10 7/8 × 18 3/4 in. Courtesy of the Amon Carter Museum, Fort Worth, Tex.

arc in front of the northwest face. For volunteers to perform such a maneuver under terrible fire was a testament to their discipline and courage. The murderous grape and solid shot rained down on the men for what must have seemed like ages. One soldier said it felt like they were in this position for thirty minutes, though the maneuver probably only lasted five minutes or less. A Mississippi private noted, "with plenty of powder I could never get out of ammunition—I could hold up my cap, and catch it full of bullets in a minute." Davis understood that if the men maintained their current position, they would all be dead before the day was over. He asked Lt. Daniel Russell, "Damn it, why do not the men get nearer to the fort? Why waste ammunition at such distance?" The colonel waited for Quitman to issue the order to charge.[42]

The Mississippians were about 180 yards from the fort, when the enemy's fire suddenly slackened. Teneria's artillerymen had ceased firing on the volunteers to deal with a new problem: Captain Backus's regulars, still perched on the roof of the tall building, were firing into the garrison. Earlier, Backus had ordered his men to retire from the roof. But when he recognized the sounds of the volunteers' rifles being fired on the fort, the captain rushed his men back to the roof to provide support. Mexican artillerymen removed a cannon from one of their platforms and pointed it toward Backus and his men.[43]

Although the Americans did not know it, the exhausted defenders were near their breaking point. Without proper cannon platforms, their guns skidded around on the slippery mud after firing. One of the fort's 8-pounders rolled off its makeshift platform with every shot. The gunners who operated the other 8-pounder were exposed to fire through a cutout in the wall, which forced them to pass ammunition through the cannon's wheels. A corporal loaded the gun while lying underneath it, a tricky feat in the heat of battle. Faulty cannon positions were not the only problems faced by the garrison. The cloth covers of the sandbags lining the parapet soon caught fire, preventing the men from using it for cover. The tired soldiers screamed "Ammunition! Water!" Manuel Balbontin recalled that "the soldiers were worn out and their lips were crusted with powder from biting cartridges, which in addition to the excitement of the combat produced a burning thirst."[44]

For the Americans, the break in fire was just what they needed. Jefferson Davis knew what to do, but he had not been ordered to do it.

"Now is the time! Great God, if I had thirty men with knives I could take that fort," the colonel screamed. His second in command, a lawyer and noted duelist with no military training, felt less constrained by military rules and regulations. Lt. Col. Alexander McClung drew his sword and shouted to his Mississippians, "Charge! Charge! Tombigbee volunteers [referring to the men of Company K] follow me!" The company, which McClung used to command, responded to his call and raced forward with him. McClung's action was illegal, since neither Davis nor Quitman had told him to charge, but his men followed anyway, eager to retaliate against the garrison that had caused them so much harm.[45]

Those who knew McClung probably were not surprised by his action. The officer had a reputation, deserved or not, for being impetuous and abrasive. He was a lawyer turned politician in Mississippi and was not afraid to defend his honor when offended. Twice he had participated in pistol duels over perceived slights against his character. Both times he killed his challengers, though in one fight he was seriously wounded. Despite his reputation, McClung had a devoted and loyal following. His popularity got him elected as Davis's deputy, even though he did not have any military experience. He knew every one of his Tombigbee volunteers by name, and they would follow him wherever he led, including straight into the teeth of Fort Teneria.[46]

McClung's heroics aside, the Mississippians were not well armed for close combat. Their long-barreled Model 1841 Whitney rifles were designed for long-distance shooting, thus essentially useless at short range, and took almost a minute to load. But the men were in no mood to care about such details. They were tired of standing in front of Fort Teneria, amid a shower of grapeshot and bullets, without advancing on it. And all of them were armed with bowie knives, swords, and other blades suitable for hand-to-hand fighting. Fortunately for the Mississippians, a large entryway into the fort opened directly in front of their line. McClung leapt on top of the fort's parapet and waved his sword to cheer his men forward. Lt. William Patterson followed him into the opening and dropped a Mexican soldier who was about to shoot his highly visible superior.[47]

Colonel Campbell also ordered his Tennesseans to charge. Armed with bayonets, they "rushed up to the cannon's mouth like very devils, in the face of a shower of balls and grape shot," one soldier remembered. They leapt across a ditch fronting the north face and scaled the

The storming of Fort Teneria by the Mississippi and Tennessee volunteers. This drawing, though it does not name him, features Lt. Col. Alexander McClung of the 1st Mississippi standing on top of the wall waving his sword to encourage his men in their assault. From Frost, *History of Mexico and Its Wars*, 301.

ramparts. Lt. George Nixon was the first Tennessean to enter the fort. Like Colonel McClung, he raised his sword over his head and shouted, "Boys come on, my brave boys, come on!" As Quitman remembered, "the charge became instantaneously general." Capt. Benjamin Cheatham of the 1st Tennessee rushed forward as well. A cannonball landed in front of him, and "as quick as lightning I dropped to my knees to let it pass over me." He recalled, "I had scarcely touched the ground when a musket ball grazed across my back just breaking the skin but it burnt me at the time as if a coat of fire had been dropped upon my back."[48]

Davis finally forgot his military discipline and screamed for all of the 1st Mississippi to charge. He galloped up to the fort on his horse, dismounted, and jumped through the embrasure. Upon entering, he ordered McClung to stay on the parapet since the animated officer had become a rallying point for the whole regiment.[49]

Most of the Mexican soldiers rushed out the back of the fort toward Fort Diablo. Some ran into the distillery building and slammed the door behind them. "I was so close behind the last [Mexican soldier] who entered," Davis remembered, "that as they closed the heavy door, I ran with all my force against it, before it could be barred and threw it open." The Mexicans fled behind a portico in the building's inner courtyard and raised their hands to surrender. An officer handed the colonel his sword. Davis closed the door to make sure no one fired on the surrendered troops. But three of the soldiers had climbed to the top of the distillery. They soon surrendered, but only after they fired one last volley, which hit Colonel McClung. One ball hit the hand that gripped his sword, cutting off two of his fingers entering his stomach, and then exiting his back. McClung crumpled to the ground. Lt. William Townsend rushed and grabbed him in his arms. McClung did not speak, and everyone thought he was dead. He soon recovered, though, and began to speak calmly to his men. Since they were still under fire, the Mississippians moved McClung to a safer position, carrying him to the ditch in front of the fort, where they dressed his grievous wound as best they could and wrapped him in a blanket. None of his men thought that he would live.[50]

By the time the Tennesseans entered Fort Teneria, it was already cleared out by the Mississippians. The Tennesseans fired on the Mexican soldiers running to Fort Diablo. Some of them also shot volleys into the fort, not knowing that by that time the Mississippians were already inside. Lt. Daniel Russell of the 1st Mississippi shouted at a Tennessee officer, "Tell your men to quit firing!" Colonel Campbell rode through his regiment yelling for his men to cease fire. Not long afterward, one Tennessean strung up his regiment's light blue flag, which could be seen throughout the city. Taylor's regulars cheered the sight, but the Mississippians fumed. Typically the first regiment to enter an enemy's fort strung up their flag. To Davis, who cared immensely about the perception of himself and his command, this was the ultimate affront, even more so than being shot at by the Tennesseans.[51]

Curiously, about this time, General Twiggs, who had apparently recovered from his medicine, appeared nearby, mounted and shouting: "Go! Go! Secure your victory!" Twiggs should have been more interested in locating his tattered division of regulars, but here he was surrounded by the successful volunteers.[52]

While the Tennesseans were attacking Fort Teneria, General Butler led the 1st Ohio across the plain to attack the city at a more central point. They entered the city farther west than Garland had earlier that morning, Butler hoping that the Mexicans would not be expecting an attack there. As soon as the Ohioans neared the city, though, all thoughts of sneaking past the defenders were erased. Mexican artillery concealed by masonry barricades and hundreds of well-protected infantrymen launched a barrage of bullets and grapeshot at the advancing volunteers—Ampudia was prepared for this move. Most of the Ohioans had never been in combat before and the intensity of the Mexican fire surprised them. Butler was unsure of his next move, and he did not have a map. "I felt my way gradually," he explained, "without any knowledge of the localities, into that part of the city bordering on the enemy's continuous line of batteries, assailed at every step by heavy fires in front and flank." Hamer, acting as the general's second in command, was not even sure what their objective was. He recalled that the men entered the north-central part of the city "with a view of attacking a Battery beyond it, or of acting according to circumstances, at some point farther up in the city, the localities of which were unknown to us."[53]

The Ohioans took cover behind a pomegranate hedge. Bullets bore through the bushes and into the men. The volunteers tried to press forward through some gardens, but the firing only seemed to get worse. Someone suggested to Hamer that they break into the houses to avoid the deadly missiles, but no one possessed the crowbars or pickaxes necessary to break down the strong doors and walls. One soldier recalled his frustration at not being able to return the enemy's fire: the brigade "entered the suburbs of the city, only to find itself raked on all sides by batteries of whose location we were ignorant, and escopette [musket] balls from the tops of the houses, whose occupants were perfectly safe, as we could neither burn nor batter down their stout walls."[54]

Mansfield, who had stayed in the city throughout the day, came forward to assist, pointing out places to attack and trying to advance the troops. After witnessing the destruction of Garland's assault, Mansfield now had more realistic views about what the American infantry could accomplish inside the city, no longer believing that they could march triumphantly through the city at their leisure. The major told Butler that if he advanced into the city, he would meet "a fire that would sweep all before it." He recommended a withdrawal. The general, knowing that Taylor was close by, galloped out to confer with the general. In the meantime his men continued to endure an unyielding fire. After what must have seemed like hours to them, Butler returned. Taylor had agreed that his men should withdraw, so they retreated into the city's suburbs.[55]

Back at Fort Teneria, the Mississippi regiment's success spurred Davis to take a party of men to seize Fort Diablo. He collected twenty soldiers, crossed the Arroyo Santa Lucia, and advanced within 100 yards of the position. The Mississippians shot at Mexican soldiers hiding behind a ten-foot wall in front of the fort. Cpl. William Grisham led the firefight until he was hit by two muskets balls. He died "calmly, silently, and with his eye upon the foe," Davis recalled. Perched on top of a small hill, Fort Diablo's cannons could not depress low enough to hit Davis's men. But dozens of Mexican soldiers on nearby rooftops poured a deadly fire into the small group. The colonel observed an embankment, which he believed could shield his men from Mexican fire while they approached the garrison. He did not consider that his men, armed only with rifles, lacked the bayonets necessary for close combat. Nevertheless, Davis waited for more men to gather before he charged the fort.[56]

Instead of following Davis, however, most of the volunteers remained on the creek's north side. Maj. Alexander Bradford collected parties of Mississippians and stragglers from other regiments. "In this lane all the troops acted with great firmness and courage," one Mississippian wrote, "being exposed to ball, grape, and canister, and musket shot from the Fort, and a heavy fire enfilading the street." The men sought to advance under the cover of some run-down buildings toward Fort Diablo, but they soon discovered that the move would not work, every angle of this approach covered by infantry behind breastworks. A charge against the fort from this point surely would fail.[57]

But General Quitman's aide de camp, and soon General Quitman himself, instructed Davis to withdraw his regiment from the city. The colonel was furious. He had collected about forty men and was ready to assault the fort, whose occupants, he believed, were "panic stricken" from the day's battle. Lt. Daniel Russell, who was organizing men for the assault, recalled his commander's reaction to the order. "You were cursing bitterly you ordered me to retire from my position to recross the creek & form in the lane, you said you had been ordered to withdraw your men, & repeated you would have taken the fort in five minutes if you had been allowed to proceed." A fuming Davis crossed his men back over the creek, and the group took cover in a small house that protected them from enemy fire. The Mississippians collapsed from exhaustion from the day's fight.[58]

General Taylor had ordered his troops out of the city after speaking with Colonel Garland, who reported to him about the same time as the volunteers' assault on Fort Teneria. The general had listened to Garland's horror story about the First Division's failed assault, not realizing all the while that Fort Teneria had fallen to the volunteers. But as Davis and the other volunteers were retreating, a messenger reached Taylor with the news that Teneria had been overrun and that the regulars had captured a distillery—the strong building guarding the fort's gorge—where the Mexicans stored their alcohol. "No doubt of it," the general told the messenger, "I thought it was by the way you fought to get into it." He ordered the distillery emptied so the men would not be tempted to imbibe.[59]

Sensing that his troops now had momentum, Taylor ordered General Butler to oversee a new assault on Fort Diablo. He also directed Colonel Garland to collect the battered remnants of the 1st, 3rd, and 4th Infantry and the Baltimore Battalion in order "to enter the town, penetrating to the right, and carry the second battery [Fort Diablo] if possible." Maybe the bloody day could be salvaged if the Americans could overrun the fort and control eastern Monterrey. "Diversion" was no longer a word the U.S. commander was using.[60]

Responding to Taylor's new orders, the Ohioans reentered the city where Garland's men had met their bloody repulse earlier that day. Evidence of that hard fight was everywhere. Wounded Americans littered the streets, begging for water or first aid. The Ohioans' canteens were empty from their earlier combat, so they had no water to give to these helpless men. One of Garland's soldiers, who was never identified, climbed orange trees while under fire in order to provide some nourishment for the wounded. Meanwhile, the attacking Ohioans fired in small groups, using the city's houses and other buildings for cover. They moved diagonally, southeast toward Fort Diablo, jumping into the waist-deep water of the Arroyo Santa Lucia and wading to the other side. Bullets zipped past them while they held their muskets high over their heads and sloshed through the creek. Some thirsty volunteers stopped for a drink from the channel— they never made it across. Once on the other side of the arroyo, the Ohioans entered the fortified lane and came under a withering fire from behind a nearby wall. "The next moment a line of flame flashed above it [the wall]," Major Giddings recalled, "and almost at the same instant the diabolical battery in its rear [Fort Diablo] saluted us with a terrible discharge of grape. . . . [W]e were now evidently in for it."[61]

Generals Butler and Hamer personally led a charge against the wall. A musket ball hit Butler below the knee, which soon bled profusely. He wrapped a cloth around the wound and retired from the action. Col. Alexander Mitchell, the commander of the 1st Ohio, approached the wall on horseback and also was hit by a ball, a wound he survived. Despite these losses, and to the Ohioans' surprise, the Mexicans retreated. The volunteers then used the excellent cover provided by the wall to pick off any soldiers who showed their heads at Diablo. It appeared that the Ohioans might finally have some success.

Ignacio Joaquin del Arenal, the artillery commander at Diablo, noticed that the Ohioans were trying to flank his position and avoid his two cannons. He therefore moved the guns outside of the walls in order to have a clear field of fire against the volunteers. The 2nd Light Infantry, which manned Diablo, continued to fire at the Ohioans to cover the artillery's move. Meanwhile, Ampudia moved his men from rooftop to rooftop, depending on where the Americans entered the city. Since the general did not have enough troops to fortify the entire city, he had to reposition his men block by block as the situation demanded.

Meanwhile, back at Fort Teneria (now occupied by U.S. troops), regulars and volunteers collected in small groups around the redoubt, looking for their comrades and seeking shelter. The regiments had attempted to stay together, but the morning's intense fire had forced them to break into smaller units. Officers scoured the area for men who had survived the carnage, forming them into improvised companies that could support the Ohioans. One American noticed an unusual sight around this time. A Mexican woman, amid bullets and artillery fire, carried food and water to wounded Mexican and American soldiers lying in the streets. She took off her handkerchief to bind the wound of a dying soldier and similarly helped two other wounded men. Then he heard the crack of a few guns, and the woman fell dead in the street. It was something the soldier would never forget: "Oh God, and this is war!"[62]

But Capt. Randolph Ridgley, Taylor's most respected artillerist, enjoyed his time at the captured fort. He quickly built a small cannon platform in Teneria from which to fire one of the captured guns. While the Ohioans were shooting at Fort Diablo from the protective wall, Ridgley poured cannon fire into the enemy position. He seemed to relish the moment, aiming the gun himself (a task usually carried out by a soldier of lower rank) and standing atop the platform—plainly visible to the enemy—so to see the effects of each shot with his spyglass. The captain cheered each time his cannon hit its target.

Optimism spread throughout the Ohioans' ranks as Ridgley's fire began to take effect. In all of the smoke and noise, however, the men had not noticed the Purisima Bridge tête du pont down the lane and off to their right. "We were beginning to hope that we might ere long silence the guns of Fort El Diablo," Giddings remembered, "when, suddenly as the lightning's flash, and loud as the thunder's peal, a battery was opened close upon our right, and swept the regiment with grape shot from flank to flank." The enfilading fire cut down many Buckeyes.[63]

Jefferson Davis, who had collected a handful of Mississippians, tried to assist the Ohioans by assaulting the offending battery. Taking a page from the Mexicans' tactics, he ordered Captain Douglas Cooper to hide inside a building and snipe at the Mexicans manning the bridge position. The colonel also discovered a road that he thought his men could use to advance on the breastwork. He asked Butler for permission, but the general was "preoccupied" and ignored the request. (Butler might have been preoccupied with his wound, which occurred around this time.) Davis suggested the idea to another general, probably Hamer, but he too ignored him. Then he saw Col. Albert Sidney Johnston, who thought it a good idea and suggested that he collect some men and commence the action immediately. Davis began marching his men down the road when Major Mansfield approached with some men from the 1st Infantry. Mansfield liked the plan as well and placed his men on the opposite side of the street from Davis.[64]

Butler's men, despite being shot at from three sides, had advanced to within a hundred yards of Fort Diablo. Despite never having been in combat, they performed like seasoned regulars, proving that volunteers could fight with equal discipline and courage. But courage could not get the volunteers through this situation. As Butler noted in his official report, "the men were falling fast under the converging fires of at least three distinct batteries, that continually swept the intervening space through which it was necessary to pass." Hamer realized that it would be madness to storm Diablo with only one regiment. Major Giddings agreed. The general therefore ordered all the volunteers—including Davis's Mississippians—to withdraw.[65]

While the Ohioans groped their way through Monterrey's streets, Garland had collected as many men of his division (who had been hovering around Fort Teneria) as he could and ordered them to take Fort Diablo by bayonet. It was around noon, and the fatigued soldiers had been fighting for almost four hours straight. Garland was asking a lot from men who already had witnessed the deaths of many of their comrades and their best officers. But the colonel, with half of his original force, thought his men could enter Diablo from the rear. Major Mansfield had suggested such a strategy when Garland assaulted Fort Teneria only hours earlier, which had resulted in most of his division being destroyed. Garland should have thought twice about trying to enter the rear of Fort Diablo.

Capt. L. N. Morris, one of the few remaining officers of the regiment, led the men along the canal's north side. "The moment we left the cover of the work [Fort Teneria]," Captain Henry of the 3rd Infantry wrote, "we were exposed to a galling fire of musketry, escopets, and artillery. . . . Every street was blockaded, and every house a fortification; and on all sides our gallant officers and men were shot down" The movement must have seemed like déjà vu to Garland, who once again did not have a map and was blindly searching for somewhere to cross the canal. Soon his men met a nasty surprise. "We unluckily ran foul of a *tete de pont* [the Purisima Bridge]," Garland recalled, "the strongest defence of the city, and from the opposite side of the bridge two pieces of artillery were brought to bear upon us at a little more than a hundred yards' distance." The command, ignorant of its location, had stumbled upon the Purisima Bridge defenses. Garland's men neared the bridge on the canal's north side when Mexican artillery there opened fire. "The fire from it was perfectly awful," Henry remembered. Captain Morris, West Point class of 1820, was hit by a musket ball that killed him instantly. Robert Hazlitt, his close friend and an 1843 graduate of West Point, carried him into a house. A musket ball struck Hazlitt while he was tending to his friend. He would no longer need to worry about whether or not his mother thought he was a "chicken," for he would not be returning home alive.[66]

General Mejía, the former commander of the Army of the North, personally oversaw the tête du pont at the bridge. His men had already contributed to Garland's earlier whipping and had annihilated most of the Ohio regiment. Now Garland was back, once again advancing blindly through the perilous streets of Monterrey. General Mejía's artillery commander, Lieutenant Colonel Gutiérrez, moved his 12-pound cannon out into the open (away from the breastwork) and fired directly into the Americans. The Aguascalientes Battalion under Col. José Ferro arrived at this critical moment to reinforce the defenders. Henry's men fired on the arriving Mexicans with little effect. Ferro's men kneeled behind the breastwork and unleashed a torrent of fire against the Americans. Mejía darted from soldier to soldier, shouting words of encouragement to each.[67]

"Going into action with five seniors, at this critical moment the command of the Third Infantry devolved upon myself," Henry recalled. He formed his remaining troops and led them in an effort to drive the Mexicans from the bridge. The men advanced by file, reloading, aiming, and firing. Henry handled his unexpected duties with vigor. Nevertheless, his men had to funnel onto the narrow bridge in order to cross it, providing excellent targets for Mexican infantrymen and artillerists.[68]

Purisima Bridge. Note the statue of the Virgin Mary standing on top of the spire on the far side of the bridge. It was undamaged during the regulars' bloody assault on the 21st. From Henry, *Campaign Sketches*, 199. Courtesy of Special Collections, The University of Texas at Arlington Library.

Bodies began to pile up on the bridge. Thick smoke settled in between the two sides, making it difficult for Americans or Mexicans to see anyone. Nevertheless, guns and artillery continued blazing. Ridgley's battery rushed from Teneria to the assistance of Garland's men. Like Bragg's earlier failed effort to use light artillery in the streets, Ridgley fired several rounds that did little or no damage to the enemy. Masonry barricades protected the Mexican cannon, and enemy troops hid safely behind sandbags or parapets on the city's rooftops. Finding that his guns were "perfectly useless," Ridgley retreated. Throughout the ordeal, a large statue of the Virgin Mary remained standing on the side of the bridge, a perfect vantage point from which to observe the carnage.

Around this time Ulysses Grant volunteered to report the 4th Infantry's position to General Twiggs and to ask that ammunition be brought to their location. "My ride back was an exposed one," he simply wrote later. The lieutenant wrapped one arm around the horse's neck, put one foot in the saddle's cantle, and slid down the animal's side to shield his body from Mexican fire. "It was only at street crossings that my horse was under fire," Grant recalled, "but these I crossed at such a flying rate that generally I was past and under cover of the next block of houses before the enemy fired." Such expert horsemanship made him a tough target. But before Grant returned, the regiment's commander ordered his men to retire, their ammunition nearly exhausted and no progress made in crossing the bridge. Captain Henry did the same with the 3rd Infantry. The Americans retreated to Fort Teneria, the only safe spot for them anywhere in the city. On their way, though, intense fire forced them to lie down in a road for an hour before continuing.[69]

It was a humiliating end to the day for the regulars. Garland probably hung his head low as his troops took refuge at Fort Teneria. Twice he had tried to attack the city's defenses, and both times his regiment had been smashed with little to show for it. But the colonel could be forgiven for much of the failure. In the morning he had followed Taylor's order to locate Major Mansfield and trail the engineer into the city. In the second assault no U.S. regiment, volunteer or regular, overran Fort Diablo. Until the Americans assumed different tactics in the city, they would have little success no matter what road they took.

About this time the 1st Ohio, with remnants of the 1st Mississippi, began withdrawing across the plain. Some of the exhausted volunteers could not keep up with their units and lagged behind the others. "Our men were tired down," a Mississippian wrote, "some of them wounded, some of them, 50 yards from the rear of the close column."[70]

After the retreating volunteers had gotten about a half mile into the open, the 3rd and 7th Mexican Lancers under General don José García Conde darted out of the Citadel to attack the retreating force. The fatigued and disorderly Americans were prime victims for a cavalry strike. Ampudia had planned to use his cavalry exactly this way—to attack and finish off defeated troops retreating across the plain underneath the Citadel's fire. The lancers first came upon and speared the wounded Americans in the suburbs and the straggling volunteers strung out on the plain. Doctors who were treating the injured fled for their lives.

At the sight of the lancers, some of the volunteers in the main column—confused, tired, and scared—threw down their arms and fled. "All organization was lost," recalled Joseph Hooker, "and our men were flying to the left in the direction of a cornfield a few hundred yards off." Artillery fire rained down on those in the cornfield, making wicked sounds as the shot and shells raked the stalks' leaves. General Hamer did nothing to prepare his men to receive the cavalry charge, and it appeared that the dispersed troops would be slaughtered by the lancers. Into this leadership void stepped Butler's unpaid inspector general, Albert Sidney Johnston. He galloped through the cornfield among the scared men and, with a loud and commanding voice, told them to organize themselves along a nearby chaparral fence. The men obeyed, abandoning the corn and posting themselves as ordered. Johnston continued to ride up and down the line, shouting words of encouragement and making final alterations to their placement.[71]

Not long after Johnston established his line, the lancers attacked. "They advanced boldly and beautifully," Giddings remembered, "their long lances gleaming brightly in the sun, and their whole line decorated with bandrol and flag." One soldier said the lancers reminded him of the "knights of olden times." The Ohioans lined up along the fence unleashed a concerted volley, and the horsemen withdrew. Jefferson Davis, noting that the Mexicans had divided into two groups, repositioned his men to face south and receive the second group's charge. "They [the lancers] came up gallantly," Lt. Daniel Russell of the 1st Mississippi recalled, "their fiery little chargers prancing and rearing, handsomely." Two of the lancers rode within sixty or seventy yards and were quickly dropped by the accurate Mississippi marksmen. Indeed, the Mississippians' rifles might not have been useful in close, urban combat, but they were ideal against mounted horsemen a few hundred yards away.[72]

The volunteers had been saved from disaster by the quick actions of an unpaid soldier with no rank, Albert Sidney Johnston, and the colonel of the Mississippi Rifles, Jefferson Davis. Joseph Hooker, Hamer's chief of staff, was probably also a steadying influence on the troops. The general praised Hooker in his official report for his "coolness and self possession in battle" and for his "soldierly conduct." Hooker, however, was quick to praise Johnston. He wrote to the colonel's son thirty years later, saying, "it was through his [Johnston's] agency, mainly, that our division was saved from cruel slaughter. . . . [T]he coolness and magnificent presence your father displayed on the field, brief as it was, left an impression on my mind that I have never forgotten."[73]

After their repulse, some of the lancers veered off toward the mortar battery, where the 1st Kentucky, which guarded the gunners, formed a protective square. Captain Bragg, who had retreated with the volunteers, hid his battery in a cornfield and opened up on the lancers' flank. The horsemen fled.[74]

Toward the evening, the surviving volunteers and regulars returned to Walnut Springs. It was a somber scene. Bloodied and fatigued soldiers collected around campfires or stretched out in their tents. Some looked for wills in the trunks of their dead comrades. Others collected the belongings of their fallen friends and wrote letters to their dead friends' relatives. Capt. Henry Bainbridge, a good friend of Major Barbour, wrote Mattie Barbour about her husband's death. "Would to God my feelings could have permitted me ere this to have expressed to you my heartfelt sorrow for the loss you have sustained—this loss to yourself is alike irreparable to the regiment and country. May God grant you support and consolation under the weighty affliction which has befallen you." A heavy downpour commenced at about 5 P.M., and many of the men, lacking tents, slept in the rain.[75]

The atmosphere was quite a contrast to the cheerful first night at the camp. After the fight of the 21st, the towering pecan trees at Walnut Springs had, as Samuel Reid described, "lost their lustrous glow," and the cool springs "murmured forth a lay of sorrow." Most of the Americans collapsed from exhaustion after eight hours of fighting and waited for the battle to begin anew the next day. They knew that Taylor would never accept the day's result as final.[76]

Surgeons worked throughout the night in makeshift hospitals to save the injured soldiers. As one soldier described, "The surgeons were busy amputating limbs, extracting balls, dressing wounds; and all who had walked unmoved through the carnage of the field, then found time to weep for the groaning sufferers." Doctor Chamberlain described his experiences after the fighting that day:

> I was, therefore, ordered into camp, and performed eight amputations, as fast as I could get along, with Doctor George, my only assistant. My work of extracting, and excising balls, securing blood-vessels, and dressing contused wounds, continued during the livelong night, and recommenced with the return of the day. I have amputated for the Tennessee, the

Mississippi, and my own regiment, and three regulars,—besides, there are a number of limbs, that, in all probability, must yet come off. It seems all blood,—blood,—blood!—and I am heartily sick of it. Oh! what a dreadful sight is a battlefield—particularly one where death is produced by artillery and the bursting of shells.[77]

Colonel Davis had other pressing duties. He remembered that Alexander McClung, his second in command, was still lying in a ditch in front of Fort Teneria and called for volunteers to find the lieutenant colonel and bring him back to camp. It would not be an easy task since it was dark and the Citadel continued to fire upon anything that moved on the plain. Despite the danger, Davis had no shortage of volunteers. Lt. William Patterson, who had earlier saved McClung's life, immediately stepped forward as did four others of the Tombigbee Company. The men dodged fire from the Citadel and reached Teneria's ditch. They found McClung, cold and stiff from hours of suffering and exposure, and put him on a crude stretcher that they hoisted on top of their shoulders. McClung groaned in agony as rain poured on the desperate group, moving as fast as possible across the plain. Citadel gunners spotted them and fired several cannonballs, one of which passed directly under the stretcher. The Mississippians reached camp safely and took McClung to a doctor. Miraculously, he survived.[78]

General Taylor's concerns centered on Fort Teneria. He believed that the Mexicans would try to retake his hard-gained toehold in the city that night. The general posted the 3rd Infantry and two companies of the 1st Kentucky in and around the fort. Lt. Jeremiah Scarritt of the engineers erected a traverse inside the walls to shield the men from the Citadel's cannon fire. It was an wretched experience for the hungry, tired men guarding Teneria. "The night set in cold, and, to complete our misery, it rained; the men had neither dinner nor supper, and, without even a blanket, were forced to lie down in the mud."[79]

The diversion against eastern Monterrey proved to be one of the deadliest actions of the Mexican War. About 14 percent of the total American force engaged, 394 men, were killed or wounded. The Tennessee regiment, thereafter known as the "Bloody First," alone lost 29 killed and 76 wounded. Colonel Campbell wrote his cousin a few days after the battle, "I do not fear danger when it is necessary to expose one's self, and I was exposed enough on the 21st for the exposure of 20 battles." And if Taylor had another day like this one, he would no longer have much of an army.[80]

For West Pointers, September 21, 1846, was one of the most tragic days in the academy's history. Eleven graduates were killed in eastern Monterrey, six lost in the 3rd Infantry alone. These officers led their men from the front and died for their effort. Any doubt that Taylor or his fellow countrymen had about the courage of the bookish academy men was erased after that day.

Nevertheless, the commanding general seemed pleased with his operations, at least as indicated by his official report. "The main object proposed in the morning had been effected. A powerful diversion had been made to favor the operations of the Second Division." Colonel Garland, the First Division's commander that day, wrote quite differently. Eight days after the carnage, he struggled to write his first official statement regarding the battle. Garland had lost many friends and brave soldiers in the deadly assaults, but his division had made little progress. Referring to the need, as was custom in an official report, to write about the gallant actions of his fallen men, he finally stated, "this must be done by others, whose grief is less profound."[81]

6

WORTH'S HOOK

"That was by all odds the hottest fire I have seen, and I have seen it pretty warm."

Lt. Napoleon Jackson Tecumseh Dana

When Zachary Taylor had just started forming his troops for the "diversion" into eastern Monterrey on the morning of September 21, William Worth's men awoke wet and hungry from a short sleep. Throughout the night, they listened to the roar of Taylor's mortar and howitzer to the east. The sounds told them their commanding general had something planned for the 21st and was trying to soften the city's defenses. Worth formed his usual line of march, with Ben McCulloch's Company A in the lead, then the rest of the Texans, and finally the remainder of the division. The Americans marched for a mile and a half without any opposition and began to think that they might reach the Saltillo road without a fight. The Mexicans had retreated from Marin, Ramos, and other towns, so perhaps they would withdraw from here too.

McCulloch's company rounded a bend in the road and learned that this time would be different. In front of them, 1,500 Mexican cavalry and infantry stood ready for battle near a hacienda called San Jerónimo. The horsemen looked dashing as usual, carrying their long lances, wearing bright red uniforms, and sitting on decorated silver saddles. The infantrymen took shelter in the cornfields around the Saltillo road.

Jack Hays, commanding the mounted Texans, shouted for his men to dismount and form in a small gulley. James Duncan's light artillery and some light infantry companies under Capt. Charles Smith and Lt. James Longstreet joined the Texans to form a battle line. For a moment the two sides observed each other, without firing a shot, from about two hundred yards away. Then the two lines began exchanging sporadic fire. Hays ordered his men to remount and take position by a fence near the road. From this vantage point they could shoot flanking fire into the cavalry while Duncan and the infantry could fire directly against the Mexican line. The Guanajuato Active Militia Cavalry charged straight toward Duncan's position. The cavalry's commander, Col. Juan Nájera, sporting a long and curly mustache, finely pressed blue uniform, and ornamented hat, led the way. Most of the Mexican infantry, who should have provided support to the attack, stayed in the cornfields away from the action. The colonel and his men were on their own.[1]

Nájera soon received an unwelcome surprise. McCulloch did not hear Hays's command to hide behind the fence and instead ordered his company to charge directly into the oncoming horsemen. As strange as the move was, McCulloch probably did not think twice about rushing pell-mell into the lancers. A common tactic used by Texas Rangers against Comanches was to execute an almost suicidal charge against a larger group of Indians to scare them away from the fight. The Texans leading the advance from Camargo to Monterrey had used this tactic also against Carrasco's cavalry with success. But the situation was different now. A daring and respected soldier, Colonel Nájera had no intention of retreating. The Mexican cavalry outnumbered McCulloch's company ten to one. The Texans fired one rifle shot before the two groups became intermingled. The Mexicans fired carbines, swung their swords and spurred their horses to lance the Texans.

But this was not the first time Texans had faced such a dire situation. Only two years earlier at Walker's Creek on the plains of West Texas, many of these same men had faced certain death. Jack Hays then led a group of thirteen Rangers to chase down some Comanches who had earlier raided a farm. His men caught up with the Indians, who outnumbered the Texans five to one. Hays should have retreated,

This drawing best depicts McCulloch's haphazard charge into the Mexican cavalry at San Jerónimo on September 21. Notice the horseman in the front center of the picture wielding a pistol, the weapon that ultimately helped the Texans survive this engagement. From Frost, *Mexican War and Its Warriors*, 87. Courtesy of Special Collections, The University of Texas at Arlington Library.

but for the first time his men were armed with new Paterson Colt revolvers, which could fire five shots in rapid fashion before being reloaded. The Rangers formed a circle with their horses, with each horse facing outward to receive the impending charge. The Indians bore down on the group, firing muskets, shooting arrows, and some leveling lances. They speared Samuel Walker, the volunteer who had ridden into Fort Brown for Taylor, and R. A. Gillespie, the latter receiving a vicious wound. The Rangers blazed away with their revolvers and eventually forced the Indians to retreat. The Texans pursued, and the fight continued on and off for miles across the plain.[2]

San Jerónimo was a similar situation against an adversary using similar weapons and tactics, and McCulloch's men knew not to panic. They unholstered their Colts and rattled off ten shots each within the tightly packed group of horsemen. Mexican cavalrymen began dropping from their saddles. Hays's men did not rush out to join the fray but instead stayed along the fence and picked off loose Mexican horsemen with their rifles. Duncan's artillery and the infantry also opened fire.[3]

Colonel Nájera urged his men on until he was killed. "We saw their lieutenant colonel fall," remembered Samuel Reid of Company A, "while in the thickest of the fight, and exhorting his men to rally and stand firm." Many of Worth's men remembered the courage and bravery that Nájera showed on this day. He gained their utmost respect, and after the battle his body was carefully tended. After Nájera fell, most of the lancers retreated. McCulloch's men, however, remained entangled with the group as the Mexicans withdrew. "Then it was that the hardest struggle took place," Reid remembered, as the men tried to fight their way back to friendly lines. The remaining Mexican cavalrymen stabbed some of the Texans with their lances as McCulloch's men tried to extricate themselves from the mass of men and horses. Most of the captain's men made it out. But McCulloch remained stuck in the pack of lancers until, as Reid remembered, "he put his horse to his speed, running everything down in his way, and regained his command without a scratch!"[4]

Duncan fired his artillery over the heads of the returning horsemen. The infantry also fired over the Texans, though accidentally killing one of them. A few of the bravest Mexicans, including Capt. José Gutiérrez de Villanueva, continued to fight as the rest of the lancers retreated. That officer received three wounds and died "fighting to the last, one of the most courageous of his race." Christopher Haile, a *Picayune* reporter, was probably referring to Gutiérrez when he wrote: "The Captain was wounded in three places, the last shot hitting him in the forehead. He fought gallantly to the last, and I am sorry that I cannot learn his name." Most of the lancers moved south, up the side of Independence Hill, while others departed the city, moving west on the Saltillo road. The Texans and some light infantry sprinted after them and shot some of the retreating horsemen from their saddles.[5]

The battle lasted about fifteen minutes. One hundred and fifty Mexicans were killed and wounded, while one Texan died from friendly fire. The battle proved, if nothing else, that the lancer could not compete with the Colt revolver in close combat, nor could Mexican lancers charge directly into a well-armed battle line. Mexico's cavalry were more successful when they flanked or encircled an enemy from the rear, not when they assaulted head on. The Mexican infantry provided no support to the brave lancers, staying hidden in the cornfield and retreating once the charge was repulsed. Unfortunately for the Mexican army, it lost some of its bravest men in this misguided fight.

The battlefield was littered with not only the Mexican dead but also Mexican saddles, carbines, and lances. "Amid the scene of carnage," Reid remembered, "lay stretched out some of their bravest men in gaudy uniforms, and many a broken lance lay here and there, while the road and hill-side were lined with their dead horses, beautifully caparisoned, the saddles ornamented with silver mountings, presenting a wild and ghastly scene." The Americans buried thirty-two cavalrymen in one pit. They also collected Mexican accouterments, weapons, and some of their healthy horses. The Texans gave away the ornate, silver saddles as gifts because they were too heavy and would wear out their galloping horses in minutes.[6]

After the battle most of the Mexican infantry retreated to the western foot of Independence Hill. A party of Texans and regulars snuck through nearby cornfields and posted themselves along a fence to fire on the group. Duncan and William Mackall advanced with them, dragging their artillery along in order to fire into the redoubt that sat on the western edge of Independence Hill. Worth set his sights on the Bishop's Palace, the position that appeared to be the key to controlling western Monterrey. Suddenly, unexpected cannon shot rained down on the Texan advance from the southeast. A battery of two cannons on Federation Hill, a work unrecorded in any engineer's reports, fired across the Santa Catarina River into the men.

Worth, who had been focused on storming Independence Hill and the Bishop's Palace, did not have much time to consider what to do because the fire was starting to take a toll on his men. Skilled artillerymen on Independence Hill fired their 9-pounder at Duncan and Mackall's guns, killing one of the horses, while Duncan's light artillery could do little damage against the strong redoubt. "The first and second shots passed over our heads," Mackall recalled, "the next struck a rock close by Irvin [McDowell] and myself, who were sitting on our horses talking about the affair, threw pieces of rock and sand in our faces and bounding over the heads of our men and horses buried itself in the mountain side. This was getting a little too warm."[7]

In the thick of this bombardment, Colonel Hays asked a junior Texan soldier to ascend a lone tree in a cornfield to observe the enemy's infantry. The Americans needed to know if the Mexicans, who were partially hidden behind Independence Hill, were advancing. The soldier climbed the tree but soon asked Hays if he could come down. "No, sir," said the colonel, "wait for orders." Some time passed, and the Texans began to move out of the area, but they forgot about the soldier in the tree. Hays ran back for him. "Holloa, there—where are the Mexicans," he asked. "Going back up the hill," the young man told him, though he did not realize who he was addressing. "Well, then, had not you better come down from there," the colonel replied. "I don't know," the soldier responded, "I am waiting for orders!" Hays shouted up, "Well, then, I *order* you down." Now realizing he had been talking to his colonel, the young man scrambled down the tree and out of harm's way (as fast as a raccoon, some said).[8]

Meanwhile, General Worth decided to move his men away from the fire of Independence and Federation hills and marched them double-time to the Saltillo road. The cannons on Independence opened up on the troops as they weaved through the cornfields and fences back toward the Saltillo road. The Americans marched under a torrent of shot and shells. Mexican gunners paid particular attention to the wagons trailing the column, possibly suspecting them to be full of infantry. The Irish teamsters driving the wagons whipped their scared horses to trot forward as fast as possible.

One of the cannonballs launched against Worth's column ripped Capt. Henry McKavett in half. McKavett, a U.S. Military Academy graduate of 1834, had the unenviable distinction of being the first West Pointer killed at Monterrey. The officer had a premonition while marching to Monterrey that he might die in battle. On September 13 he wrote a friend: "Possibly, I may write you next from Monterrey; but no one can foresee the result if our movement should be obstructed. Please remember me kindly to ——." The captain willed all of his money to the New York City's Orphan Asylum, which had raised him as a boy. The determined McKavett, though raised in an orphanage, had worked hard through his young life and eventually received an appointment to West Point, graduating twenty-fourth in his class. At Resaca de la Palma, he had led a daring charge against a Mexican artillery position. He was one of Taylor's most respected soldiers.[9]

The rest of Worth's men arrived at the Saltillo road, then moved west (away from the city) until they were out of artillery range. The general now had to decide whether he should attack Federation Hill

The heights west of Monterrey. Capt. Daniel Whiting, a West Point graduate in the 7th Infantry, produced five of the rarest lithographs of the war. Three of these depict scenes of Monterrey, including this one, which shows Worth's men marching west down the Saltillo road to move out of range of Mexican artillery on Federation and Independence hills. Notice the "flying artillery" cannon with its complement of six horses and five men (bottom right). *Heights of Monterey, from the Saltillo Road Looking towards the City. (From the West).* Lithograph by Frederick Swinton, after Daniel P Whiting, 1847. Toned lithograph (hand colored), 12 11/16 × 19 1/2 in. Courtesy of the Amon Carter Museum, Fort Worth, Tex.

or Independence Hill or deploy his men in the Rinconada Pass—
where they were then located—in order to block any Mexican reinforcements should they arrive. Santa Anna was expected to arrive
with a strong army any day from Saltillo. If those troops appeared
while Worth was attacking one of the heights, the Americans would
be surrounded and probably destroyed. Pvt. Zenith Matthews saw the
situation clearly: "Nothing could be done toward attacking the city
without taking the two heights and the Bishop's Palace."[10]

General Worth scanned the Mexican works with his spyglass.
Federation Hill contained a small redoubt on its western end (Fort
Federation) and on its eastern end a larger stronghold known as Fort
Soldado. Worth remarked to his Texan aide-de-camp, Maj. Edward
Burleson, that he must have "the heights," referring to Federation
Hill, but wondered what the best way was to achieve this. "Easy thing
General," Burleson replied, "send the Rangers to take them." Burle-
son knew the Mexican army well, being one of the few Texans in
Taylor's army who had fought against it at San Antonio de Bexar in
late 1835. He also led the backbone of Sam Houston's army at San
Jacinto, the 1st Regiment, which charged directly into Santa Anna's
position and routed the Mexicans.[11]

Regardless of Burleson's Texan heroics, Worth was not sure about
his advice. He first ordered Capt. Charles Smith's three companies of
the artillery battalion to assault the hill. Maj. Michael Chevalier from
Hays's regiment asked the general if his Texans could accompany the
storming party. "No, sir," Worth told him, "I wish Capt. Smith especially to command that expedition." Major Chevalier outranked
Smith and would by regulations have command of the group if he
accompanied the men. "There shall be no difficulty about that," Chevalier replied, "I'll go *under* Capt. Smith." "Very well," Worth replied,
"you can go sir."[12]

In this assault Major Chevalier would lead a veritable "who's
who" of Texan heroes, including R. A. Gillespie, William Wallace,
Samuel Walker, and Ben McCulloch. In addition to their Colts, the
Texans possessed another weapon that would serve them well in the
assault up the steep hill—their plains rifles. This weapon, like all
rifles of the time, fired more accurately at a greater range (up to 300
yards) than the regulars' smoothbores (which were not accurate beyond 50 yards). A rifle's barrel contains spiraled grooves, known as
"rifling," which spin the ball as it exits the barrel. Rifling allows a

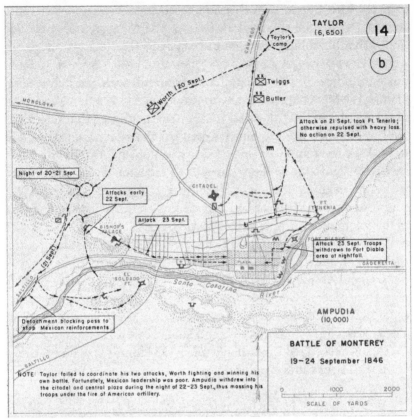

American attacks against Monterrey, September 19–24. This map shows the Americans' western attack on Federation and Independence hills. Worth was worried that Santa Anna would arrive in his rear on the Saltillo road during the attack, putting his division in jeopardy. Map courtesy of the Department of History, United States Military Academy.

gun's projectile to maintain a level trajectory for greater distances than those shot from a smoothbore barrel. The rifles would allow the Texans to pick off soldiers perched above them on the hill.[13]

Worth formed his men—half Texan volunteers and half regulars— and pointed at the hill. The 400-foot-tall height contained at least two cannons and hundreds of Mexican soldiers. Small shrubs and thorny chaparral lined its slope. As Reid recalled, the men thought it would only be taken with great sacrifice, a "forlorn hope" they called it. "Men, you are to take that hill—and I know you will do it," Worth yelled to his troops. They responded, "We will," and huzzahs erupted from the line. Captain Smith marched his men on a circuitous route west down the Saltillo road away from the Mexican positions. He hoped that his soldiers, hidden in corn and sugarcane, would go unnoticed by the expert gunners on Federation Hill. They left at noon, during the heat of the day, and clambered through the fields. Soon enough the Mexican artillerists saw them and fired cannons and musketry down into the group. But the crops camouflaged the Americans well, and no one was hit. Smith's men left the safety of the cornfield to ford the river and were exposed to a vicious bombardment. "The men rushed into the sweeping current," Reid later wrote, "waist deep, while the enemy's shot, as it struck the water, sent forth a hissing sound, and made the river boil and foam with the whistling windage of their venomous copper balls." Surprisingly, no one was hurt in the crossing. The men hid in thick chaparral on the other side to catch their breath and let water drain from their shoes and clothes.[14]

General Ampudia, now realizing that Federation Hill was Worth's objective, ordered General Conde's brigade to support the defenders there. But he recalled Conde before his men even reached the hill. The soldiers at Forts Federation and Soldado were on their own. The Mexicans descended the hillside and hid behind rocks and bushes. From the lower vantage point, they could better aim at the approaching enemy.

Worth, observing this movement, ordered Capt. Dixon Miles to take seven companies and divert the defenders' attention from Smith's main attack. He was probably worried that the Texans and regulars would be cut down before they even made it to the base of Federation. Unlike Smith, Miles had no need to conceal his movements and took a more direct route to the hill. Lt. Napoleon Dana described what happened as they crossed the Santa Catarina River: "We put into the river, and the depression being now too great for them to use their cannon any longer, the infantry rose, about five hundred of them, and poured in their lead as fast as they could send it. . . . Their bullets showered on us literally like hail. They struck the water all around us, between us, before and behind, everywhere. It appeared impossible that we could escape being shot. That was by all odds the hottest fire I have seen, and I have seen it pretty warm."[15]

Miles's men continued through the chaparral to the base of the hill, arriving before Smith did. Miles then carried out his diversion by sending some his men away from the safety of the hill's base, where they would attract the attention of the Mexican soldiers above. It worked. The enemy sent musketry and artillery against the exposed men, while Smith maneuvered his troops through cornfields and linked up with Miles's main body. Here they were safe from the cannons perched on the steep slope above them.

Although there is no record of a discussion, the two captains probably discussed how best to assault the hill before deciding that the Texans should start climbing first. Armed with their rifles these men would be able to pick off soldiers hiding among brush and rocks, clearing the way for the regulars. Considering the steep incline, the regulars would be lucky to hit anyone with their smoothbores at any distance exceeding a few paces. Smith's men would have to somehow lug their long muskets, which were more than 57 inches long (including a 42-inch barrel) to the top of the mountain and wait for the moment when they could charge the Mexicans with bayonets.[16]

Whatever the reason, the Texans started ascending the hill first—"ahead like devils," Dana recalled. The regulars, including men from Miles's 7th Infantry, began climbing soon after. The men grabbed thorn bushes, chaparral, and rocks to pull themselves up. "Inch by inch they disputed our ascent," recalled Texan Reid. Although the Americans thought that the steep incline would lead to their deaths, in reality it saved many of their lives. The Mexicans fired downhill, and as so often happens in such situations, most of them overshot their mark. They also could not depress their cannons enough to hit the soldiers clinging to the steep hillside's vegetation. Chaparral bushes and rocks further obscured the Americans as they crept up the slope.[17]

General Worth anxiously watched the attack from the road. Although he could no longer see his men, hidden among the hill's chaparral and rocks, he could see the hundreds of Mexicans unleashing a withering fire against his soldiers. Journalist George Wilkins Kendall remembered, "it was a trying moment for all; for an incessant firing of both grape and musketry, was pouring upon the storming parties, while not a solitary shot was returned." Worried, Worth ordered Col. Persifor Smith to take his 5th Infantry and Capt. Albert Sidney Blanchard's Louisiana volunteers to support the assault. Colonel Smith collected his men and marched right away.[18]

Captain Smith's storming party continued its ascent and met a torrential fire as the men neared the summit, which was almost perpendicular. The Mexican soldiers finally could see their enemy, and they unleashed the most accurate volley of musketry since the assault started. The Americans climbed on, with the Texans picking off any Mexican soldier who showed himself and the regulars firing orchestrated volleys from their muskets. Soon they arrived at the summit, shouted "huzzahs," brandished bayonets, and streamed over the top. The Mexicans scrambled out of Fort Federation and sprinted eastward along the hilltop toward El Soldado—a stone fort on the eastern end of the hill. The fleeing troops tried to throw a 9-pound cannon down the hillside, but in their haste, they only overturned the gun's carriage. Lt. Edward Deas remounted the cannon and began firing on Soldado. According to multiple accounts, incredibly, one of his first shots hit a Mexican cannon head on and spun it around. Wild cheers erupted from the Americans.

While the attack on the redoubt was occurring, Colonel Smith ordered his supporting column to advance up the south side of Federation Hill in order to take a different approach to the summit. The colonel's men snaked their way up the side and soon emerged on the top. When he arrived at there, Smith shouted, "Men, take that other fort!" The command was "hardly necessary," as Reid recalled, because the Texans, the artillery battalion, Colonel Smith's 5th and 7th Infantry, and Blanchard's Phoenix Company were already in hot pursuit of the enemy. Captain Smith's men too were sprinting across the top of the hill toward Fort Soldado. William Worth did not care who was the first to enter the main fort; he was simply elated that his men were able to storm the redoubt so quickly. The anxious general had already sent for Jack Hays to take a hundred men to reinforce both Smiths because he thought the storming party needed help to continue their attack. But he applauded their initiative to rush to the second fort without waiting for his orders. Worth was an aggressive, sometimes impetuous general, and his men were acting just as he wished.

Texans, Louisianans, and regulars rushed headlong toward Fort Soldado. The Mexican garrison fired their muskets at the oncoming Americans, while the 9-pound cannon belched canister and grapeshot, wounding many of the attackers. But the Americans continued forward, almost as if they were obsessed with taking Soldado. "On we went," said S. D. Allis of Blanchard's company, "loading and forming as we advanced, until within fifty yards, when we rushed up as fast as

our legs would carry us, driving the Mexican down the other side."
The Texans ran with a wild-eyed look, giving the "Texan yell" as they
plowed through the fire in a mad rush to be the first into the walls.
Gillespie's company was the first to enter, followed closely by the 5th
Infantry, Blanchard's Louisianans, and the 7th Infantry. But according
to reporter Christopher Haile, "The three commands may be said to
have come out even in the race." The surviving Mexicans fled down
the hill toward Monterrey or across the valley to the Bishop's Palace.
Lt. Thomas Pitcher of the 5th Infantry, one of the first men to enter
the fort, saw a group of Texans near the fort's cannon and said, "Well,
boys, we liked to have beaten you." He pulled out a piece of chalk and
scrawled "Texas Rangers and Fifth Infantry" on the gun. A sergeant
from the 5th Infantry strung up their regimental flag, and an officer
from the 7th did the same.[19]

It was no surprise to the Texans that Gillespie jumped into the fort
first, probably followed closely by his friend Bigfoot Wallace. Gillespie was a fearless fighter whose daring exploits were known throughout the state. He had served under Jack Hays from 1841 to 1845—a
period that contained some of the most intense fighting between the
Texas Rangers and the Comanches in a battle for control of the West
Texas plains. He was also part of a group of Texans that had clashed
with Mexican troops under Gen. Adrian Woll at the Battle of Salado
Creek. Gillespie was the same Ranger who had earlier in Matamoros
insulted Robert Hazlitt, a brave regular who died while leading his
men into action on September 21. If Gillespie and Hazlitt had fought
alongside each other, the regular probably would have earned the
Texan's respect, perhaps even his friendship. For now, though, the
Texans and regulars stood within the captured Mexican fort, shaking
hands with their friends and inquiring about the health of others. Reid
later described the moment: "It was indeed a most animated scene.
Men flushed with victory, and begrimed with powder, stood holding
with a firm grasp the hands of their companions in arms, while relat-
ing some little incident or adventure of the fight, and then a loud peal
of laughter would burst forth from the different groups, at some ludi-
crous description of the runaway Mexicans."[20]

The Texans were not the only volunteers who behaved well under
fire. The assault was the Phoenix Company's first mission, and Blanchard's Louisianans acted with aplomb. "Captain Blanchard's company of Louisiana volunteers," one soldier recalled, "fought bravely,

as well as did the regulars, who tried hard to get into the works before the Texans." Haile, who probably wrote with some exaggeration to excite his audience back home, agreed: "Capt. Blanchard and his company have already made a reputation that will not soon be forgotten." Casualties for the Americans were eighteen wounded, of whom two later died; Mexican losses are unknown.[21]

The speed with which the Americans approached Fort Soldado must have surprised the Mexicans, who left behind most of their supplies in their haste to abandon the place. Worth's men captured a small bonanza of equipment and weapons, including a 9-pound cannon, tents, mules, ammunition, and entrenching tools. The soldiers also dragged the 9-pound cannon from the western redoubt and established it at Soldado.

Soon afterward Lieutenant Dana's artillerists began lobbing cannonballs across the Santa Catarina valley toward the Bishop's Palace, but most missed their target. The Mexicans returned fire, but their shots flew high over the Americans' heads. The soldiers watched the artillery exchange with awe. Flaming cannonballs arched high across the beautiful, deep valley between Federation and Independence hills. This hilltop-to-hilltop duel did not last long, however, because a massive thunderstorm quickly descended on the area. Lightning snapped across the sky and rain poured down on the tired men. Most of them had not eaten in thirty-six hours and chewed on raw corncobs for nourishment. Many were still wet from wading the river but could not make fires to dry their clothes. Nightfall brought an end to the firing, and most of the men on Federation Hill curled up and slept in the rain. A few lucky ones slept in captured tents.

Worth wasted no time in deciding his next move. He organized an assault party of 470 men, under the command of Lt. Col. Thomas Childs of the artillery battalion, to assault Independence Hill the next morning. The attack order was textbook Worth—maintain the momentum, be aggressive, and surprise the enemy. The assault party consisted of three companies from Childs's own battalion, three companies of the 8th Infantry (including one under Lieutenant Longstreet), and seven Texan companies belonging to Jack Hays and Samuel Walker.

Thomas Childs was one of the oldest West Point graduates in Taylor's army, having graduated seventh in the Class of 1814. He was not a lieutenant colonel but a captain who had received two brevets to that rank. To some in his unit, it seemed strange that a captain was commanding such an important storming party. D. H. Hill, 4th Artillery, thought it a "queer state of things" when a captain commanded a brigade. "Our worthless old officers have generally been laid on the shelf," he observed. Such was the state of affairs in the nineteenth-century U.S. Army, though, when it took over twenty years to obtain the rank of captain and another twenty years to become a major. Less than one-third of the active colonels, lieutenant colonels, and majors in the 1846 army were on duty with their regiments in Mexico; the others were too old, too sick, or too disinterested to bother.[22]

The Texans had just finished tending to their horses when they were ordered to be ready for their second assault in twelve hours. A soldier in McCulloch's company recorded in his diary, "went to camp —fed our horses—got supper—and expected to get a good nights rest but we had just retired to take a rest, when the order came for Capt McCulloch and Capt Gillespie's comp[anies] to be ready to march to the attack of Independence Height." Regulars and Texans alike awoke at 3 A.M. to storm the hill. The early morning weather was crisp and refreshing, though the previous night's storm had left a thick fog in the valley. Reid noted that the men were "invigorated from the fresh air." At camp word passed through the ranks to move cautiously and keep silent. Engineers John Sanders and George Meade led the assault column through fog-covered cornfields and chaparral toward Independence Hill.[23]

Since being assigned to Worth's division, Lieutenant Meade had found plenty of work to do. Earlier in the campaign, Meade had believed that engineers rarely played a big role in combat, complaining to his wife that there had been no opportunities for him to "perform brilliant feats" at Palo Alto or Resaca de la Palma. On this cool morning, while guiding 500 men to the base of a fortified hill through fog, cornfields, and chaparral, he probably would have taken back that statement. A successful surprise attack now depended on Meade and Sanders getting the troops to the base of Independence Hill undetected. The Mexican general who planned the hill's defenses believed that the Americans would attack from its eastern, more gradual slope rather than the steep western incline they now approached and had structured his forces accordingly. If the Mexicans learned of their presence, they could reinforce the redoubt there (Fort Libertad) and put up stiffer resistance. But Meade and Sanders successfully guided the assault troops quietly into position. Childs then divided the command between himself and Capt. John Vinton. One group would attack the hill from the southwest, while the other would ascend the northwestern slope.[24]

The Texans were also divided, with Hays commanding one portion and Walker the other. Both groups of men were from the "western regiment" of Texas volunteers—officially known as the 1st Mounted Regiment of Texas Volunteers—which contained hardened frontiersmen like Walker, Hays, Gillespie, McCulloch, and Wallace. They were the best fighters Texas had to offer. Among them, "Bigfoot" Wallace had a more interesting story than most. He had come to Texas from Virginia in 1836 after learning that his brother and cousin had been massacred at Goliad in order to "take pay out of the Mexicans," as he put it. He fought against the Mexican army twice before coming to Monterrey, once at Salado and again at Mier, where his accurate rifle took down many soldiers. Even so, he had yet to take enough "pay" from the Mexicans and had vengeance on his mind while waiting at the bottom of Independence Hill. Other Texan volunteers probably muttered stanzas of the Rangers fight song "Cry Vengeance for Texas!" under their breath. In their eyes they would be righting many wrongs this chilly September day.[25]

After finalizing the command arrangements, Texans and regulars alike began to grope their way up the steep, seven-hundred-foot hill in pitch-black darkness. Like Federation Hill, the slope of Independence was covered with thorny shrubs and giant, four- to five-foot-high crags of rock. The men pulled themselves up by grasping the trunks of thorn bushes or by hanging onto cracks in the rock formations. The slippery mist-coated rocks left more than one man tumbling down the hill. The soldiers climbed to within a hundred feet of the crest when small-arms fire rained down from above.[26]

Seventy Mexican soldiers from the 4th Light Infantry manned Fort Libertad. General Conde did not provide reinforcements to the redoubt because he did not believe that anyone could climb the steep slope below it. The small garrison detected the assault party, though they could barely see in the darkness, probably by hearing noises from the soldiers clambering up the slippery hill—a rifle barrel clinking against the side, rocks tumbling down the hill, or perhaps the grunt of a man pulling himself up the steep slope. For the Mexicans, it must have been nerve-wracking to remain in the small redoubt, unable to see the enemy below or to depress their artillery far enough for use against them. The soldiers probably cursed Conde and Ampudia for not supplying them with more men. Despite these fears, they used their muskets and pistols with spirit and determination. Shooting downhill against men hidden by rocks and mist was almost futile, but they did come close to hitting their adversaries. "They now commenced a rattling fire" as the Americans got close to the top, a Texan private remembered, "one ball hit the rock, chipping off a piece, my hand was on." Just below the summit, a virtual cliff extended for about twenty yards. Under this steady fire, the men pulled each other up over rocks and bushes to scale the sheer face. "My worthy frontier friend," the Texan recalled, "ever ready to help me, gave me a boost up over a big rock, in return I helped to pull him up." They tried to select bushes with sturdy roots since weak shrubs would uproot and send men tumbling.[27]

Around this time, Captain Miles with three companies of the 8th Infantry descended the north side of Federation Hill toward the palace. The regulars, hearing the firing from Independence Hill, gave three cheers to distract the Mexican defenders. One gunner turned his howitzer on Miles's men and showered them with grapeshot. The Americans took cover behind some rocks and an old fence, then continued down the hill so they would be in position to stop any reinforcements that tried to approach the hill from the south.

Before scaling the western face of Independence Hill, Childs had instructed his men to hold their fire until the order went out. Soon after clearing the cliff, an order to fire echoed throughout the ranks: "Now Men! Give them Hell." Shots erupted from both sides of the hill against the Mexicans in the redoubt. "When we raised the [Texan] *yell* and made a charge they poured their fire into us for ten minutes," remembered a soldier in Hays's regiment. By this time the sun had begun to rise, and the Texans could see the silhouettes of Mexican soldiers above them and aimed carefully at the moving shadows. Reid describes what happened next: "Panting and breathless, men and officers strove to gain the height, contending with the rocky steep as well as with the enemy—peal after peal, and shout and cry, rang wildly forth for victory—onward they rushed, braving the storm of hail until they gained the brow, and with a loud huzza bore back the foe."[28]

Gillespie was one of the first to reach the summit. He jumped over the redoubt's sandbags, and a bullet struck his pistol lock and

The Bishop's Palace and Monterrey. This illustration provides an excellent representation of the Bishop's Palace following its capture, though it does omit some of the additional defensive measures that the Mexicans undertook to fortify the palace, including cutting out loopholes, stacking sandbags, and erecting makeshift breastworks. *Monterey, from Independence Hill, in the Rear of the Bishop's Palace, As it Appeared on the 23d, September, 1846. (Looking East).* Lithograph by Frederick Swinton, after Daniel P. Whiting, 1847. Toned lithograph (hand colored), 12 7/16 × 19 7/16 in. Courtesy of the Amon Carter Museum, Fort Worth, Tex.

ricocheted into his stomach. He fell and called to 1st Lt. G. H. Nelson. Gillespie gave Nelson his sword, told him to wear it, and instructed him not to tell anyone about his wound until the palace was taken. Then he shouted, "Rush to the fort!" Bigfoot Wallace picked up his wounded friend and helped him to safety. Pvt. Henry Thomas, a friendly young Texan, was also shot at Fort Libertad. Despite the heavy gunfire, James Longstreet and the other regulars brandished bayonets and swords and charged into the redoubt. The Mexicans fled, running east along the top of the hill to the much stronger Bishop's Palace. Unlike their comrades on Federation Hill, they took their cannon with them.[29]

The Americans collapsed from exhaustion. "We found shelter and took it easy," a Texan remembered. They saw the Mexicans dragging the cannon to the palace but were too tired to give chase. Worth sent three more companies of the 8th Infantry to the summit to reinforce his victorious men. The general did not want to lose their hard-fought toehold. After catching their breath, Lieutenant Longstreet's company and some Texans moved out of Fort Libertad and advanced within firing range of the Bishop's Palace, about 350 yards east of the redoubt. A giant Mexican flag flew from its rooftop, and from their position they could see that the Mexicans had built breastworks surrounding the abandoned two-story structure. The only entrance into the palace was a fortified door, which would be impossible to batter in while exposed to heavy fire. Longstreet's men were not in position long before a large group of Mexican infantry sallied from the palace against them. The two sides exchanged fire, and the Mexicans eventually retired. Musket fire from the palace thereafter began to take a toll on Longstreet's command, so he and the Texans returned to the redoubt.[30]

Don Francisco Berra, commander of the garrison, had two hundred men and three cannons to defend the Bishop's Palace. The defenders posted themselves at the windows and at loopholes cut out of the walls. Berra also stationed men outside the palace, behind large boulders, bushes, rocks, and anything else they could use. The general moved some of the cannons from the Priest Cap so they could fire west against Worth's troops instead of east toward Taylor's men. The elaborately constructed Priest Cap, a position designed to defeat an enemy approaching from the city, would be of little use in the upcoming contest.

The Bishop's Palace. This view shows the palace and the Priest Cap from the east, the direction from which General Ampudia believed that the Americans would assault. Today the Bishop's Palace contains a city museum; bullet holes from the battle can still be found in its walls. Author's collection.

Worth sent Maj. Martin Scott's 5th Infantry and Blanchard's Louisiana volunteers to reinforce the men on the hill. While these troops could help Childs storm the palace, what the colonel really needed was artillery. If he could somehow get a cannon onto the hill, it could provide crucial support from the captured redoubt. A howitzer would be an ideal gun, since it fired in an arched trajectory that could pass over the palace's walls and descend on the garrison from above the roofless structure. The short-barreled howitzer fired spherical case shot (shells filled with musket balls and an explosive charge) that was timed to detonate over the heads of exposed enemy troops.

The problem was how Childs's men might get a howitzer up a steep seven-hundred-foot slope. General Worth challenged James Duncan and John Sanders to make it happen. Duncan tasked one of his best officers, Lt. John Roland, to bring a 12-pound howitzer to the base of Independence Hill. Sanders chose what he believed was the most practical route for the gun to travel up the hill, then he and

Duncan picked fifty men to drag the piece with ropes. Men on the summit would pull the cannon up while others below steered it along the chosen route. This was quite a feat, considering that the howitzer weighed 1,700 pounds and that the perpendicular slope was covered with rocks and bushes. But the howitzer reached the summit ready for action.

Lieutenant Roland mounted the howitzer on a small platform and built a small breastwork around the cannon. By this time a small group of Americans under Captain Vinton had moved closer to the Mexican position and were hiding behind a line of rocks and chaparral crossing the hill about halfway between the redoubt and the palace. Lieutenant Roland screamed to the soldiers, "clear the way gentlemen I am going to fire." All of the men fell flat to the ground. The howitzer's shells screeched as they arched over their heads and landed in the palace as intended. "I assure you I have never heard a more agreeable sound," one American wrote. The first and second shots landed just outside the walls, and the third landed in the middle of the roofless palace itself. George Wilkins Kendall wrote, "The effects of the howitzer . . . were at once visible: with remarkable accuracy the shells were thrown directly into the windows and other openings of the enemy's works." But the Mexican soldiers, though unnerved by the development, did not consider yielding. Colonel Childs raised a white flag to suggest that the garrison surrender. The Mexicans gave their response by firing on the flag bearer.[31]

It was now around noon. The high sun dissipated the morning mist and beat down upon the soldiers lying behind the outcroppings. "[T]he sun poured down red hot amid the rocks of the slope," a Texas private recalled, "and we were being slowly roasted." Many of the Americans had been on the hill since dawn, and they wondered how this day would end. Some worried that Worth might sacrifice these men in a frontal assault to regain his reputation. The general might have considered this, but he wanted to give Childs and Vinton a chance to determine the best way to attack the palace. Vinton considered his options, none of which were good. He probably figured that although a frontal assault would be costly, it might be the only viable one. Then Jack Hays suggested a better plan: coaxing the Mexican garrison out of the palace with a ruse de guerre. If they sent a small party forward toward the palace, perhaps the garrison would charge out, leaving the door open and the fort unguarded. Meanwhile, the

Texans and regular infantry would hide on the side of the hill, surprise the exposed soldiers, and rush into the palace. Vinton liked the
idea and called for Samuel Walker and Captain Blanchard to prepare
the ruse.[32]

Lieutenant Colonel Berra was determined to regain all of Independence Hill. The artillery fire from the redoubt's howitzer and
Dana's guns on Federation Hill made holding the palace untenable.
Exploding shells raked the inside the palace, and the garrison could
only hold out for so long. Around this time General Ampudia finally
decided to send more than fifty men under General Torrejón to support Berra. As Reid described, "Battalions of infantry formed in front
of the Palace, their crowded ranks and glistening bayonets presenting
a bold and fearless front, while squadrons of light-horsemen, with
lances bright and fluttering flags, and heavy cavalry, with scopets
(carbines) and broadswords gleaming in the sun, richly contrasting
with the gaudy Mexican uniforms, made a most imposing sight."[33]

Into this "imposing sight" marched Blanchard's ninety Louisianans. They advanced across the hill and took position about fifty yards
from the palace. "Balls began to fly thick as we advance;" Sgt. S. D.
Allis remembered in a letter to his uncle, "every bush has a Mexican
in it. . . . We get under cover of nooks, bushes, and low places, and
whenever we get a good shot at a fellow in or near the castle, cut loose.
Volley after volley is fired at us, but we lay low and they shoot high."
Aside from the scattered musket fire from Blanchard's men and the
howitzer, the hilltop was silent. Worth's men waited for what seemed
like hours to see if the ruse would work and Berra's men emerged.
Patience paid off, for the Mexicans could not resist the bait. Berra
probably yearned to go at the Americans ever since they appeared on
the hill.[34]

A Mexican bugle sounded, and hundreds of cavalry sallied from
the palace after Blanchard's men. "They are coming out of the castle,
about 500 strong, to make an attack on us," Allis continued in the
letter to his uncle, "One of our 12-pound howitzers has been hoisted
on the hill in the rear, and the shells commence whizzing over our
heads . . . They advance on us; we are ordered to close at the right on
the top of the hill, and fall back into a ravine one hundred yards
distant. We did so in great order, firing several times as we retreated.
The Mexicans came at us with a yell; the battle grew hot." The un-
flappable Blanchard recalled the Mexicans' appearance more plainly

in his diary: "we advanced to 50 yds—& commenced a galling fire on the Castle & on the troops below—Movement among them—they came around our left flank & showered their shot on us, by which I lost one killed and two wounded—it is a wonder why more were not hit."[35]

Blanchard's men did not panic but withdrew slowly while firing their weapons. The Louisianans arrived at the small rock outcropping that ran across the hill. As instructed they stopped, turned around, and formed a line. Vinton then gave the signal, and regulars from the 5th and 8th Infantry and the artillery battalion filled out the line on the left- and right-hand sides. "They suddenly rose before the enemy," Reid described, "like an apparition, to oppose their progress." Now the Mexican cavalry, trailed by their infantry, faced a wall of glistening muskets and bayonets. They approached to within twenty yards of the line before the Americans opened fire.

But for the Mexican soldiers on Independence Hill, the worst was yet to come. The words "fire" and "charge" rang throughout the hill, and the Texans and regulars hidden along the sides jumped from their positions and fired their rifles and muskets into the bunched-up horsemen. Scores of Mexican horses, crammed together on the narrow hilltop, scrambled wildly in retreat. They galloped back past the Bishop's Palace and down into western Monterrey. The infantrymen did the same, though some ran into the palace seeking shelter. But the Texans and regulars were right on their heels and poured through a hole in the palace door created by a well-aimed shot from Roland's howitzer. "The Texans were invaluable and brave as lions," Dana recalled. "They pursed so hotly that they entered pell-mell with the enemy into the palace." One Mexican soldier tried to blow up the palace by igniting the ammunition, but his plan was thwarted by the onrushing Americans. Duncan and Mackall rushed their light cannons to the east side of the hill to fire at the Mexicans retreating into the city. One officer found a spiked howitzer, but his men drove the spike through and were soon firing upon the fleeing soldiers. One group of Mexicans, unconcerned about the developments on the hill, casually strolled near a cemetery in western Monterrey. To their surprise one well-aimed shell from the howitzer landed in their midst, sending them darting east to get out of the range.[36]

For the first time the Americans beheld the beautiful view of Monterrey from the palace. The towering hill overlooked the entire

Storming of the Bishop's Palace. Shown center left is the main door through which the Americans ultimately entered. U.S. forces captured four pieces of artillery at the palace, including a beautiful 12-pound brass piece made in Liverpool in 1842 and etched with the words "Republica Mexicana." *Storming of the Bishop's Palace, At the Siege of Monterey Sept. 22nd, 1846*. Lithograph by the firm of Nathaniel Currier, 1847. Toned lithograph (hand colored), 8 5/16 × 12 13/16 in. Courtesy of the Amon Carter Museum, Fort Worth, Tex.

city. Orange groves and sugar cane dotted the plain to the north. The
beautiful plazas, lined with statues, fountains, and other embellish-
ments, stretched out before them. And although few if any recognized it, they could also see General Arista's palatial house, replete
with fountains and orange groves, in northwest Monterrey. The Sierra Madres rose to the south, and they could make out the Santa
Catarina River winding its way along the city's south side. When
Mackall planted his cannon here, he could hardly take his eyes off the
beautiful view long enough to fire them. "[B]ut not even the hurry and
excitement of the fight could distract attention from the gorgeous
magnificence of the scene that here burst upon the eye," he wrote to
his son. Surgeon William Withers, who visited the spot after the battle, admitted, "I have never beheld such scenery and if I should live a
thousand years I never expect to behold such again."[37]

Lt. George Ayres of the 3rd Artillery had the honor of bringing
down the giant Mexican flag atop the palace and raising the Stars and
Stripes. Cheers erupted from the men. Samuel Walker cut down the
signal flags in front near the door, giving one of them to a Texas
private who had fought with him since Palo Alto.[38]

It was now around 4 P.M., and the Mexican and American wounded
were collected and brought to the palace for treatment. The injured
Mexicans thought that they were going to be killed and were surprised to learn otherwise as American medics treated their injuries as
they did those of their own men. Some of the Americans comforted
their wounded adversaries, providing cigars and water, and staying
with them throughout the afternoon. One Texan met a Mexican who
was shot in the stomach. He brought him down to the river so he
could relax under a small tree and drink some water. The dying man
asked him to deliver some money to a Juanita Sanchez in Monterrey.
The Texan, true to his word, found her after the battle and delivered
the money as well as some coat buttons from the dead soldier's jacket.

The Americans captured thirty prisoners, a howitzer, two 9-pound
cannons, many muskets, several lances, and ample ammunition. Perhaps the biggest prize was a beautiful 18-pound brass cannon manufactured in England. General Worth lost only six men killed and
seventeen wounded. Gillespie and Thomas, who were wounded that
morning, died the next day. Bigfoot Wallace stayed with his friend
in his final hours, providing him water and tending to his wounds,
surely a painful experience, even for a rock-hard frontiersman like

Bigfoot. Gillespie's death even shook Jack Hays, who had seen count-less men die in battle. Hays wanted to ensure that his commanding general knew just how much Gillespie meant to Texas and to his new country. "In the various conflicts which had taken place Capt. Gilles-pie had been ever most conspicuous," he informed General Worth in his final report. "He was the first man who mounted the summit in storming 'Independence Hill' and among the first when he fell. In his death I deplore the loss of an intimate and long cherished friend, and the country that of a noble and most gallant soldier long identified with the defence of the Texan frontier." Thomas and Gillespie were buried at the redoubt where they fell. Worth renamed Independence Hill "Mount Gillespie" in honor of the Texan.[39]

Reporters Christopher Haile and George Wilkins Kendall had ob-served the fight from the hilltop, determined to provide their readers an accurate eyewitness view of events. Often this meant getting close to the deadly action. "I saw Haile several times during the fight," one soldier recalled, "riding about quite indifferent to the balls which fell around him. Although he did not run into danger, he did not appear to try to avoid it when it visited him."[40] Kendall and Haile wrote de-tailed first-person accounts of the events that day. Haile scribbled a quick note about the battle to his editor that was printed in an extra on October 4. These were the first words read by any in the States concerning the clash on Independence Hill:

> I have but a few moments but left to write in, and must there-fore defer the particulars of the storming of the palace until I have more time. Col [Thomas] Staniford went up at day-light with the balance of the Eight, and Maj Scott led up the Fifth. The Louisiana boys were on the hill with the Fifth, at 8 o'clock A.M. One of Duncan's howitzers, in charge of Lieut. Rowland, was dragged up, or rather *lifted* up, and opened up on the palace, which was filled with troops. The Mexicans charged on the howitzer but were driven back. A constant firing was kept up for several hours particularly by Blan-chard's men, who left a dozen Mexicans dead upon the hill-side. At length a charge was ordered, and our men rushed down upon the palace, entered a hole in the door that had been blocked up but opened by the howitzer, and soon cleared the work of the few Mexicans who remained.[41]

For two days the Texans and the regulars under Worth had fought side by side in difficult conditions. They assaulted two hills under fire and successfully overran four strongly prepared positions. For each assault the Texans composed almost half of the total force. Worth placed his faith in these eccentric soldiers, and they paid him back in blood, courage, and results. Many regulars disliked the Texans' careless ways, detesting their dirty campsites, undisciplined manners, and ruffian physical appearance. But none of these quirks mattered during combat, for they showed plenty of courage and ability once on the battlefield. Even Napoleon Dana, a hardened regular, admitted that the Texans fought bravely. Jack Hays was especially proud of his men. "The action of the two forces [the regulars and Texans] upon this occasion [storming of the Independence Hill redoubt]," he wrote Worth, "was marked with generous emulation and perfect confidence in each other."[42]

Worth had more to be grateful for than just his brave Texans. His troops—regulars and volunteers alike—had assaulted two seemingly impregnable positions with little loss of life. The men had feared the general for his "grade or grave" motto, but instead he had showed that he would not needlessly throw away lives to achieve personal grandeur. He sent his best men to assault the strong points and reinforced them with other troops from the division. If Worth had any leadership defect, it was that he was a perennial worrier; he continued to throw troops into battle if there was even the slightest chance he might lose.

Off to the north and east of Monterrey, Zachary Taylor spent September 22 solidifying his hold on Fort Teneria and conducting small probes into the city. He did not provide Worth another "diversion" on the 22nd—one had been enough for his remaining men. Instead Taylor ordered his troops to stay put. He wanted them to recover from the bruising of the 21st and to fortify his tenuous hold in northeastern Monterrey while waiting for Worth to cut off Ampudia's line of retreat to the west. The men with Taylor gave three loud cheers on the afternoon of the 22nd when they saw the Stars and Stripes flying over the Bishop's Palace.

Taylor was pleased with Worth's actions. He had given him the most important mission on the battlefield, and Worth rose to the challenge. Taylor correctly judged that the general was the right man to carry out the operation. Worth's reputation catapulted to national prominence once the articles about his attack were published throughout the United States. "Worth has won all the laurels at this siege," a surgeon with the army recalled, "and he deserves them." He continued: "It [Monterrey] has before been besieged by powerful forces, but was never before taken. Nor could it have been taken now, by any man other than General Worth."[43]

Ampudia, for his part, felt the noose tightening around his command. His army was surrounded with no prospect of reinforcements forthcoming. The general was not ready to give up the city, though. The success he had enjoyed on the 21st probably gave him some confidence that the Americans could not take Monterrey. And perhaps Santa Anna would arrive soon with additional troops and artillery. But probably foremost in Ampudia's mind was the political calculation that he did not want to surrender too early and be branded a "coward" by the Mexican leadership. Regardless, the Mexican commander decided that the contest was not over. The Americans would need to root out his army block by block before he would capitulate.

7

STREET FIGHT

"It was indeed a most strange and novel scene of warfare."
Pvt. Samuel Reid

The sun rose on September 23 with General Worth in control of western Monterrey. He had cut off General Ampudia from Saltillo and Mexico City. But even if the Mexican government had known about Ampudia's predicament, it probably would have left him to deal with the Americans himself. To rescue Monterrey now would cost too many lives since Worth controlled the Molinas of Jesús María, mills located just outside the city, and Independence and Federation hills.

Worth pondered his next move. He had not received any orders from General Taylor during the night of the 22nd. He considered the possibility of starving Ampudia into submission. A siege was not a bad idea militarily, given how many Americans had died on the 21st trying to root the Mexicans from the city. Politically, however, James K. Polk needed quick victories not long, drawn-out sieges. Plus, neither Taylor nor Worth had the requisite patience for a siege, preferring a quick, hard fight instead to decide the matter.

While considering his strategic options, Worth ordered the 5th Infantry to move a captured 9-pound cannon to a new hill, south of the river, where the gun could fire into more central parts of Monterrey. The men steered the cannon down Federation Hill and dragged it up the steep slope of a neighboring height. A group of Mexican lancers, oblivious to the gun's placement, allowed their horses to graze almost directly below it. As soon as the cannon was ready, the Americans fired on the group, killing many men and horses. The general next ordered Maj. Harvey Brown to take five companies and a section of William Mackall's battery and assume a blocking position in the Rinconada Pass in case Santa Anna or other reinforcements approached. Rumors abounded that Santa Anna was on his way to Monterrey with thousands of reinforcements, and this possibility continued to worry Worth. D. H. Hill, an officer in one of Brown's five companies, was upset at being shoved to the rear before what appeared to be an imminent fight for the city. "Of all things in the world," he wrote in his diary, "I was most desirous to be engaged in a street fight on account of the novelty and excitement."[1]

With the pass secure, the general focused his attention on the city itself. He still had not received any direction from Taylor about whether he should storm the city or stay in his current position. But Worth grew impatient waiting and ordered the 5th and 7th Infantry down from Federation and Independence hills to enter the city. The general also sent George Gordon Meade and Ben McCulloch to reconnoiter western Monterrey so he would know what opposition his men might encounter.

As Meade entered the city, he probably reflected on the last few days. He had written his wife on September 17, "I believe they [the Mexican army] are evacuating the town at this moment, and we shall march in without firing a gun." But the intense fighting on the 21st and 22nd had probably changed his views on Mexican bravery. Now he was entering the city, surveying the area for what was sure to be a bloody climax to the fighting. Meade and McCulloch returned to provide an informative report to their commander. They told him that the Mexicans had abandoned the far western part of the city, including a fortified cemetery, and had moved to another square closer to the center. The cemetery was within range of Worth's light artillery on Independence Hill, so despite his preparations, Ampudia had decided to abandon the area for more defensible positions.[2]

Worth's decision to send his troops into Monterrey without orders was, strangely enough, one of the reasons that Taylor selected him to command the hook movement in the first place. Taylor knew that the general could operate independently and that he would seize the initiative and not let up until he had won or lost. Taylor probably anticipated how Worth would proceed on the 23rd in the absence of orders, though that still did not excuse him for not providing guidance to his subordinate at such a critical juncture in the battle. Around 10 A.M. Worth finally received an indication of his commander's intentions indirectly—cannon and musket fire erupted from eastern Monterrey, a clear sign that Taylor was advancing into that part of the city. By attacking from the east and west simultaneously, the Americans could squeeze Ampudia from both sides, straining his limited resources perhaps to the breaking point.[3]

Worth formed his men. He created two columns to advance eastward toward the city's center. A southern column, which would travel near the Santa Catarina River, contained four companies of the 7th Infantry and a 12-pound howitzer from Mackall's battery; James Duncan would later join this wing with his light artillery. The northern column included four companies of the 8th Infantry and two 6-pounders from Mackall's battery. The general divided 300 Texans between the two columns, with Jack Hays leading those to the south and Samuel Walker leading those to the north.

Samuel Walker and the other Mier Texans probably looked forward to what they may have considered a final reckoning. Their hated nemesis, Pedro de Ampudia, awaited them in the city's center. For years they had sought the opportunity to settle accounts with the general, who they regarded as a dishonorable scoundrel. Walker was one of the few Texans fighting at Monterrey who had met Ampudia. The Mexican commander had interviewed Walker when he was captured early in the fighting at Mier. When he asked him how many Texans were in the town, Ampudia could not believe Walker's answer: "Surely," he told Walker, "they [the Texans] do not have the audacity to pursue and attack me in the town!" Walker reportedly replied: "Yes, General, you needn't have any doubt about that. The Texans will pursue and attack you in hell!" Soon after, Ampudia marched the Texan prisoners to Mexico City, where many spent two miserable years imprisoned, some in Mexico's infamous Perote Castle. On the way he and Santa Anna had imposed on them the "Lottery of Death" after some Texans attempted to escape. Bigfoot Wallace remembered that he searched for the smallest bean he could find when it was his turn to draw because he thought that the white beans, which meant survival, were smaller than the black beans, which

Western Monterrey. In this Daniel Whiting lithograph, one can see how valuable rooftops were in the fighting for the city's squares, including the Plaza del Carne. The small parapet edging the roof provided effective cover, and the commanding view allowed soldiers to fire on enemy troops in multiple directions. This view is to the west, with the Bishop's Palace in the distance (center right). The road to Saltillo ran through the valley in the center of this view. *Monterey, As Seen from a House-Top in the Main Plaza, (To the West.) October, 1846.* Lithograph by Charles H. B. Fenderich, after Daniel P. Whiting, 1847. Toned lithograph (hand colored), 13 × 18 13/16 in. Courtesy of the Amon Carter Museum, Fort Worth, Tex.

meant death. Although he drew a white one, Wallace's heart had sunk when he saw a black bean in the hand of his good friend Jim Ogden, who simply replied, "I am ready." But instead of a quick execution, the Mexicans had shot the condemned multiple times from many paces away. The firing went on for 10–12 minutes, during which Wallace, Walker, and the other survivors, who could not see the execution, listened to the groans of agony from their friends. The Texans never forgot this painful moment. The storming of Independence and Federation hills had provided a measure of revenge for them, but only by subduing Pedro de Ampudia could they close this painful chapter in their lives.[4]

In addition to revenge, the Texans brought something else to this third day of fighting at Monterrey: experience. Men like Wallace, Walker, Thomas Green, and others had learned how to fight in a city based on their experiences at Mier. Like Monterrey, that town had narrow streets laid out in a grid-like pattern and lined with sturdy limestone-constructed houses. Mier's dwellings also contained flat roofs edged by a small wall. The Texans' experience there gave them unique insights into urban combat. Green, for example, remembered trying to climb a scaffold at Mier and thereby exposing himself to enemy fire. Rather than continue the exercise, he determined that "it would be better to make farther breaches in the wall than expose the men to the enemy's fire." He and his fellow veterans knew to avoid open spaces at all costs and to never charge down the narrow streets, as Taylor's men had done on the 21st. They understood this firsthand because the Mexicans at Mier had also marched down an open street, trying to root the Texans out of two houses. The Texans waited until they were within firing range, and after one discharge from their rifles, the Mexican soldiers were "swept into the eternal night." Neither General Worth nor any U.S. regular had fought in a city as well defended as Monterrey. But Worth had grown to trust his senior Texan subordinates, including Walker, Hays, and Edward Burleson.[5]

Major Burleson was perhaps Worth's closest Texan advisor. As the general's aide de camp, he was Worth's principal military assistant and confidant. When the general decided to attack Federation and Independence hills Burleson had recommended that the Texans accompany the regulars in their assault on the former. Burleson was one of the few Texans in Taylor's army who was at San Antonio de Bexar in 1835 when the Texans assaulted that town's Mexican garrison, the first time any Texans had fought a military force inside a city. At that battle, as at Mier, the men quickly adapted to the unique combat environment, digging trenches across San Antonio's streets in order to avoid the blasts of Mexican artillery. They also busted holes through the walls of the town's adobe houses, dropped through roofs into rooms, and cleared the rooftops of Mexican soldiers. Although he made no record of it, Burleson probably suggested such tactics to Worth as a means to avoid the carnage that had occurred on the 21st in eastern Monterrey. But regardless of who actually made this recommendation, Worth listened, because he directed engineer John Sanders to accompany Samuel Walker with a group of pioneers to help the Texans cut holes in the sides of the city's houses. The men collected all of the pickaxes and crowbars they could find; a few also carried ladders. Sanders had retrieved many tools from Fort Soldado left behind by the fleeing Mexican soldiers.[6]

Around 2 P.M. Walker's Texans and the 8th Infantry advanced down Iturbide Street into the Plaza de Capilla, the westernmost plaza in Monterrey. Here sandbags had been stacked inside the city's cemetery and loopholes had been cut out of the graveyard's wall as defensive measures. But as Meade discovered, the Mexican defenders had already fled the area. Walker's Texans, the 7th and 8th Infantry, and Sanders's pioneers continued past the cemetery, under sporadic fire, until they came to the Plaza del Carne. As the Americans approached the square, hundreds of Mexican soldiers appeared on the surrounding buildings' rooftops. Musket barrels seemingly protruded from every possible spot in the area. Stacked sandbags provided additional cover to the anxious defenders. A large cannon, covered by a masonry barricade, guarded the main street from the plaza into the center of the city.

Worth, desiring an up-close view of the fighting, descended from the Bishop's Palace with the 5th Infantry and Duncan's light artillery. When he arrived near the Plaza del Carne, the general, ever-meddling during the heat of battle, redirected the command of his troops. He placed Col. Persifor Smith in charge of the southern column with two new companies from the 5th Infantry. Worth also added five more companies to the northern column, including three from the 7th Infantry under Dixon Miles. Worth's officers directed the infantry to cut through houses, yards, and walls and to seize the rooftops.[7]

At 3 or 4 P.M., enemy musket fire in the plaza seemed to strengthen. Mexican troops poured in from the east, and the rooftops became crammed with soldiers. Something must have happened in the eastern part of the city that allowed Ampudia to refocus his limited manpower on Worth's advance.

In eastern Monterrey that morning, Taylor's Fort Teneria garrison awoke to find Fort Diablo evacuated. This surprised the men, who thought that Ampudia would use Diablo as a launching point to retake Fort Teneria. Instead, the Mexican commander had retreated deeper into the city. Learning of this, General Quitman ordered Jefferson Davis (1st Mississippi) and Lt. Col. Samuel Anderson (1st Tennessee) to occupy the empty fort. They did so with little fanfare, capturing a few prisoners and some ammunition. Mexican soldiers stationed in a half-moon redoubt about 150 yards toward the cathedral fired on Davis's men as they entered.

Once Taylor was apprised of the situation, he ordered Quitman to advance westward into the city. Davis briefly reconnoitered the half-moon redoubt, then collected three companies of Mississippians and one company of Tennesseans to move on that position. As they approached the breastwork, rooftop sharpshooters fired at Davis's men while Mexicans behind the redoubt sent musket and artillery fire toward the Americans. The Mississippians' rifles could not hit the well-hidden soldiers, and Quitman directed Davis to move to a safer place lest his companies be destroyed. He also ordered the remainder of the Mississippi regiment forward to reinforce the small assault team.

Mirabeau Lamar, a former president of the Republic of Texas, had accompanied Davis that the morning. He believed that Quitman would need soldiers who were familiar with street fighting and recommended that the general ask for Texan reinforcements. Quitman agreed and sent for Henderson's Texans, who were stationed on the opposite side of the city to investigate reports that some Mexican soldiers were retreating. Once he received the orders, Henderson collected his men and sent them galloping as fast as they could back to eastern Monterrey. The East Texas Rangers, unlike their comrades with General Worth, had not yet seen any fighting and were eager to participate. They rushed to the city's suburbs, leapt off their horses, and hitched the animals in a sheltered area. The Texans then sprinted into the city, dodging bullets and shells until they reached Davis's position.

Davis, Henderson, and Lamar probably discussed how to attack the redoubt. Although no record of any conversation exists, Lamar and Henderson probably recommended breaking into the nearby buildings and moving house to house to advance around the Mexican position. Davis later acknowledged, "I derived great support from them [Henderson and Lamar]; as well as from their gallantry, as their better knowledge of the construction of Mexican houses." To Col. George Wood, commander of the 2nd Regiment of Texas Mounted Rifles, the objective was clear. "From this point the attack commenced," Wood later wrote in his official report, "the immediate object being to dislodge the enemy from the battlements of the adjacent houses, from which they poured down upon us—themselves in comparative security—an incessant fire." Any discussion between the commanders probably did not last long, for the Texans rushed into the street like "unchained lions," as many soldiers later described. Along with the Mississippians, they began to smash in doors, break holes in the sides of houses, and climb onto rooftops. "We continued to advance and drive the enemy," Davis later wrote, "by passing through courts, gardens, and houses, taking every favorable position to fire from the house tops, which from their style of architecture furnishes a good defence against Musketry."[8]

To get into a house, the Texans and Mississippians would locate a weak spot in a wall or door. The porous limestone walls of the homes chipped away easily with a strong, pointed tool, and the men used axes to beat down the tough wooden doors of the homes. This was the most hazardous part of the operation because the men had to expose themselves in the thoroughfare while attempting to cut the hole or bash in the door. The Texans, Tennesseans, and Mississippians distracted the enemy during these operations by providing cover fire with their rifles. After a passageway was created, the rest of the group crossed the street and entered the house. "Whatever other troops may accomplish in the field or in the charge," a Tennessee volunteer stated, "yet in this mode of fighting the Texans are infinitely superior to every other corps." While the Texans were barging into houses, Lamar, dressed in a bright red vest and perched on a beautiful white horse, waved his sword over his head and shouted, "Brave boys, Americans are never afraid," and, "Remember Goliad, Remember the Alamo!" Even Davis, who was rarely impressed with anyone outside of his regiment, was surprised by Lamar's courage:

"with a bright red vest, heedless of danger, [Lamar] rushed into the thickest of the fray."[9]

After gaining access to the buildings, the Texans then poured onto the rooftops and fired their accurate rifles at Mexican soldiers on the tops of neighboring houses or at those shooting from the street. From these heights, they could strike many of the soldiers who had thus far eluded them when the Americans were advancing down the street earlier in the day. Many of the Texans carried plains rifles that could hit an enemy soldier positioned two or three houses away. The rifle's large-caliber bullet ensured that any Mexican who was hit would not be returning to the fight.

The Mississippians carried even better rifles than the Texans. Davis had battled hard in Washington to ensure that his men were armed with the best rifles made. He believed that the army's standard-issue musket was an outdated weapon for modern warfare. By 1846 a new ignition system, the percussion cap, had been developed that was superior to the flintlock ignition system then used by the army smoothbore. Davis believed that arming his men with new technology was critical to their success, so much so that he had refused to raise a regiment earlier in the year because his men would not have received these rifles: "Knowing that the Mississippians would have no confidence in the old flint-lock muskets, I insisted on their being armed with a new kind of rifle." Davis liked the model 1841 rifle manufactured by the Eli Whitney company. It had a shorter barrel than the army's musket, making it a lighter weapon so that the men had more mobility in battle, and it used percussion caps. Since the rifle could not be fitted with a bayonet, Davis authorized his men to carry knives, swords, revolvers, and other weapons for close combat.[10]

As for the Mexicans, their old English Tower muskets failed them this day. The smoothbores had worked well on the 21st, when Mexican soldiers had rained down musket balls on a massed enemy groping through narrow city streets. But now the Americans were fighting a different type of battle. Hidden behind parapets, firing from rooftops, the Texans, Mississippians, and Tennesseans aimed carefully and only pulled the trigger when they had a target within their sights. The Texans "commenced the work of sharp-shooting from one house-top to another," one volunteer remembered, "killing every Mexican as they would a squirrel." Every hit the Americans made was fatal since only the heads of Mexican soldiers were visible, peering over the top of a roof's parapet. Using these methods, the Americans gained control of all of the houses and buildings around the half-moon redoubt. "By a hard fought track through the houses," one soldier recalled, "of blood and death, [we] round[ed] the barricades on either side." The Americans fired down on the redoubt from windows and roofs, forcing the Mexican garrison to evacuate. This position would have made bloody work of Taylor's men had the Americans used the tactics of the 21st. But now they were using new techniques that allowed them to capture the redoubt with few casualties.[11]

As the Americans were making their move around the redoubt, General Taylor ordered Captain Bragg's battery to support Quitman's advance. He also ordered the 3rd Infantry, which had lost five of its officers on the 21st, to protect the battery once in the city. Protecting artillery was probably the last thing the infantrymen wished to do. Some of their best officers had been killed on the 21st. The leadership of the regiment had been decimated with the deaths of Barbour, Lear, Morris, and others. The men had also lost many friends with whom they had trained with at Jefferson Barracks and endured the encampment at Corpus Christi. They wanted something to show for these losses.

Bragg arrived at a narrow street that led toward the cathedral. The captain was as fearless as ever, even though the carnage of the 21st must have been fresh in his mind. The soldiers were thrilled to have artillery support. "The scene was exceedingly inspiring," one soldier remembered, "when Lieut. Bragg entered the city, late in the evening, with his train of Flying Artillery, & commenced firing along the streets." Bragg's men unlimbered one cannon and began firing. Musket balls soon zipped all around his exposed men. There were no barricades to masque the cannon or to provide cover to the men and horses; all were fully visible in the open street. A brave first sergeant steadily aimed the gun until he was shot, and soon other men and some of the horses began to drop. For Bragg's men, this day was starting to look like the 21st all over again.[12]

Lt. Samuel French, one of Bragg's officers, unlimbered a 12-pound howitzer and fired down a different street. This action elicited an immediate response. "A volley [was] fired at us that rattled like hail on the stones," French recalled. Four out of his seven men operating the piece were killed or wounded, as were most of his horses. French knew that his men would not survive if they remained in the middle of the narrow street, but he recalled a method that a mob had used during riots in Philadelphia. He tied ropes to the front and back of the gun and ordered his men to take cover on both sides of the street. They loaded the gun from a hidden location, then pulled the cannon into its exposed firing position with the ropes. French worked his cannon for two hours using this method. Unknown to the lieutenant, the Mexicans at Mier also lassoed their cannon out of harm's way when they were fired on by Texans from inside the town's houses.[13]

General Quitman soon arrived on the scene with George Henry Thomas, Bragg's second-in-command. Quitman told French to reposition his howitzer down another street and continue the attack. The lieutenant subtly reminded the general that Thomas had yet to fire his cannon and was Bragg's second in command. Quitman understood French's implication. "No, you remain here, and let Thomas pass over when you fire," Quitman replied. As French fired and smoke poured out of his cannon, Thomas moved his gun, men, and horses through the thick screen, unlimbered his gun in the new position, and went into action.[14]

The Texans, Mississippians, and 3rd Infantry also used the artillerists' smoke to disguise their movements. Soldiers sprinted through the thick, white smoke floating in the narrow streets to beat down a door or to pick a hole in a wall. It provided terrific cover. The infantry also took advantage of Bragg's cannons to maneuver through Monterrey's streets. After a gun fired, Mexican soldiers had to take cover to avoid any grapeshot. This provided time for the American infantrymen to cross or move down the street. "Go it, my boys!" one officer would shout, and everyone in his group would sprint to their objective.

General Taylor could not resist getting a closer view of the action. He galloped into the heart of the fighting on his white horse, dismounted, and began issuing commands as if he were a captain or lieutenant. He crossed one particularly dangerous street that was amply covered by Mexican soldiers who fired their muskets at anyone who exposed themselves. "There he was, almost alone," French recalled. Taylor tried to open the door to a nearby house but found it locked. The general yelled at the owner to open the door, but he refused. The two began arguing, the homeowner probably unaware that he was denying entrance to a major general of the U.S. Army. Capt. William Seaton Henry, whose 3rd Infantry was supporting Bragg, observed Taylor crossing a different street and recalled that "by every chance [he] should have been shot." He chased down the general to remind him how much he was exposed to enemy fire. Taylor's reply was simple and to the point: "Take that ax and knock in that door." The captain, a little stunned by these words, nevertheless grabbed the axe and began chopping at the door. "When we commenced on the door," he remembered, "the occupant signified, by putting the key in and unlocking it, if we had no objection, he would save us the trouble. It turned out to be quite an extensive apothecary shop." The store-owner offered the two Americans water and limes. One soldier re-called seeing Taylor casually munching on a piece of gingerbread and sugar, which he probably found in the store.[15]

Taylor was in his element wandering the streets of Monterrey, rallying the men through his actions. News of his bold behavior spread like wildfire through the ranks. Taylor probably did not think much about this, simply wanting to be on the scene to encourage his soldiers fighting with the enemy. He likely also wanted to ensure that he could keep up with the flow of the battle, as he had not on the 21st, and be able to help his troops achieve victory. In many ways Taylor's approach to combat had not changed from his younger days. In September 1812, when he was a captain in the frontier army, the Pota-watomi Indians attacked a small, remote army outpost called Fort Harrison, which Taylor commanded. The Indians outnumbered the garrison, and his troops thought that they would be overrun. Flaming arrows set fire to the barracks which soon whipped through the struc-ture, igniting many other buildings. The men feared they would burn to death, but Taylor, sensing that the men might be ready to capitu-late, jumped onto the barracks and began to put out the fire with the help of some others. He was successful, his men rallied, and even-tually the Indians retreated. Taylor's inclination to personal and deci-sive action had not altered much since September 1812, and most of his men, especially the volunteers, loved him for his bravery. His presence, his casual demeanor, and his incredible calmness under fire inspired them to go to great lengths in doing what their commander asked of them.

The general's first decision once he arrived in the city was to order Bragg to withdraw his cannons. The flying artillery, so effective in the open field, could do little against an enemy hidden behind limestone walls and masonry barricades. Bragg and his men seethed over the order. Once again the artillerists were thwarted in their efforts to turn the tide of the battle. Bragg probably wanted some revenge against the Mexican soldiers who had been so elusive to his guns since his arrival at Monterrey. George Thomas fired a "farewell shot at the foe" in frustration as he retreated.[16]

The volunteers were not the only soldiers learning how to fight in the city. Captain Henry's 3rd Infantry beat in the doors and walls of houses leading toward the Grand Plaza. They burst into one house containing five women and some children. These civilians screamed "Capitano! Capitano!" believing that they would all be killed. Henry shook their hands to reassure them that there was no danger. While the captain's men continued to move through houses, Davis and some Texans advanced to within one block of the Grand Plaza. A strong Mexican battery, about fifty feet from them, guarded a road leading to the square. They wanted to cross Santa Rita Street, the last major thoroughfare before entering the plaza. The Americans began stacking horse saddles and baggage to construct a makeshift barricade to protect them from the artillery and small-arms fire that they surely would encounter.

Now the troops were only blocks from the cathedral, the greatest prize for the Americans. They knew that General Ampudia was head-quartered in the building and that if they could advance to the edges of the Grand Plaza, the battle would soon be over, for Ampudia would have no choice but to capitulate. Maj. William Scurry of the Texas regiment rushed down Morelos Street and darted to the west side of Santa Rita Street with eleven men. Intense musket and cannon fire greeted his small group as they rushed closer to Ampudia's lair. The fighting intensified further around the cathedral, where Mexican soldiers prepared for a last stand. Hundreds of civilians, including women, children, and priests, huddled anxiously in the plaza while Taylor's men moved closer and closer. They knew that the fighting was close. Many of them probably believed that if the Americans made it into the plaza, they would die. Mexican priests and politi-cians had spread rumors throughout the region that the Americans slaughtered soldiers and civilians alike, hoping to deter the popu-lace from aiding Taylor's army. Now those rumors probably fed wide-spread panic throughout the plaza.

While Monterrey's civilians pondered their fate, Jefferson Davis asked one of his men to run to Taylor to request artillery support. If he could move a few cannons into the area, he might be able to break the stalemate that existed on the corner of Santa Rita and Morelos. Scurry and his men could not advance farther against the heavy fire. If nothing else, the smoke and grapeshot from any artillery support would provide the soldiers cover so they could sneak into nearby houses or buildings and continue to creep closer. But Davis did not get the answer he wanted, the messenger informing him that Taylor had already ordered Bragg out of the area. As the colonel pondered his next move, he received more unwelcome news—Taylor was ordering all Americans out of the eastern part of the city. This made little sense to Davis. They were so close to victory, why should they retreat now? Two days prior he had thought that his men could overrun Fort Diablo and advance close to the city's center, but Taylor had ordered him to retreat. Now he again was told to withdraw when his objective was so near his reach. Davis probably muttered a few choice words regarding his former father-in-law as he obediently began to pull his men back. The only soldiers whose rage matched Davis's were the Texans. They believed that it was only a matter of time before they could have entered the Grand Plaza and forced Ampudia to surrender.[17]

Back in western Monterrey Worth's men could hear the slackening fire to the east. They could also see hundreds of additional Mexican soldiers lining the rooftops in the Plaza del Carne and nearby parts of the city. With Taylor's men retreating, Ampudia shifted his men west, and now, as Samuel Reid said, "the street fight became appalling."[18]

Taylor's retreat gave the Mexican commander new hope. Before, troops were closing in on him from both sides, and even the arrogant Ampudia had to believe that his fate was sealed. Taylor's withdrawal allowed him to focus solely on defending against Worth's western attack. Ampudia sent a few men to harass Taylor's retreating men as they withdrew from the city so as to keep them moving out. The rest shifted west. In the Plaza del Carne, Mexican soldiers "showered down a hurricane of balls" on the Americans. Walker's Texans and Sanders's pioneers found shelter in a building in the square and assessed the situation. Fortunately for the Americans, officers like Worth, Childs, Vinton, Hays, and Walker fought a different kind of urban battle than Taylor had on the 21st. "Had we attempted to advance up the streets, as our poor fellows had done previously [on the 21st]," Lieutenant Meade later wrote, "all would have been cut to pieces; but we were more skillfully directed."[19]

Worth's Mier veterans knew that the best way to fight in an urban environment was to move building to building rather than rushing pell-mell down the open streets. At Mier these Texans had learned to scrutinize the location of the town's buildings in order to determine which ones provided the best positions for firing into enemy troops and artillery positions. Those at street corners were ideal since a soldier inside could fire in two, possibly three different directions. At one such location in Mier, the Texans had carved out a loophole and put Bigfoot Wallace there. "I always waited for a good chance," Wallace said about his time at that post, "and had a bead on a Mexican every time I touched the trigger." The Texans drew upon these lessons at Monterrey. They picked holes toward the most strategic structures in the city. In addition to corner homes, they sought to utilize the tallest buildings, such as one on the southeast corner of the Plaza del Carne, which afforded an excellent view of western Monterrey. But storming the building would not be easy. Dozens of Mexican soldiers covered the top of the structure, and many others hid inside.[20]

Instead of assaulting the position directly, the Mier veterans understood that they would need to seize a neighboring rooftop from where they could better fire into the soldiers who manned the top of the building. They could also burrow through nearby houses until they could pick a hole in the wall to access its interior. One of their favorite techniques, which they had used at Mier and San Antonio de Bexar, was to overtake the rooftop of a house filled with enemy soldiers. They would then pick a hole in the roof of the dwelling and drop into the group of soldiers, wildly firing their pistols and shotguns. It was hazardous work since only one person could fit through the hole at a time, so the first person had to survive long enough to be joined by his comrades.

Captain Sanders and his pioneers embraced these new techniques and executed them brilliantly. As instructed by Worth, his men accompanied Samuel Walker's Texans as they moved down Iturbide Street toward the plaza. The pioneers laid ladders against the sides of houses so the Texans could climb onto roofs in the square. They also picked holes in the sides of adobe homes with crowbars so Walker's men could crawl inside. "In crossing a street that was raked by the enemy's cannon and infantry on housetops and houses," a Texan recalled, " a few men would rush across with crow bars and picks, burst into the doors, while others kept up a heavy fire from behind the parapets on the house tops." One regular was surprised at how easy it was to carve out a hole with a pickaxe in the thin-clayed walls. He noted that these were so soft that he could cut through a two-foot wall in twenty minutes.[21]

For Sanders, a successful regular soldier, learning new fighting techniques from nonprofessional soldiers was at odds with many of the lessons he had learned twelve years earlier at West Point. The academy's science-based curriculum taught its soldiers to think logically, one step at a time, in order to dissect problems from start to finish, not how to develop novel solutions in unpredictable situations. Teaching soldiers how to think "out of the box" was not the goal of West Point's instructors. If anyone should have been influenced by West Point, it was Sanders. He graduated second in the Class of 1834. He mastered mathematics, science, and engineering and excelled on the two examinations given each year in those topics. One of his instructors boasted that he was one of the quickest mathematicians ever to attend the school. For a soldier steeped in the academy's curriculum, and for one who had never seen battle, Sanders adapted quickly to this strange combat environment and was one of Worth's best soldiers on the 23rd.[22]

With Sanders support, Walker's Texans pressed ahead. Reid described the scene: "Doors were forced open, walls were battered down —entrances made through longitudinal walls, and the enemy driven from room to room, and from house to house, followed by the shrieks of women, and the sharp crack of Texian rifles. Cheer after cheer was heard in proud and exulting defiance, as the Texians or regulars gained the house-tops by means of ladders, while they poured in a rain of bullets upon the enemy on the opposite houses. It was indeed a most strange and novel scene of warfare." Mexican soldiers waited silently inside the homes so they could surprise the intruders with gunfire. "When we broke through the wall," remembered one Texas volunteer, "we received a heavy volley from the room right in our faces that broke the wall above us and knocked off one hat. We fired into the room, then piled into it, and the Mexicans left in a hurry."

Sometimes the men fought hand to hand with rifle butts, bayonets, knives, and other implements.[23]

A regular entered one house to find two dozen women hiding from the gunfire. "As the hinges of the door were about to give way," he remembered, "a tremulous voice on the inside beseeched me not to break the door down, it should be opened. When unlocked, I rushed in as well as I could, over beds, chairs, cushions, etc., etc., and to my surprise found the room occupied by about twenty-five women!" The women screamed and pleaded for their lives. The American assured them that they would be fine, but one woman, disbelieving him, begged him to at least spare her one-year-old child. "In spite of me, tears rushed to my eyes," the soldier recalled, "and I could only speak with a full heart as I told her to rise, and assured her that she and her child were perfectly safe." To reassure them, he guarded the house all night so that no soldiers would bother the group.[24]

Up to this point, Lt. Abner Doubleday of the 1st Artillery, a "red-legged" infantryman, had been sitting in the rear of the division, away from the battle, until he decided to enter the city to locate his commander, Colonel Childs, and ask for orders. Instead he found Captain Vinton of the 3rd Artillery, who also commanded part of the artillery battalion. Vinton directed the lieutenant to place his company in line and wait for orders. Doubleday feared that he would not see any fighting, until James Duncan rode up to Vinton and Doubleday and said, "You can save a large number of men, if you shelter them behind some projecting houses," pointing them toward the dwellings, which were farther east and much closer to the battle. Doubleday was thrilled since, as he put it, his men would soon have "warm work." The lieutenant and his men marched double-time down a sidewalk toward their new location while musket and cannon fire flew all around them; Doubleday recalled hearing the "whiff! whir!" of the grapeshot and the "tsing" of the musket balls. Men fell dead and wounded onto the sidewalk, the wounded dragged by their comrades to the safety of a nearby store.[25]

Captain Vinton ordered Doubleday to shelter his men inside the store. As he entered the establishment, Doubleday turned around and saw one of his men get struck in the head by a musket ball and drop to the ground. Two musket balls then hit the wall next to the lieutenant's face and another went through the coat of a soldier to his left. A dying artilleryman was dragged inside and bled to death on the floor. Doubleday was certainly having "warm work" of it now. At this violent juncture, a soldier in Doubleday's regiment decided he wanted a light for his pipe but could not find one inside. He sauntered across the street under heavy fire and lit his pipe at a match used to light a 6-pound cannon. He then puffed away as he strolled back while grapeshot and musket balls poured down around him, arriving unharmed.

Most of Doubleday's men were safe inside the store, but they were also pinned down and not advancing into the city as Vinton had hoped. The captain ordered the artillerists to dash to a nearby bakery and take shelter under a wall there. They did so and hid for an hour while the Texans overtook nearby rooftops. Vinton soon ordered them to storm a house near the wall. Doubleday had discovered earlier that two to three men should cross the street in a group rather than one at a time, two providing covering fire while the other swung an axe against the door or picked a hole in the wall. (He also learned that these groups should always run rather than walk across the street). In one instance, Doubleday's men entered a house that contained a delightful orange grove in the backyard. Vinton had ordered the men not to touch the oranges without approval from the owners. Doubleday was furious: "For men tired, hungry, and thirsty I think this was carrying respect for private property rather too far." Doubleday could be angry at the captain, but he could not criticize Vinton's performance on this day. Vinton, a career artillery officer, adapted to the new environment as quickly as Sanders had, part of the small group of officers under Worth who ensured that they would not repeat Taylor's mistakes on the 21st. Vinton safely guided many American soldiers through the streets of Monterrey. Doubleday was lucky to have found him.[26]

Soon enough Doubleday and his men were on the run again. Vinton ordered them to storm another house. The lieutenant ran across the street with two men, but the door was locked. "Weld [one of the men] had luckily picked up an axe at one of the houses," Doubleday recalled, "and we set to work to force the fastenings but owing to the immense thickness of the panels it was a long time before we could succeed." Doubleday and his men had particular trouble getting into another house. Once the family inside realized that it was hopeless to keep the door locked, they opened it, believing that they would all be killed. A little boy held up a picture of Jesus to the officer and said, "It is our Lord, sir." Instead of killing them as the boy expected, Doubleday asked them to make some coffee and took some of their grapes.[27]

Throughout the battle, the animated Baille Peyton, a personable Louisiana volunteer, rode around with his name written in large letters on his straw hat. "How goes the battle?" he asked Doubleday, having just come from Taylor's camp. He soon moseyed off on his horse to observe the rest of the fighting. Ultimately Baille spoke to many soldiers throughout the day, and his wit and humor, delivered in such a dire situation, was appreciated by everyone he met.

While Doubleday's company moved forward, the Texans were scampering across rooftops. The top of one house offered a commanding view of the city, and its parapets were ideal for firing at Mexican soldiers hidden on the top of buildings or inside another house. One of the men recalled that he would watch an embrasure until he saw it darken (meaning that a Mexican soldier was hiding there) and then shoot through the hole. The Texans took their time when firing their guns. Flintlock rifles took around one minute to load, and the men wanted to make sure that they hit their target after that effort. They also used their ammunition sparingly. Since some of them had been Rangers before the war, it was engrained in their psyche to treasure every bullet. In a month-long ride across the Texas plains, a Ranger could only carry a small pouch of ammunition and could not count on any logistical support. He needed to make every shot count. At one point in western Monterrey, so the story goes, a Texan became detached from his company and fell in with a bunch of regulars. Two Mexicans, an old man and a boy, had been firing their muskets at the regulars, wounding the soldiers and preventing them from advancing. The regulars fired volley after volley but could not hit the concealed assailants. Then the Texan had his turn. He waited until the boy and the old man raised their heads above the parapet and fired once. They both dropped. "Dubs," said the Texan, who then went his own way.[28]

Not long into the fight, Mackall's artillery rolled into the plaza and began firing canister at a Mexican cannon. The projectiles embedded harmlessly into a concrete barricade. Meanwhile, Mexican soldiers took advantage of one of the few exposed targets they could find. "The top of every house was covered with snipers," Mackall wrote his son, "and a perfect shower of musket balls fell in every direction, then showers of grape, and I assure you I never wish to be in as hot a place again." Mackall maneuvered his guns skillfully through-

U.S. artillery in western Monterrey, September 23. This illustration shows
either Mackall's or Duncan's cannons deploying in the middle of a street to
fire on Mexican positions. A dead horse lies in the foreground, killed by the
dozens of enemy soldiers lining the rooftops, safe from the fire of the light
artillery. From Frost, *Mexican War and Its Warriors,* 273. Courtesy of Special
Collections, The University of Texas at Arlington Library.

out the narrow streets, unlimbering them quickly and efficiently.
"Our artillery [Mackall's] was heard rumbling over the paved streets,
galloping here or there as the emergency required and pouring forth
a blazing fire of grape and ball," Reid remembered. Mackall's guns,
like other American light artillery units at Monterrey, accomplished
little during the battle.[29]

Worth's Texans knew there was a better way to stop Ampudia's
artillery: to make it unhealthy for anyone to use it. Many of them had
faced the same problem with a cannon at Mier in 1842. Instead of advancing straight toward the gun, the Texans had crawled through
houses until they were within fifty yards of the position and had carved
out a loophole in a facing wall. Another group did the same thing on the
other side of the street. When the loopholes were manned, the Texans
poured a vicious crossfire into the enemy artillerists, effectively si-
lencing the gun. "Round the gun at the nearest angle of the square,"
remembered on Mier veteran, "the dead and desperately wounded
were literally heaped in piles." On Iturbide Street the Texans used
these techniques to defeat well-placed Mexican artillery. "Captain

Miles with three companies of the Seventh and Captain Merrill with two companies of the Fifth now joined us," one Texan recalled. "Some mounted the roofs and picked off the men who manned the [Mexican] guns at the barricade and closing around them in the rear to capture the guns. . . . [Captain] Sanders . . . had come up with ladders, picks and crowbars . . . and helped to break through the house walls." Just as they were about to fire on the senior Mexican officer at the battery, a Texan yelled out: "Boys don't kill that officer on the pinto, he treated us kindly while we were prisoners. I don't want to see him killed. I am going to knock his hat off, to try and scare him, and make him retreat." The Texan shot off the Mexican's hat. But the officer simply asked a nearby soldier to hand it to him, examined the hole, and then put the hat back on his head. Soldiers continued to fall all around him, but the officer never considered leaving the cannon. He survived the battle and afterward was told by the Texans why he had survived. The Mexican looked at the hole in his hat and thanked them for their kindness.[30]

Only two blocks south from Walker's and Sanders's group, Worth's second column, under Persifor Smith, advanced along the river. The colonel stood in the open, directing his men forward. Despite the danger, he placed himself near a Mexican barricade and raised his spyglass to observe enemy movements. At one point Lieutenant Doubleday ran out to the street and asked Smith if he could use his spyglass, which "brought the swarthy faces of the Mexican gunners into a most interesting proximity," he remembered. Smith's soldiers fought their way to a line of houses just blocks from the cathedral. They had advanced more quickly than Vinton's troops because Ampudia posted most of his men on Iturbide Street. Worth's decision to split his columns thus provided the riverside troops a much-needed advantage in the march toward the plaza. The men rushed into a plaza four blocks from the cathedral and reached a deserted barricade. Once there the Mexicans opened up a vicious fire. Capt. Frank Gardner of the 7th Infantry screamed to his men to raise ladders on the sides of nearby houses and pick holes in the walls. They carried ladders, under fire, to a few houses but were shot as they tried to climb them. All of Gardner's men except for himself and his quartermaster sergeant were wounded in the endeavor.[31]

Napoleon D. T. Sherman, who had earlier thought that the Americans would give the Mexicans an easy whipping, took cover inside a house as galling musket fire poured down around him. He later recalled that three men in his company of the 7th Infantry were wounded in "less time than you could count three." His unit built ladders so they could assault the rooftops of nearby homes. As with Gardner's men, Dana's soldiers provided covering fire while three or four brave souls ran into the street, propped the ladder onto the side of another house, and scaled them to the roof. Mexican soldiers, perched along nearby rooftops, unleashed withering musketry at the Americans. Since the fighting had started, the defenders had yearned for easy targets and now finally had some. "We had nothing to do but fight them their own way," Dana wrote his wife. His views on Mexican gallantry had come a long way since his days at Camargo: "The enemy fought very obstinately [in Monterrey], and we had to fight them by inches and advance upon them from house to house."[32]

Two officers from the 7th Infantry crossed to the south side of the Santa Catarina River and reached a small redoubt overlooking south-central Monterrey. Under a heavy fire they held the position and fired into the city to assist their comrades. Meanwhile, Capt. Theophilus Holmes of the 7th Infantry, working with Hays and his Texans, picked through houses and garden walls until his men got within firing distance of the plaza. James Duncan was with these men. He tried to use his flying artillery against the Mexicans but had no more luck than Mackall. Duncan had to get creative with his cannon fire in order to displace the enemy. "A fire of shells and shrapnel was opened with effect," Duncan recalled, "wherever the enemy showed themselves in the streets or upon the house tops within range. Wherever any effect could be produced, either by direct fire, horizontal ricochet, a reduced charge, both the piece and howitzer, were kept industriously employed 'till nightfall." In one street Duncan unlimbered his gun without realizing that a Mexican cannon had him in its sights. He lost six men and six horses to a single blast from that gun. He ordered the dead horses cut away, reattached his cannon, and moved into an alley to seek cover.[33]

The Texans and regulars in both columns continued to press forward toward the central plaza. "Inch after inch was taken, but not an inch was given," Kendall wrote for the New Orleans Picayune. It was slow and bloody work, and the men became worn down from fatigue and hunger. The Mexicans fought bravely, "better than we expected," admitted one Texan, "and we began to have more respect for them."[34]

Ampudia had put his soldiers in a difficult position. Holing up in Monterrey's central plaza while the Americans closed in on both sides gave his men little chance for victory. Ampudia should have taken the initiative on the 21st or 22nd and tried to retake some of the northeastern forts, but instead he gathered his men and ammunition in the city's center. It was only a matter of time before the noose closed in around him. The men's faith in their commander must have been at an all-time low. Most of the Army of the North's soldiers disliked Ampudia before the battle started. Now that the general had put them in a losing position, the competent officers in the army had little reason to fight for him. But the soldiers did fight, and they fought well. They defended Monterrey block by block, even when they knew that their chance for victory was slim. They fought for pride, for *la patria*, and for their fallen comrades. Mexican weaponry failed them on the 23rd. Their antiquated English Tower muskets could do little to stem the advance of men who crawled through houses and fired from rooftops. The inaccurate smoothbore could not hit a distant shape sprinting across a rooftop or a head peeking out from a parapet. Doña María Josefa Zozaya did not care about their technological limitations. She rallied the men at one prominent house to defend the city. She ran food and ammunition up to Mexican soldiers on a rooftop during the middle of the battle, emblazoning herself on her nation's psyche as a heroine. "The beauty and rank of this young lady," recorded a Mexican historian after the war, "communicated new attractions; it was requisite to conquer to admire her, or to perish before her eyes to be made worthy of her smiles."[35]

The Mexican soldiers continued to fight hard. Mackall and his men, along with some infantrymen, sheltered themselves inside a house to escape a barrage of musket balls and grapeshot. Mackall had earlier acquired some oranges, probably against orders, from a grove across the street. He and his men were devouring the precious fruit when a young officer approached the group and asked where they had found their oranges. They pointed to a yard on the opposite side of the street. The officer pushed the door open with his foot as grapeshot splintered the wood. He was unharmed. An Irish soldier quipped, "Faith, Lieut, that was likely to prove a sour orange." Mackall could not help but chuckle.[36]

Worth, worried and anxious as always, called for additional Texans to reinforce the troops in the city. Pvt. Zenith Matthews's company had been guarding a mill in the Rinconada Pass when it received the order and dashed into the city. "Our troops cut their way through the houses to the Mexicans then commenced firing upon one another from the tops of the houses," he remembered.[37]

The Texans and regulars pressed on toward the city's center until they reached the home of Don Jose Maria Gajar, who owned one of the nicest houses in Monterrey. Gajar was terrified that the Americans would ransack his home and kill him. To persuade the soldiers to spare him, Gajar laid out a "sumptuous collation" of food and his finest china on a long table. "As they [the Texans] came near," Gajar remembered, "my heart almost failed me, for the Texians, with their coarse hickory shirts, and trowsers confined by a leathern strap to their hip, their slouched hats, and their sweat and powder-begrimed faces, certainly presented a most brigandish appearance. . . . They came along, yelling like Indians, and discharging their rifles at the Mexicans on the house-tops, a few of whom still continued to fire upon them, as they passed along the street." Gajar opened his large folding doors and invited the Texans inside. For these men, who had not eaten anything but raw corn for four days, the bounty offered them was a delightful site. After Gajar introduced himself in English, one of the Texans responded, "Hello! The old fellow speaks English!" Noticing the table another cried, "Look there, boys! [T]here's a sight good for an empty stomach!" Gajar invited, "Walk in!—walk in, gentlemen," declaring to the Texans, "help yourselves; my house and all it contains is at your service!" The hungry men rushed in and gorged on the feast, though they did so with the "utmost decorum," as Gajar recalled. The owner told them that he was a native of Spain. "Well, I reckoned you warn't a Mexican, and you may always count on the friendship of the Texan boys."[38]

Gajar kept his house open for three or four days, and many of Worth's soldiers enjoyed his food and wine. Samuel Walker posted a sentry at his door so no Texans or regulars would disturb the place. "I did not lose so much as a spoon," Gajar remembered, "of the valuable amount of plate which had been all the time exposed upon my tables." After the feast, the new Texans took over the Hidalgo Hotel, one of the nicer lodges in the city. All of the Mexicans inside had departed except for the cooks. The men rounded up some sheep and cows so the cooks could make dinner for any soldier who passed by.[39]

Back at the Plaza del Carne, the men were still trying to overrun the tall building on the southeast corner. They had taken over many nearby dwellings and were closing in on their objective. The companies of Capt. Richard Screven (8th Infantry) and Capt. Moses Merrill (5th Infantry) burrowed through limestone walls until they gained the entire line of buildings on the eastern side of the square. They finally overtook the tall building by surrounding it on all sides. The Mexicans inside fled. Engineer Sanders not long after entered the building to fortify and prepare it to host two howitzers. Worth had ordered the guns placed on its roof in order to fire into the Grand Plaza. Troops dragged the cannons up the stairs and into position. The pioneers also created more loopholes from which the infantry could fire.[40]

More regulars poured into the plaza, cutting off the principal thoroughfare from the Citadel on the northern plain and the Grand Plaza. The Citadel still held more than four hundred Mexican soldiers who could potentially reinforce the defenders in the city. Walker's men continued to jump from roof to roof toward the main plaza. The houses near the square were closer together than those in the outskirts, allowing the men to hop from one to another with ease. They began to find inside these buildings increasing numbers of women, who screamed and called on the saints to save them as the Americans broke through a wall or ceiling. "Opening the hole I dropped into the room," one Texan recalled, "and taking off my hat, told them in the best Spanish I could muster, that we were American soldiers and gentlemen and they were perfectly safe, that they were safest to remain where they were." A man was stationed in the room to protect the ladies.[41]

Nightfall offered a temporary reprieve to the fighting. Hays's Texans withdrew from the city to feed their horses. The Americans carried wounded men from the streets up to the Bishop's Palace, which had been turned into a temporary hospital. Lt. Charles Hanson, under orders from Colonel Smith, baked bread in a captured bakery for the hungry troops. All night long the young lieutenant doled out fresh loaves to the hungry soldiers as every American soldier in western Monterrey stopped by the Panadería del Gallo.

Earlier in the day Worth had ordered a 10-inch mortar, sent to him by General Taylor, established in the cemetery. Once night fell the gun began launching shells in a high, arched trajectory at the Mexicans hiding in the cathedral. The first few shots landed short of their mark. One fell in a kitchen near Abner Doubleday and some other Americans. Doubleday recalled that "the next attempt also fell short among our own troops who were very much annoyed at being bombarded in rear as well as front." The Mexicans in the Grand Plaza nervously watched the shells get closer to their positions. Priests pleaded with Ampudia to surrender in order to save the hundreds of civilians congregated there. While the Mexicans worried, Zenith Matthews sat down at the cemetery's gate to rest his aching feet and to watch the blazing shells rise high into the dark sky to explode over the Grand Plaza. It was a beautiful sight to him and other Americans. They were "gleaming through the air like fiery comets . . . and bursting with a loud report," Samuel Reid recalled.[42]

Other sights, however, were not so appealing. The city had been ravaged by the day's fighting, and evidence of the intense combat was everywhere. Corpses littered the rooftops, and giant holes and indentations ruined the city's walls and roofs. Blood and bodies marred the floors of the city's once-beautiful buildings. "Below lay the city, wrapped in the drapery of darkness," Reid poetically recalled, "whose folds covered the dreadful scene of the carnage and ruin of its streets, where lay dead horses, demolished masonry, broken arms and cast-off accoutrements of soldiers." The governor's house, one of the most elaborate residences in the city, was virtually destroyed. Shells and shot bent the iron bars covering the windows. Bayonet slices and musket holes ruined the beautiful stuccoed ceilings, and soldiers used the intricately carved wooden doors for firewood. The city's precious artwork was destroyed by gunfire or artillery rounds. Well-kept orange and pomegranate groves were shredded by cannon fire. Chips of limestone covered the city's streets, and dust hung in the air for days. Some of the town's best villas were no more than crumbing heaps on the ground. A Mexican historian wrote of the battle: "Monterrey was converted into a vast cemetery. The unburied bodies, the dead and putrid mules, the silence of the streets, all gave a fearful aspect to the city." Mexico's most beautiful city was now a ruin of death and destruction.[43]

Samuel Walker did not have time to consider the ugliness of war. Two hundred of his Texans remained in the city's post office near the plaza. He readied his men to fight the next morning by collecting all of the crowbars they could find. One hour before daylight Walker ordered his men to pick a hole in the wall of a house whose roof offered a direct view into the Grand Plaza. He posted Texans on nearby buildings to provide cover. In the distance they could see the flag of the Spanish counsel, which had been "pierced in a hundred places," as George Kendall wrote. At daylight the men picked the final stone away and prepared to enter the house. The front door opened, and a group of Mexican soldiers tried to sprint to safety. Texans on the roof cut down the men with their rifles. From their new perch, the volunteers unleashed a withering attack against the soldiers who surrounded the cathedral. "We were now behind the roof barricades and were beating the Mexicans at their own game," a Texan remarked. The Mexicans placed a cannon in a nearby street to push back the Americans' advanced line, but anyone who tried to load the gun was shot down.[44]

Not long after, Walker's Texans spotted a Mexican soldier bearing a white flag. "What do you want?" Walker asked the man. "To capitulate," he responded. Bigfoot Wallace recognized the man carrying the flag and leveled his rifle to shoot him. "Lieutenant, don't you know a parley when you hear it blowed?" a Texan asked Wallace, who replied, "No. Not when I am in front of *that* man." He recognized the flag's bearer, Col. Manuel Moreno, as one of the officers at Salado when the Americans were forced to undergo the "Lottery of Death." Moreno had laughed whenever a man drew a black bean, signifying execution, and had grabbed Wallace's giant hand to show it off before the Texan could see what color bean he had drawn. Wallace was determined to kill him. "Look at this *hand*," Wallace yelled at Moreno. "Do you know it? Ever see it before?" The scared Moreno said no, and Wallace began shouting curses at him. At some point Walker probably intervened to stop Wallace from acting on his desire for revenge. Being the senior officer present, he agreed to Moreno's request and escorted him and another Mexican to see General Taylor.[45]

Once the emissaries reached the American commander, the two sides agreed to a ceasefire. The Texans and regulars were enraged when they were told. They had closed in on the plaza and believed it was only a matter of time before they could demand unconditional surrender from Ampudia. "Hays and Walker were very much chagrined," Private Matthews wrote, "and the men almost savage about it." After lengthy negotiations between Taylor and Mexican officers, the battle of Monterrey was over. Taylor allowed Ampudia's soldiers to keep their small arms, six batteries of light artillery, and twenty-one rounds of ammunition. This was quite an impressive arsenal allowed to a defeated army. The Mexicans agreed to withdraw within seven days to a negotiated line past the Rinconada Pass. The two armies also agreed to a general ceasefire for eight weeks.[46]

On September 25 the surrender ceremony took place. The large Mexican flag in the Black Fort, the last bastion still filled with Mexican soldiers, was lowered and replaced by the Stars and Stripes. All of the confiscated cannons and guns were stacked in the main plaza. Many Mexican generals met with Generals Worth and Taylor over the next few days. Maj. Gen. José María Ortega, while drinking with Worth, toasted everyone in the room, saying, "I drink to the perpetual peace of the two Republics, and may we hereafter ever be as brothers joined in one cause, and let us show to foreign nations the greatness of our power." Meanwhile, McCulloch, Hays, and Walker had other matters to attend to. They went back to Gajar's house to thank him for his hospitality. While there they mentioned that some Texans had thought of asking him if they could purchase one of his silver spoons as a souvenir. Gajar immediately offered them the spoons for free, which the Texans declined to accept because they did not want to take his silverware without proper compensation.[47]

Mexican soldiers soon began marching out of the city in a long line. Their bands played each day as the infantry and cavalry staggered out of the city over a week-long period. Some American officers were concerned that the Texans would act recklessly when Ampudia finally passed in front of them, but they followed orders and did not utter a word (or fire a shot). They did, however, recover one of McCulloch's horses as it was being led out by a Mexican soldier. Some of the regulars recognized their old comrades in the surrender procession. John Riley, who led the American deserters at Monterrey, kept his head down and tried to remain inconspicuous as he passed. But he was spotted by his old comrades as he rode on top of an artillery caisson, and they hissed and jeered him. "Lend me a pistol," one soldier in Riley's old company declared, "and I'll shoot the cowardly cur." Over 100 American deserters followed the Mexicans out of the city.[48]

Monterrey was on the lips of every American when news of the battle arrived in the States. Newspapers dedicated whole sections to the three-day action, and some, like the *New Orleans Picayune*, published special extras to cover the action in detail. They printed maps depicting the fighting and maneuvering and published accounts written by soldiers in the field. And those with embedded journalists published their lengthy stories based on their personal observations of the campaign and combat.

The battle of Monterrey made an indelible impression on the soldiers who fought it. Taylor had rooted out Ampudia from his "Perfect Gibraltar," though not without serious loss. He reported losses of sixteen officers, 120 men killed, and 368 wounded, some of whom later died. Ampudia wrote the Mexican secretary of war that his command had suffered losses of 122 killed and 316 wounded. Skeptics believe that casualties for both sides were much higher than either general admitted. Regardless, Mexican and American soldiers who fought there would probably agree with the statement made by one U.S. general present at the battle: "I do not believe that, for downright, straight forward, hard fighting, the battle of Monterrey has ever been surpassed."[49]

8

ON TO MEXICO CITY

"The old Monterey game . . . was adopted."
George Wilkins Kendall

After the battle, Pedro de Ampudia's men marched west out of Monterrey past the armistice line in Rinconada Pass, arriving in San Luis Potosi in mid-October. Upon their arrival they found Santa Anna, who had been appointed commander of all Mexican military forces after his return from exile. The bedraggled soldiers were probably happy to see the generalissimo, believing that he was the only man who could stop the Americans. The generals of the Army of the North—Arista, Mejía, Ampudia, and Torrejón—had been disgraced by defeat. The country needed a new commander, one who could rally the men to fight an army that appeared unbeatable.

Zachary Taylor, meanwhile, settled into new quarters at Monterrey. He appointed William Worth governor of the city. Worth instituted strict measures to ensure respect for the city's property and inhabitants. He placed the Second Division (regulars) inside the city and sent the volunteers back to Walnut Springs. The general did not want the volunteers to bring their bad habits to Monterrey.

At his new headquarters Worth was paid a visit by the Texas volunteers, who were returning to the United States because their enlistments had expired. He offered each man a drink and bid him good luck, later issuing a general order thanking the Texans for their efforts: "Hereafter they and we [the regulars] are brothers, and we can desire no better guarantee of success than by their association." For their part, the Texans were awed by the valor of the West Pointers. These frontiersmen had learned from experience rather than books and classroom lectures, and many of them probably thought that these well-educated regular officers would fold under pressure. Monterrey showed the Texans, and many others, that the West Pointers always led from the front. "It was fortunate for the service that we had so many West Point graduates to bravely lead the men," one Texan later wrote. "It was 'Come on men,' and we knew who led us."[1]

Back in Washington, President Polk was not reveling in Taylor's victory. Once word of the armistice reached Polk, he cursed Taylor for giving Ampudia such lenient terms, expecting nothing less than an unconditional surrender from the Mexican general. The president believed, with good reason, that if Mexican forces were allowed to keep their arms and supplies, they would simply regroup and return to fight again. "He [Taylor] had the enemy in his power & should have taken them prisoners, deprived them of their arms, . . . and preserved the advantage which he had obtained by pushing on without delay," Polk scrawled in his diary. The president instructed Taylor to cancel the ceasefire at once. The general was surprised, believing that he had acted in accordance with his instructions and the president's intentions for the campaign. He had treated the locals and the Mexican army with courtesy in order to leave the window open for negotiations. The general surely doubted that Mexican authorities would be inclined to negotiate if he detained their soldiers while seizing foodstuffs and other supplies from the population.[2]

What Taylor did not know was that Polk's stance toward the Mexican government was changing. In mid-September the president received a letter from Santa Anna in which he refused to enter negotiations with the United States to end hostilities. This message particularly upset Polk because he had allowed the former dictator to depart Cuba for Mexico under the agreement that Santa Anna would seek peace once he returned to his country. He was now reneging on that deal. Polk responded by ordering Maj. Gen. Robert Patterson, a general of volunteers and Taylor's subordinate, to overrun the Mexican state of Tamaulipas, occupying its capital, Victoria, and its largest port, Tampico. Seizing the state would allow the Americans to control almost all of northern Mexico. Polk hoped that by doing so, the locals, who had a history of rebelling against the national authorities, would rise up against Santa Anna. A widespread revolt might finally prompt the Mexican government to negotiate an end to the war. But Santa Anna undercut this strategy when he declared that he would embrace a federalist form of government, which meant that he would allow Mexico's states more autonomy from the central government. Armed with newfound freedoms, the country's northern states would now be more reluctant to rebel.[3]

Polk again changed his approach to forcing negotiations. The cabinet had been debating a possible campaign against Mexico City for some time, and Polk now decided that this would be the only way to force Mexico to cede territory and end the war. He ordered that a second American army land at Veracruz and march west to overrun Mexico City. The general commanding the expedition would need men, so Secretary of War William Marcy instructed Taylor to provide 2,000 regulars and 2,000 volunteers for the campaign. He also told the general to stay in Monterrey and not to march on Saltillo as Taylor had intended. Marcy did not want him to risk a fight after stripping his command of some of its best men. Taylor fumed over Marcy's directive. Santa Anna was supposedly gathering an army at San Luis Potosi, and now Washington wanted to deprive him of his men. Taylor wanted to arrive in Saltillo before Santa Anna because it served as an important crossroads to three major northern Mexican cities. Once entrenched there, it would be difficult to root out Santa Anna.[4]

While Taylor was considering his next steps, he received a message from Brig. Gen. John Wool. Wool had departed San Antonio in late September to seize the city of Chihuahua, 350 miles northwest of Monterrey. Taylor had lost communication with him during his own campaign and was surprised to learn that the general was in Monclova, only 100 miles northwest of Saltillo. Wool begged him for permission to move his men farther south because the long march and drawn-out encampments were making his volunteers restless. Taylor agreed and sent Wool to Parras, located near Saltillo and 180 miles past the line that Marcy had ordered him not to cross. Taylor further ignored Marcy's orders and sent Worth with 1,200 men from Monterrey to Saltillo, which surrendered without a fight.[5]

Meanwhile, Winfield Scott, the newly appointed commander of the Veracruz expedition, arrived at the Rio Grande to appropriate 9,000 of Taylor's men. This would leave in northern Mexico some

7,000 men, only 800 of whom were regulars. Although Taylor refused to meet with him at Camargo, Scott nevertheless tried to soften the blow with rare diplomatic flattery: "But, my dear general," he wrote, "I shall be obliged to take from you most of the gallant officers and men (regulars and volunteers) whom you have so long and so nobly commanded." Ultimately Scott acquired 4,000 regulars and 3,200 volunteers from Taylor. Generals Quitman and Worth joined the expedition, as did Twiggs and others. Taylor retained Jefferson Davis's Mississippians and Braxton Bragg's artillery. The bulk of this reconstituted army were untested volunteers from Illinois and Arkansas, most of them Wool's men. Although they lacked discipline and training, Taylor would have to rely on them soon. A jittery General Worth had already sounded one false alarm from Saltillo, but few doubted Santa Anna's intention to march northward.[6]

Intelligence suggested that Santa Anna was gathering forces in San Luis Potosí and would soon march north. Indeed, Santa Anna soon collected almost 15,000 men for his army: some from neighboring garrisons, some newly recruited from the populace, and the rest from the remnants of Ampudia's Monterrey army. He marched his command in record time from San Luis Potosí across the desert to La Encarnación, a hacienda roughly sixty miles south of Saltillo, where his forces skirmished with some American cavalry. When reports of these clashes filtered in to Taylor, he refused to believe them. How could Santa Anna march 15,000 men across the desert that quickly? Not until Ben McCulloch rode undetected throughout the Mexican camp and estimated that the army totaled 20,000 soldiers did Taylor finally acknowledge that Santa Anna was indeed at his doorstep.[7]

With Wool's men, Taylor possessed about 4,500 troops, almost all volunteers. He positioned his army at a point known as La Angostura, or "The Narrows," in a deep valley running just south of Saltillo. Wool had scouted the location earlier and recommended it as an excellent defensive position. Taylor posted his men at points throughout this valley, including at a small hacienda known as Buena Vista, one mile north of the Narrows. Dozens of deep ravines extended like fingers from the mountain into the center of the valley, making it difficult to move men and artillery quickly around the battlefield. Taylor posted his green volunteers on La Angostura's slopes, hoping that the incline would steady their nerves under fire. He also placed artillery on the road that bisected the valley.

With only a day's rest for his men at La Encarnación, Santa Anna rushed his soldiers 35 miles to Agua Nueva, a hacienda where he had heard Taylor's men were encamped. The Mexicans observed smoldering buildings and houses and some overturned American carts. Santa Anna, seeing the carts and fires, believed that he was behind an American Army that was wildly retreating for its life, so he ordered his men to pack three rations and rushed them to the Narrows. There, to his surprise, he found Taylor's army, turned toward him and massed in a strong defensive position. Despite the turn of events, Santa Anna still held the advantage: he had three men for every one of Taylor's.[8]

Around 11 A.M. on February 22, 1847, Santa Anna employed a small diversion on the valley's road while General Ampudia, who quickly violated the terms of his parole by commanding troops against the Americans again, led the main attack through ravines and gorges to take a prominent knoll on Taylor's left. The Mexicans did not take the knoll that day, but they did climb to a better position above it. Both sides ceased fighting after sunset. During the night Santa Anna reinforced Ampudia's men on the high point and moved some artillery to the road to divert the Americans from his true objective. The diversions tricked Taylor into believing that the enemy's main effort would focus on advancing down the valley's main road. Not until Joseph Mansfield reported that Mexican forces were gathering to overwhelm his left flank did Taylor think otherwise. The general sent Major Mansfield on a wild gallop across ravines and hills to gather reinforcements. Taylor's weak left could not withstand a massive attack.[9]

Fighting soon developed on the American left, atop an extended plateau, and threatened to turn the entire flank. If that happened, Taylor knew that his green volunteers would flee and the battle would be lost. The general scrambled to assemble a makeshift line that could hold long enough for his infantry to move into position. Sam French and George Thomas, who were still with Bragg's Company E, 3rd Artillery, rumbled their gun caissons across deep ravines and around boulders to join the men on the left flank. Bragg's other lieutenant, John Reynolds, soon arrived as well. French received a musket ball in his thigh and entrusted his 12-pounder to one of his lieutenants. He stayed on his horse and hovered near Lieutenant Reynolds, who was pumping canister into oncoming Mexican cavalry. Supported by some American infantry, Bragg's guns kept Santa Anna at bay and prevented Taylor's flank from collapsing. Bragg's artillery would finally play its intended role in battle: lobbing canister and grape into oncoming enemy horsemen or infantrymen who had nowhere to hide.[10]

It was only 9 A.M., but Santa Anna smelled victory. He knew that the American left flank was under duress and sent a mixed group of cavalry and infantry to attack the weak point. Taylor now needed his best infantry to save the day, ordering Colonel Davis and his Mississippians to the plateau. Taylor's faith in these men had risen since their valiant display at Fort Teneria in Monterrey and knew that he could count on them. Davis did not disappoint. Along with the 2nd and 3rd Indiana, the colonel formed his men into a giant "V," with the open end facing the enemy and acting as a funnel. The American volunteers successfully cut down the advancing cavalrymen and secured Taylor's left. The famous V, which might have been more of a makeshift arch than an actual V, made Davis a national military hero.[11]

Santa Anna then sent thousands of infantry to continue the cavalry's efforts against the American left. Bragg, who had been on that flank since morning, commanded three cannons that fired at the oncoming Mexicans. Taylor, desiring to be in the thick of the action, rode up just behind the captain as the infantry advanced. Bragg finally had the moment he been waiting for since the campaign began—his guns were about to play a momentous role in battle. His men rapidly fired their cannons at the approaching Mexicans, forcing them to withdraw and again saving the American left. During this assault Taylor reportedly uttered the famous words, "A little more grape, please, Captain Bragg!"[12]

Once the fighting ended, Taylor and his men tried to recuperate and prepare for a continuation of the battle the next day. The officers were not excited about the prospect of more fighting, as wounded men crowded the army's makeshift field hospitals. But to everyone's surprise, when dawn broke, Santa Anna's army was no longer in sight, having retreated during the night.[13]

Taylor owed his success at Buena Vista to his Monterrey veterans. Davis's Mississippi Rifles and Bragg's Company E had saved the army from defeat. If Santa Anna had turned the American left flank, Taylor's green volunteers—who were not handpicked like before the Monterrey campaign—would have fled toward Saltillo. The Mexican commander already had his cavalry in place to cut down any retreating Americans, which would have resulted in a terrible slaughter and an overwhelming Mexican victory. Other volunteers, including some Texans, also contributed to the American victory, but none could equal the role that Davis's and Bragg's commands played during the battle.

While Taylor's volunteers were battling Santa Anna, Winfield Scott was landing at Veracruz with 9,000 men. On March 9, 1847, Scott and his navy counterpart, Commodore David Connor, executed the largest amphibious landing of U.S. troops in the country's history. The general gave his old protégé, William Worth, who attended Scott's expedition, the honor of being the first man to step onto the beach.

With all of his men ashore, Scott decided to bombard Veracruz into submission with siege artillery rather than charging the fortified city with infantry. A bombardment would take more time, but the general needed all of the men he could muster for the upcoming campaign. Some of his soldiers disapproved of this patient approach, including General Worth, who openly voiced his disapproval of the strategy. Monterrey had been overrun in just three days, so why not do the same at Veracruz? The siege was ultimately successful, and few Americans died in the effort. One unlucky Monterrey veteran, Capt. John Vinton, who had been critical to Worth's success in taking Independence Hill and overrunning the city, received a direct hit from a cannonball and was killed instantly.[14]

Scott soon ordered his men to march west from Veracruz along the national highway toward Mexico City. This time he put David Twiggs, Worth's old rival, in charge of the advance and held Worth in reserve. Worth was upset because he believed (rightly so) that he was Scott's best general and that his success at Monterrey had earned him the privilege of leading the army into battle. And Twiggs would probably have a chance at action. After the Battle of Buena Vista, Santa Anna miraculously retained the support of Mexico's leaders and formed another army. His engineers found a strong position on the national highway where the road descended into a deep pass known as Cerro Gordo, which was lined by a large hill and plateau. This time, like Taylor at Buena Vista, Santa Anna would be on the defensive, which he probably hoped would steady the nerves of his men, few of whom had seen combat.[15]

Scott's decision to put Twiggs in the lead was almost a tragic mistake. Twiggs advanced straight toward the Mexican defenses on the highway, instead of stopping to consider possible flanking movements or waiting for reinforcements. This was exactly what Santa Anna hoped the Americans would do. Twiggs ignored the advice of his West Pointers to pause and consider an alternative path. Fortunately a sick General Patterson, who was senior to Twiggs, lumbered to the front in time to call off the ill-conceived assault. Eventually Scott reached the front lines and prepared a better plan of attack. He listened to his West Point engineers and decided to flank the Mexican position by sending men on a small path that led to the rear of Santa Anna's troops. The consequent battle was a gory one.[16]

Some of Monterrey's distinguished veterans were on the field that day. Napoleon Dana Tecumseh Sherman, whose attitude regarding the Mexican army had changed after Monterrey, was left for dead by his men after being wounded in a charge on the hill. He was found by a burial party a day and a half later and eventually made a full recovery. Another veteran, volunteer William Campbell, the commander of the 1st Tennessee who had led his men at Fort Teneria, was placed in charge of one of Scott's brigades at an inopportune time during the battle. His superior, Gideon Pillow, had ordered a charge against a fortified hill without reinforcements. The general was wounded and handed his brigade to Campbell in the middle of the fight. The colonel had never commanded a military unit larger than a regiment, but he did not have time to argue the point. He pushed his men forward until the Mexicans raised a white flag and retreated. Many soldiers in his brigade died in the assault.[17]

Following the battle, Scott ordered Worth's division to Puebla, roughly seventy miles from Mexico City. The Americans entered the city without a fight and assumed control of 80,000 presumably hostile Mexican citizens. A jittery Worth called his men to arms at the slightest rumor of an attack, the men referred to these roll-outs as Worth's "scarecrows." At one point the general issued a circular that warned his men to avoid all local food because it had been poisoned, an allegation that later proved to be false. When Scott entered Puebla, he publicly rebuked these actions in a banquet that Worth prepared for the general. The commanding general found fault with all of Worth's actions in the city, including the generous concessions that he gave the city council upon his arrival. Scott forced him to retract these concessions as well as the poison circular, concerned that the latter's derogatory language concerning Mexicans might inflame their resentment and put the Americans in more peril.[18]

Worth, believing he had acted properly in administering Puebla, demanded a court of inquiry to examine his conduct. He had previously been governor in Monterrey, Saltillo, and Veracruz, so he was surprised that Scott was questioning his management of the city. Worth had more experience and ability than anyone in the army to govern a hostile citizenry. The three officers selected for the court were not an impartial group. David Twiggs, a rival, was probably eager for some retribution against Worth dating from the previous spring, when the two had been at loggerheads in South Texas over who was second in command to Taylor. General Quitman, another member of the court, also sought fame in battle so he could reap the political benefits back home, and his successful efforts at Fort Teneria had been largely overshadowed in the press by Worth's operations in western Monterrey. Perhaps the only person on the tribunal who would reflect objectively over the court's proceedings was Persifor Smith, who retained a high degree of military professionalism and probably would weigh the facts neutrally. Ultimately, the court voted unanimously against Worth, though Scott, perhaps trying to salvage some sort of relationship with Worth, downplayed the findings. Relations between the two lifelong friends were at an all-time low. They could not even get along during dinner. At banquets held for the officers, Worth rudely continued conversations with his dinner partners as Scott gave long monologues regarding his many famous exploits. During one meal, Scott halted his story and remarked, "I'll not say another word— my host [Worth] is engaged in a private tete a tete & I'll not interrupt him." Tension filled the air afterward.[19]

Worth must have been surprised at the turn of events. Since the campaign in northern Mexico, he had been eager to serve under Scott, his old mentor and friend, and was excited to participate in the Veracruz campaign. The general believed that his success at Monterrey entitled him to be in the van of Scott's forces all the way to Mexico City.

After ten weeks in Puebla, Scott ordered his men to march toward Mexico City. The city was situated in a giant dried lakebed, surrounded by marshland and lakes, with the only approaches on ele-

vated highways and causeways. After his engineers conducted reconnaissance of the possible approaches, Scott decided to attack the
capital from the south, where Worth was then located, by moving
along the south side of Lake Chalco and turning north up a main road.
The American commander had discounted this route early on when
he had heard that the thoroughfare was not practical for artillery. But
further reconnaissance by James Duncan suggested that it could handle artillery and was not well fortified. All along Worth had been
lobbying Scott to approach Mexico City from this direction, but the
general had ignored his request. Relations were so bad between the
men that Worth begged Gideon Pillow to persuade Scott to reconsider
the Chalco route, knowing that Scott would not listen to him.[20]

As engineers investigated a fortified position at San Antonio that
lay along this route, Maj. Gen. Gabriel Valencia moved his entire
command into position about four miles from Santa Anna's main
army to establish a fortification on a commanding bluff overlooking a
farm. Santa Anna ordered him to withdraw to the main body, but the
general ignored him and kept his men on the bluff. Scott ordered
Twiggs and his division to assault Valencia's position. The Americans skirted a massive lava field to prepare for their assault. Persifor
Smith, who had previously led his men against Federation Hill and
commanded so ably inside Monterrey on the third day, led a brigade
under Twiggs. Upon surveying the strong front of the Mexican position, Smith decided to flank the enemy by sneaking his men through a
ravine that led to Valencia's rear. He believed that his troops would
never make it across the deep ravine in front of the bluff. Valencia's
position soon was covered from three different directions by three
brigades. At dawn Smith, now reinforced, ordered his men to creep
through the ravine and charge with bayonets. The Mexicans fled in
seventeen minutes, and the battle, known as Contreras, became one
of the biggest routs of a Mexican force during the campaign. Smith had
few casualties in the assault, though one of them was a Monterrey
notable. Capt. Charles Hanson of the 7th Infantry, who had baked
bread for hungry men during the fighting on the third day at Monterey,
died at Contreras when he was struck by musket fire while climbing a
hill with the Second Division. Smith's wisdom to flank the position,
rather than attack it directly, saved many lives that day. He chose a
better option that shattered the Mexican troops with minimal casualties to his own. Some soldiers said that Smith was second only to

Scott in his ability to command, and his conduct at Contreras sug-
gests that they might have been correct.[21]

After the battle Twiggs's men, flushed with victory, raced northeast toward Churubusco, a fortified church and convent where Santa
Anna was regrouping. The convent, with walls four feet thick and
twelve feet high, sat along a deep river crossed by a fortified bridge. It
was a strong position, the convent also having parapets on its roof and
an irrigation ditch running in front of it. Twiggs's men rushed to the
attack, but the Mexican defenders unleashed a withering barrage of
gunfire, forcing them back. General Worth, who was still south of the
area at Contreras, moved quickly to assist. First he needed to overrun
a smaller Mexican position at San Antonio, which stood between his
army and Churubusco. The general sent Charles Smith, who had
helped him assault Federation Hill, to pick his way through the lava
field and flank the position, while John Garland, who had fought so
hard on the first day in eastern Monterrey, pressed forward on the
highway. The combination of Worth's advance and the sight of their
comrades fleeing from Contreras caused the San Antonio defenders
to flee northeast for Churubusco. Santa Anna added the retreating
troops to his forces at Churubusco, hoping that his army could stop
the Americans from marching into Mexico City.[22]

Worth sent Garland and Captain Smith to attack Santa Anna's
left flank at Churubusco, but the men could not make headway
against the strong position. James Duncan could not move his guns
within firing range due to the heavy mud from rains that forced water
levels over nearby dikes. Mexican soldiers showered musket fire on
Garland's men, who were plainly visible as they trudged through a
cornfield. Worth should have looked for a way to flank these troops,
but instead he continued sending his men directly into the fray believing that someone would be successful. The fears his men possessed at Monterrey—that the general would throw them into battle
without first scouting the best route of approach—became reality
at Churubusco. Worth was probably aggravated by recent events at
Puebla and had not had a chance yet to prove that he was Scott's best
general. He also knew that Twiggs was attacking the same position
from the west and probably sought to outperform his old rival by
breaking the enemy before he did. Whatever the reason, the general
sent his best regiment, the 6th Infantry, against the bridge, where
the regulars were cut down rapidly. Worth continued sending in wave

after wave of troops against the bridge until they finally took it through hand-to-hand fighting. One wonders if Worth recalled Taylor's operations in northeast Monterrey and the difficulty that the First Division had in advancing across the Puente Purisima. Unlike Garland, however, who sensed the futility of trying to cross that bridge, here Worth pressed on until his men were successful, though at a fearful cost in lives. James Longstreet, who led the assault on the redoubt at Federation Hill, carried the colors of the 8th Infantry across the bridge under fire. Eventually, some soldiers under Brig. Gen. James Shields got behind the Mexicans, and the combination of this maneuver and Worth's assault spread panic throughout Santa Anna's lines, causing his soldiers to evacuate the position. The Battle of Churubusco was not one of Worth's best moments.[23]

After a short ceasefire (which Santa Anna used to resupply his men and prepare Mexico City for attack), Scott ordered Worth to carry a position southwest of the capital called the Molino del Rey ("King's Mill"), where reports indicated cannons were being produced. Scott could have bypassed the fortifications there and still entered Mexico City from the south, but he wanted the position taken. At Molino del Rey a line of concrete buildings ran from north to south for three hundred yards, most of them lined with parapets. A drainage ditch ran parallel to the buildings on their left and then curved west to a strong stone building known as Casa Mata. Santa Anna posted here 8,000–9,000 men, many of whom hid behind the parapets or sandbags on the rooftops. Worth reconnoitered the position and became concerned after finding the Mexican defenses much more powerful than he had anticipated. He recommended to Scott that the Americans wait until daylight to attack and also requested permission to assault another strong fortification, the castle of Chapultepec, which lay just beyond Molino del Rey in the southern part of Mexico City. Scott agreed to the daylight attack but denied permission to take the castle. Worth's men attacked in the morning, but they were pushed back by the strong infantry and artillery, sustaining heavy casualties. George Ayres of the 3rd Artillery, who had been brevetted for his actions at Monterrey, died during the engagement; he had been one of the first men to enter the Bishop's Palace and grab the Mexican colors. John Garland brought his brigade into the battle but was forced back by vicious Mexican fire. Only after reinforcements arrived was the position taken. Garland's brigade, which attacked from the south and southeast, eventually stormed Molino's gates. Duncan brought his artillery into the heaviest of the fighting and battered down Casa Mata. Over 800 Americans were killed or wounded, Worth losing 25 percent of his division. He and Scott blamed each other for the disaster. The tension between the two, which had boiled over a few times since the campaign began, now intensified further.[24]

Four days later Scott sent troops against Chapultepec. Because Scott had previously rejected Worth's request to attack the stronghold after taking Molino del Rey, Santa Anna had had time to fortify the already formidable position. The castle, which housed a military college, sat atop a hill two hundred feet high that was protected by irrigation ditches, a swamp, and a minefield. An aqueduct and a high wall on the slopes of the hill protected three sides of the castle.

Scott ordered General Quitman and his volunteers to advance on the castle from the south. Quitman, like Worth, had longed for battle since he joined the army at Veracruz, but his division had yet to play a major role in combat. Notable at Monterrey when his men successfully overran a position that the regulars were unable to seize, Quitman wanted a chance to show his ability to Scott. He also was a major general but did not have the number of troops under him normally assigned to a general of that rank. Since the campaign, he had been asking Scott for larger roles in upcoming actions, which the commander had denied him. Chapultepec would be his chance. Quitman's men approached on a road from the south flanked on both sides by ditches and vast meadows beyond. Heavy musketry and artillery fire greeted Quitman's men, who continued to march up the road into the teeth of the Mexican defenses. The attack stalled, and Quitman sheltered his men at a small bend in the road. He ordered General Shields to take three volunteer regiments and cross the open fields to reach a fifteen-foot-high wall guarding the castle. Shields did so, but his men took heavy casualties before reaching the wall. Quitman's division, which now contained volunteers from New York, Pennsylvania, and South Carolina, found a breach in the wall and assaulted the castle. They eventually took the castle, though not until after intense hand-to-hand fighting within the walls.[25]

Elated by his victory, Quitman ordered his men to pursue the fleeing troops into Mexico City itself. Scott only wanted him to perform a small feint against the city because he intended to attack the capital from a different point. But Quitman ordered a general pursuit. His men assaulted the Belén Gate, which guarded one of the entrances into the city. Mexican soldiers in the gate's blockhouse, along a nearby causeway, and throughout a promenade running to the north offered stiff resistance to the volunteers. Santa Anna arrived to oversee the battle in person, bringing with him additional artillery and infantry. Quitman's troops began to make headway by hiding along roadside arches and inching their way forward. Once near the gate, Quitman himself grabbed a rifle, fired a shot, and tied a handkerchief to the end of the weapon. He waved it over his head and yelled for his men to rush the gate. Perhaps Quitman sought to emulate Lt. Col. Alexander McClung, who had done something similar for his brigade at Fort Teneria and changed the course of that fight. The volunteers eventually routed the Mexicans at the gate, though not without serious bloodshed. Quitman's men, now without ammunition and completely fatigued, were halted by Mexican fire from an old tobacco company. Almost every member of the general's staff was wounded, as were all of his artillery officers. Scott criticized Quitman after the war for his rashness in entering the city, where his quest for glory led to appalling casualties.[26]

While Quitman attacked the Belén Gate, Scott sent General Worth with Monterrey veterans John Garland, Charles Smith, and James Duncan to assault the San Cosme Gate to the north. Scott had intended this to be his main approach into the capital: he wanted Quitman only to carry out a diversion while Worth directed the real attack. Mexican soldiers posted themselves throughout a line of roadside buildings and houses near San Cosme. After surveying the situation, Worth decided to utilize his newfound understanding of urban-warfare tactics. "The old Monterey game . . . was adopted," George Kendall recalled. The general ordered his men to burrow through the area's buildings rather than advance down the middle of the street. His sappers busted holes in the walls using pickaxes and crowbars to slowly advance into the city. Ulysses S. Grant, who accompanied Worth, also relied on his experience of urban warfare at Monterrey. "I found a church off to the south of the road," he later wrote, "which looked to me as if the belfry would command the ground back of the garita San Cosme." With some men, he disassembled a howitzer and dragged it into the church's bell tower. Once reassembled, the gun lobbed shells onto Mexican positions 100–

200 yards away. Although Grant does not record it in his memoirs, at the time he may have been thinking about the howitzer hoisted onto the top of the tall building in the Plaza de Carne, whose shells could reach the Grand Plaza in Monterrey.[27]

Eventually Santa Anna surrendered the capital. The American soldiers gathered in the city's Grand Plaza. As Worth's men started for the square to join their colleagues, sniper fire badly wounded Colonel Garland. The shot was probably meant for Worth but hit Garland, who was standing by his side. After all that the colonel had been through at Monterrey, Churubusco, and Molino del Rey, he had the misfortune of being grievously wounded after the surrender of Mexico City. In retaliation Worth ordered every house, palace, and convent in the area shelled with an 8-inch howitzer. Scott soon appointed Quitman governor of Mexico City.[28]

U.S. newspapers printed headline after headline about the conquest. Articles highlighted the exploits of certain generals. One article said that General Pillow, Polk's old law partner, was the main reason for Scott's success, while another declared that Worth and Duncan had found the route south of Chalco that led to the army's success. General Scott detested the articles and implicitly blamed Worth for leaking the army's operations and "self puffing" in order to achieve fame. He issued a famous general order, circulated throughout the army, that blamed Worth (though not by name) for inflating his role in the campaign. Worth demanded that Scott call him out by name and vehemently denied leaking any information to the papers. Their tit-for-tat continued until Worth upped the ante by writing President Polk that Scott was acting in a manner "unbecoming of an officer and a gentleman." He then asked the president to investigate his old friend's behavior. When Scott learned about the letter to the president, he placed Worth, Duncan, and Pillow under arrest for insubordination. Pillow and Scott had been at odds since the fighting ended, and Scott believed that Pillow was also leaking information for self-aggrandizement. When word reached Polk of the general's actions, he ordered Scott relieved of command and ordered Worth, Duncan, and Pillow released. He also demanded that a court of inquiry examine Worth's earlier charges against Scott. Now the tables were turned, and Scott was on trial for his actions. Worth and Duncan eventually agreed to retract their charges, but Pillow insisted on launching the court of inquiry. The trial became a highly publicized

showdown, where Scott offered tirade after tirade in front of his colleagues. In one episode he told Worth that he was "done with him
forever." The trial tarnished what was otherwise a brilliant campaign
in which Garland and Monterrey's veterans, including Worth, Quitman, and Persifor Smith, played vital roles.[29]

EPILOGUE

After the war William Worth returned to the United States and was eventually transferred to San Antonio, where he commanded the Department of Texas and New Mexico. He later contracted cholera and died at his headquarters on May 7, 1849, at the age of fifty-five.

Worth is best remembered for his performance at Monterrey—and for good reason. In just two days he defeated a large cavalry force and stormed two fortified heights. His operations trapped Ampudia inside the city and prevented him from receiving reinforcements and supplies. Worth's wise decision to first attack Federation Hill, which was less fortified than Independence Hill, gave his men a vital position from where they could direct artillery fire into both the Bishop's Palace and the city itself. Its capture gave his troops confidence while sapping the morale of the Mexicans on Independence Hill, who helplessly watched the other height being taken. But the general owed most of his success to his men. Texans and regulars alike fought with tenacity and bravery. Climbing the steep slopes of Federation and Independence hills tested their courage under fire. It helped that many of the soldiers had already served under Worth during the Seminole War, and they respected the general for his aggressive style. They probably respected him even more once they realized that he was not going to throw them into battle recklessly to achieve personal glory. Indeed Worth listened to his officers, including Capt. John Vinton, who recommended the ruse on Independence Hill, and Maj. Edward Burleson, who suggested new ways to fight inside the city.[1]

In contrast, Ampudia's record at Monterrey is not as glowing. He did little to prepare his men for success after replacing General Mejia. Prior to the battle, his constant wavering over a strategy for Monterrey's defense lowered his men's confidence and prevented the completion of key fortifications like the Citadel and Fort Teneria. Also, he knew that his only possible avenue of retreat was to the southwest, yet he did little to secure western Monterrey from attack. If he could have retained control of that part of the city, Ampudia could have retreated and regrouped in the Rinconada Pass while awaiting reinforcements. Once the battle started, Ampudia kept many of his soldiers in reserve in the main plaza. These men could have been used to support the brave defenders at Fort Teneria or to reinforce western Monterrey. The general also showed little initiative when he had an advantage over Taylor's defeated troops. He likely could have retaken Fort Teneria on the night of the 21st but instead stayed in the plaza, almost as if he were waiting for the battle to end. General Mejia, despite being relieved of command, showed passion and courage in leading his men at the Purisima Bridge on the 21st. His presence in the middle of the fight helped inspire their successful effort to repulse the First Division as the Americans tried to cross into the city.

Taylor's efforts at Monterrey were mixed. To be sure, he outperformed his counterpart, General Ampudia, but he still made serious mistakes. On the 21st he ignored his original objective and decided to overrun northeast Monterrey at any cost. He sent his men pell-mell into a bloodbath with no clear purpose. Even after the battle Taylor believed that his "diversion" had been successful, almost as if he were unaware that he had sent half of his army against the city. Colonel Garland and his men bore the brunt of the general's poor decision making as they stumbled through the streets without maps or any knowledge of the city's layout. Yet Taylor refused to give any credit to Garland, who did the best he could given the situation.[2]

Garland was not the only officer without accurate information regarding Monterrey's defenses. Prior to the battle Taylor did not disseminate such intelligence to his subordinate commanders. Between captured prisoners, defectors, and the engineers' reconnaissance, he knew where most of Monterrey's key garrisons were located and how strong they were. In just one interrogation conducted by the Texans, the Americans learned about virtually all of the fortifications in the city. Unfortunately this information was never passed on to division and brigade commanders, who stumbled upon key garrisons like Fort Diablo and Fort Federation. Taylor should have provided maps of the city to his officers and given them relevant intelligence on Ampudia's defense.

Despite these failures, Taylor did many things right at Monterrey. Prior to the Mexican War, the frontier general usually charged straight into a fight without first considering flanking approaches. His "charge first" demeanor, as displayed at the battles of Okeechobee and Resaca de la Palma, proved to his critics that he possessed limited tactical sense. In other words Taylor could not develop innovative battle plans to gain an advantage against the enemy, instead typically winning by brute force and through the courage of his men. At Monterrey, however, Taylor did pause in front of the city, spending a full day and night scouting its fortifications. He then held a council of war to hear his senior officers' opinions on the best way to attack, agreeing with their suggestion that the thrust of the army's effort should be against western Monterrey while a diversion was carried out to the east. During their council of war, Taylor and his officers decided to hit the city at its weakest point (the west), carrying out a nineteenth-century version of "maneuver warfare." This battlefield tactic—to feign attack against the most heavily defended approach and send the bulk of one's forces against the defender's weakest point—is often attributed to Winfield Scott, who used it repeatedly throughout his campaign to Mexico City. Taylor, however, was the first general in the war to embrace the tactic, and it paid dividends at Monterrey.[3]

Taylor's decision to take only a third of his volunteers to Monterrey was a risky but calculated approach that ultimately proved successful. He selected only a few units of his best volunteers to march into Mexico. Many of them were embedded with regular units so the confidence and discipline of the regulars would rub off on the citizen-soldiers. Others volunteers were commanded by former regulars. Taylor also quickly understood the unique role that the Texans could play in scouting and in battle, and he utilized them to the fullest extent. All of his volunteers, with the exception of the Baltimore Battalion, performed as well as any regulars at Monterrey.

Most of Taylor's success, though, is overshadowed by the bloody diversion of the 21st, when many of America's best soldiers died trying to march down open streets against impossible odds. The loss of so many West Point graduates that day was the worst in the academy's history, and Taylor had little to show for their sacrifice. A wellspring of poems, songs, and illustrations emerged in the aftermath of the battle, all attempting to depict the carnage and courage of the soldiers of that fateful day, one of which, T. Mayne Reid's "Monterrey," declared:

> We were not many—we who stood,
> Before the iron sleet that day,
> Yet many a gallant spirit would,
> Have been with us at Monterey.

Maj. Philip Barbour, 3rd Infantry, who was killed on that first day of fighting, was remembered, like soldiers on both sides, for his bravery and for his love of family and country. William Marvin wrote in his poem "Battle of Monterrey" a few stanzas regarding Barbour's burial in the United States:

> We laid our loved Barbour to sleep in his grave,
> Where forest trees waved o'er his head;
> Where the mocking-bird sings the sad dirge of the brave,
> And wild-flowers bloom on his bed.

> His loved one, away o'er the wide spreading main,
> May hope for his presence no more:
> He never can gladden her lone heart again,
> For he sleeps, and his marching is o'er.

> Yet oh when the last muster-roll shall unfold,
> And millions the ranks shall sustain,
> When the arch-angel wakes the last trumpet of gold,
> Oh then he will march us again.

Despite the destruction that the fighting caused, today when one visits Monterrey, there are few signs that such a vicious battle occurred there. A few bullet holes in the Bishop's Palace are all that remain visible aboveground. Under the surface, however, corpses from both sides still lie buried. During the U.S. occupation of the city from 1846 to 1848, the Americans recovered and transferred some remains, but many of the soldiers were buried during lulls in the fighting, and the survivors could not recall their locations. Many are still unknown.

To this day the most noteworthy legacy of the battle is located in Texas. Several months after General Worth's death, a cavalry major was ordered to establish a fort in North Texas to protect the area's settlers from Indians. He stopped at a bluff overlooking the Trinity River and decided that it would make a good site for a military post. During the day's journey, the officer had pondered the great campaigns of the Mexican War, specifically "about the siege of Monterey and the brilliant strategy of Gen. William J. Worth of New York, which had made possible a surprisingly easy victory. Worth was a dashing fellow and a great horseman. His personality drew his fellow officers about him in an admiring circle." As his men made camp for the night, the major "decided to call the new fort after his friend." The city that later developed around this site remains the largest in the United States with a military title in its name: Fort Worth.[4]

Notes

INTRODUCTION

1. In 1846 the city was spelled "Monterey," but it will be referred to in this book by its modern spelling.
2. Sullivan, *Field of Monterey.*
3. Henry, *Campaign Sketches,* 210; Dana, *Monterrey Is Ours,* 128.

1. PRELUDE TO BATTLE

1. Powell, *Major General Zachary Taylor,* 28–29; Marvin, *Battle of Monterey,* 56.
2. Background on Taylor's life drawn from Bauer, *Zachary Taylor;* Powell, *Major General Zachary Taylor;* Holman Hamilton, *Zachary Taylor,* vol. 1; and Mahon, *Second Seminole War,* 226.
3. Hitchcock, *Fifty Years in Camp and Field,* 192.
4. Haynes, *Polk and the Expansionist Impulse,* 97, 107; Merk, *Manifest Destiny,* 29–31, 61–62; Weems, *To Conquer a Peace,* 43; Bauer, *Mexican War,* 10–11; Borneman, *Man Who Transformed the Presidency,* 142 (quote). Polk also hoped that Mexico could repay a longstanding debt through land. In 1842 an international tribunal awarded over $2 million to the United States for losses incurred during Mexico's many revolutions or by the rash acts of its officials. Mexico defaulted on its payments two years later.
5. Ganoe, *United States Army,* 202.
6. Kluger, *Seizing Destiny,* 440–41; Borneman, *Man Who Transformed the Presidency,* 194. Also, Slidell's credentials showed that he was a minister plenipotentiary, meaning that he was in Mexico with full diplomatic credentials. Herrera's acceptance of Slidell would have been tantamount to reestablishing diplomatic relations, which had been severed in March 1845. Herrera

was in no position to do that until his government received some kind of compensation for Texas.

7. Weems, *To Conquer a Peace*, 96–97; Merk, *Manifest Destiny*, 87.

8. Borneman, *Man Who Transformed the Presidency*, 145, 191 (quote); Kluger, *Seizing Destiny*, 438–39. Polk wanted the boundary line to run along the Rio Grande to El Paso, then due west to the Pacific. Merk, *Manifest Destiny*, 82.

9. Borneman, *Man Who Transformed the Presidency*, 194; Kluger, *Seizing Destiny*, 438.

10. Zachary Taylor [hereafter referred to as ZT] to Marcy, Mar. 8, 1846, in U.S. House, *Mexican War Correspondence*, 120; Winders, *Mr. Polk's Army*, 9, 22–23, 52; Ganoe, *United States Army*, 196. When Taylor assembled his force at Corpus Christi in late 1845, he had 3,900 men, including four regiments of infantry and four regiments of artillery. Although the authorized strength of the army was much higher, most companies retained only about half of their authorized number of privates due to desertion and illness. Congress, which had neglected the army for years, tried to remedy the situation by enlarging the size of an infantry company from 42 to 100 men in May 1846. Regarding the march to the Rio Grande, Polk's order arrived at Corpus Christi on February 3, but Taylor did not depart until March 8.

11. Paredes to Arista, Apr. 18, 1846, cited in J. Smith, *War with Mexico*, 1:155.

12. Quote cited in ibid., 1:159.

13. ZT to Adjutant General (hereafter referred to as AG), Apr. 26, 1846, in U.S. House, *Mexican War Correspondence*, 141.

14. One soldier said he did not run from anything and refused to lie flat. As a shell flew toward him, though, he had a change of heart and dove to avoid the shell. His dive elicited a hearty laugh from his comrades. Thorpe, *Our Army on the Rio Grande*, 5–6.

15. Dillon, *American Artillery*, 26; Bauer, *Mexican War*, 52. Each 18-pound cannon tube weighed 4,700 pounds and was pulled by twelve oxen.

16. Artillerymen who fought as foot soldiers were called "red-legged" infantry. Bauer, *Mexican War*, 20.

17. *Niles Register*, May 30, 1846. Justin Smith colorfully observed, "the American artillery surprised him [Arista] almost as much as if Taylor had used shooting stars." J. Smith, *War with Mexico*, 1:166.

18. Forman, *West Point*, 60–63; Winders, *Mr. Polk's Army*, 55. State leaders also were concerned that the West Pointers would fill all of the army's officer slots, thus leaving none for qualified men from other schools.

19. Skelton, *American Profession of Arms*, 228–29; Morrison, *Best School in the World*, 8, 15.

20. Skelton, *American Profession of Arms*, 250–53. In 1824 an artillery school of practice was established at Fortress Monroe. The infantry and artillery schools, which existed for almost ten years, trained soldiers in specialized tactics.

21. Ibid., 193; Ripley, *War with Mexico*, 1:94–95; Winders, *Mr. Polk's Army*, 54.

22. Chaparral is a collection of dense, thorny bushes and trees.

23. Skelton, *American Profession of Arms*, 193; Coffman, *Old Army*, 49.

24. Wilcox, *History of the Mexican War*, 73; Lt. Jenks Beamen journal, in Smith and Judah, *Chronicles of the Gringos*, 71.

25. *New Orleans Picayune*, May 16, 1846; Winders, *Mr. Polk's Army*, 69–72; Campbell, "Mexican War Letters," 132. The twelve-month enrollment was important because previously volunteers were recruited for only three months. These "three-month men" could not serve abroad, were problematic for regular officers to use in combat, and were used primarily for local defense and garrisons. As for the public response, in Tennessee, for example, 30,000 men wanted to volunteer for service, but the state's quota was capped at 3,000 troops.

26. Winders, *Mr. Polk's Army*, 69–72; Weigley, *United States Army*, 183. Not all of the 11,000 men that volunteered embarked for the Rio Grande. The War Department later reaffirmed that although Gaines's men had volunteered for six months, by law they could only serve for three. Polk eventually relieved Gaines from command and ordered him to come to Washington, D.C., to face a court of inquiry.

27. Taylor had raised his voice to troublesome volunteers many times throughout his career. During the Black Hawk War, Taylor needed his militia to march to another town in order to prevent a possible siege. When the men objected because they were tired, Taylor yelled: "You are citizen soldiers and some of you may fill high offices but never unless you do your duty. Forward! March!" Hamilton, *Zachary Taylor*, 1:91–103; ZT to Atkinson, June 2, 1832, cited in Bauer, *Zachary Taylor*, 61.

28. Reid, *Scouting Expeditions*, 26, 43; Wilkins, *Highly Irregular Irregulars*, 10; Hanson, *Plains Rifle*, 2; Utley, *Lone Star Justice*, 7–8.

29. *Frontier Times*, 78; Reid, *Scouting Expeditions*, 23; Giddings, *Sketches*, 98. The famed leader of the Texas Rangers, Jack Hays, required new recruits to possess a horse whose value was at least $100 if they were to be considered for his company.

30. Morrison, *Best School in the World*, 97–98, 100; Coffman, *Old Army*, 76–77; Skelton, *American Profession of Arms*, 172, 305, 318–19. The horses were of little use for cavalry training anyway since the academy used them for both artillery and cavalry drilling, even though a very different type of animal was required by each arm.

31. Reid, *Scouting Expeditions*, 37. These are three selected stanzas of a longer song.

32. Webb, *Texas Rangers*, 73–74. In 1842 a Mexican army under Gen. Adrian Woll invaded Texas and took control of San Antonio.

33. Vestal, *Bigfoot Wallace*, 160–61.

34. Chartrand, *Santa Anna's Mexican Army*, 7, 30–31, 41. Mexico purchased 20,000 additional Tower muskets in 1842 and 1844.

35. Ibid., 13, 15, 18. Light cavalry scouted the enemy's advance and acted as skirmishers, rarely engaging in heavy combat. Medium cavalry acted as dragoons, dismounting and fighting as infantry when needed. Heavy cav-

alry units usually carried lances. The horsemen loved the lance so much that many of them acquired and armed themselves with the weapon, and many regiments often had more than the allotted one hundred lancers.

36. Ibid., 7.

2. MEXICAN PREPARATIONS

1. The First Brigade trailed behind the Second, followed by the cavalry. The First Brigade marched with the oxen and artillery, while the Second hauled wagons filled with ammunition. The cavalry was the rearguard. Taylor, *Letters*, 3.

2. Fort Paredes was a pentagonal-shaped earthwork surrounded by a deep moat that ran from the river. Arista had constructed the fort to defend Matamoros from attack. J. Smith, *War with Mexico*, 1:158.

3. One general on the march recalled: "Most of the wagons were broken, many of the oxen were stolen by the wagon masters so they could not continue forward. It was necessary to pull [by hand] some of the wagons during days by the soldiers due to the lack of oxen or because the oxen were so tired." Account by Gen. Antonio María Jáuregui, *Monitor Republicano*, Sept. 11, 1846.

4. On July 9, infantry from the 1st Regiment, the 2nd Light Infantry, the 4th and 10th of the Line Infantry, and two companies of the 6th Regiment departed the city. The 7th and 8th Cavalry regiments accompanied them. The soldiers were not excited about the prospect of moving again. One angry general wrote, "Of course he [Mejía] directed that the injured come with us, the sick, or useless[,] the pieces [of artillery] did not have any mobility and the cargo [artillery] was not accurate enough for a violent operation[,] to march to Monterrey, [these were] guarded by conscripts from the regiments of Mexico and the Morelia battalion." Ibid.

5. J. Smith, *War with Mexico*, 1:214, 215.

6. *Tampico Esperanza*, July 30, 1846; *Seminario Político del Gobierno de Nuevo León*, Aug. 6, 1846.

7. For example, Santa Anna sent troops to Texas and Zacatecas, whose leaders refused to relinquish the autonomy granted to their state under the constitution that Santa Anna had revoked. Fehrenbach, *Fire and Blood*, 382.

8. Balbontin, *Siege at Monterey*, 330.

9. *Monitor Republicano*, Aug. 11, 1846.

10. The Arroyo Santa Lucia is referred to in the writings of American soldiers as the Ojo de Agua Canal. The canal was and still is known as Santa Lucia. "Ojo de Agua" means "spring" in Spanish, but many of the soldiers were not aware of the local name. Discussions with Ahmed Valtier.

11. E. K. Chamberlain to S. C. West, Sept. 28, 1846, in S. Smith, *Chile con Carne*, 96.

12. Proclamation written by Garza y Evia, June 18, 1846 (published in the local paper, June 25, 1846), original draft, Archivo Municipal de Monterrey (hereafter referred to as AMMTY); *Monitor Republicano*, Aug. 22, 1846.

13. Elizondo to Garza y Evia, Apr. 1, 1846, Box 43, Military Group, Archivo General del Estado de Nuevo León (hereafter referred to as AGENL).

14. Mejía to Garza y Evia, Aug. 24, 1846, Box 49, Military Group, AGENL.

15. Balbontin, *Siege at Monterey*, 334.

16. Cossio, *Historia de Nuevo León*, 233.

17. Robinson, *Mexico and Her Military Chieftains*, 259.

18. Garza y Evia to the Ministry of Foreign Relations, Aug. 23, 1846, Box 49, Military Group, AGENL; Robinson, *Mexico and Her Military Chieftains*, 252.

19. *Monitor Republicano*, Aug. 27, 1846, in *El Ciudadano General Pedro de Ampudia.*

20. *Monitor Republicano*, Aug. 17, 1846; *Tampico Esperanza*, Aug. 25, 1846.

21. Balbontin, *Siege at Monterey*, 331, 332; J. Smith, *War with Mexico*, 1:230. At San Luis Potosí 100 additional infantrymen joined the brigade as did 150 lancers.

22. Balbontin, *Siege at Monterey*, 332–33; Cossio, *Historia de Nuevo León*, 234–35.

23. J. Smith, *War with Mexico*, 1:231.

24. Ampudia to Garza y Evia, Aug. 28, 1846, Box 50, Military Group, AGENL; Cossio, *Historia de Nuevo León*, 238, 242.

25. Balbontin, *Siege at Monterey*, 335.

26. Cossio, *Historia de Nuevo León*, 245; Box 1, U.S.–Mexico War, AMMTY.

27. Cossio, *Historia de Nuevo León*, 246; Ampudia to all alcaldes in Nuevo León, Sept. 3, 1846, Civil Topic, AMMTY. Ampudia told affected residents that the government would reimburse them for their loss. He also demanded that nearby alcaldes send men to help fortify the city.

28. Alcáraz et al., *Apuntes Para La Historia*, 69.

29. *Seminario Político del Gobierno de Nuevo León*, July 16, Aug. 13, Sept. 13, 1846, cited in Miguel Ángel González-Quiroga, *Nuevo León Ante La Invasión Norteamericana*, 38–39.

30. Sepulveda to Garza y Evia, Aug. 25, 1846, Box 49, Military Group, AGENL.

31. *Boletín Oficial*, Sept. 16, 1846.

3. MATAMOROS AND THE ARRIVAL OF THE VOLUNTEERS

1. But the same soldier also noted that "such conduct (of the U.S. troops) should make our countrymen proud of their army." Henry, *Campaign Sketches*, 122–23.

2. Sedgwick, *Correspondence*, 1:8. The soldiers were not allowed to slaughter cows owned by local farmers, so the men also purchased all of their beef from local markets. One volunteer killed a giant deer that reportedly field dressed at eight hundred pounds. Officers believed that the dressed deer was a cow and were going to punish the hunter unless he provided antlers to

prove that it was in fact a deer. The soldier found them and kept the animal. Thorpe, *Anecdotes and Letters*, 121–22.

3. U.S. House, *Mexican War Correspondence*, 286, 333. Marcy even provided Taylor with a proclamation written for Mexican citizens that the general should post around Matamoros. It stressed that the war was against the government of Mexico, not the Mexican people. The document read in part: "Our late effort to terminate all difficulties by peaceful negotiation has been rejected by the dictator Paredes, and our minister of peace, whom your rulers had agreed to receive, has been refused a hearing. He has been treated with indignity and insult, and Paredes has announced that war exists between us. This war, thus first proclaimed by him, has been acknowledged as an existing fact by our President and Congress, with perfect unanimity, and will be prosecuted with vigor and energy against your army and rulers, but those of the Mexican people who remain neutral will not be molested." Ibid., 286.

4. "Recollections of the Mexican War," Apr. 15, 1900, 52.

5. Jenkins, *History of the War*, 240; Henry, *Campaign Sketches*, 114; Barbour, *Journals*, 67; Reid, *Scouting Expeditions*, 162. At Fort Paredes the Americans found destroyed ammunition boxes and cannons. Col. David Twiggs, who was appointed governor of Matamoros, was told by the city's prefect that there was no war materiel hidden. A skeptical Twiggs questioned other sources in the city and eventually found a wealth of supplies, including muskets, ammunition, clothing, saddles, and cannons. His men also discovered one mortar in the bottom of a well and pulled the two cannons out of the river. The biggest prize was two gorgeous mahogany gun carriages designed to hold 32-pound tubes. American artillerists also saved the copper grape canisters for their guns. Most Mexican artillery munitions were copper, which the soldiers believed poisoned those it struck.

6. *Republic of the Rio Grande*, June 30, 1846; Wilcox, *History of the Mexican War*, 66–67. Many were aghast at the sight of the Mexicans' grotesque wounds. "In the four or five [hospitals] I visited," wrote one surgeon, "I saw 300 who were more or less severely wounded, mostly with grape and round shot." Some of the injured Mexicans did recover, however, and they perched themselves cheerfully in the doorways and smiled to passersby. A reporter wrote that he could not believe how happy such men were after all they had endured. "The Mexicans must be more tenacious of life than any other race," he wrote. Jarvis, "Army's Surgeons Notes," 102.

7. Henry, *Campaign Sketches*, 110; Barbour, *Journals*, 66. The soldiers remarked on the city's gloomy, fortress-like feel. One observed, "The flat roofs, huge, massive doors, and large grated windows, give the whole place a cold, prison-like appearance." Robertson, *Reminiscences*, 105.

8. "Recollections of the Mexican War," Apr. 15, 1900, 53.

9. Barbour, *Journals*, 85–86, 111.

10. Skelton, *American Profession of Arms*, 194–95, 200; Bauer, *Mexican War*, 35–36. Prior to 1834, an officer also could receive a brevet for ten years of service in the same grade. Brevet officers could be put in command at a grade equivalent to his brevet and receive the higher salary also under these earlier guidelines. Skelton, *American Profession of Arms*, 194.

11. Wallace, *General William Jenkins Worth*, 1–45, 52–54; Peterson, *History of the Wars*, 177–88.

12. Barbour, *Journals*, 72.

13. Weigley, *United States Army*, 183; J. Smith, *War with Mexico*, 1:205.

14. Wilkins, *Highly Irregular Irregulars*, 35; Webb, *Texas Rangers*, 94. Johnston graduated from West Point eighth in his class and was a regimental adjutant in the Black Hawk War. He left the army and moved to Texas because his wife was ill and enrolled as a private in the Texas Revolutionary army. For more on Johnston's background, see Johnston, *Life of Albert Sidney Johnston*; and Roland, *Albert Sidney Johnston*.

15. ZT to AG, July 31, 1846, in U.S. House, *Mexican War Correspondence*, 321.

16. Weigley, *United States Army*, 183.

17. One soldier recorded: "We really get but little sleep, and our camp at night is filled with men wandering about for shelter from these intolerable pests [mosquitoes], and filling the air with imprecations upon their ruthless assailants. No kind of clothing is proof or protection against their bites; they pierce through, with their stings, pantaloons, drawers, stockings, and (some deliberately assert) boots. All night long, without the slightest intermission, they continue their attacks, and the assertion of many that they are nearly driven crazy is not much exaggerated." Kenly, *Memoir*, 43.

18. Meade, *Life and Letters*, 110; John Reynolds to his sister, Sept. 3, 1846, John F. Reynolds Papers, Franklin and Marshall College Archives and Special Collections; Hill, *Fighter from Way Back*, 2.

19. Barbour, *Journals*, 89; Barna Upton to Friends, July 9, 1846, Barna N. Upton Mexican War Letters, 1842–48, Yale Collection of Western Americana, Beinecke Rare Book and Manuscript Library; *Republic of the Rio Grande*, June 1, 1846. Few records capture the wide extent of the crimes. In most instances they went unreported if the perpetrator was sent home by Taylor. Captain Henry notes that "of late there have been several disgraceful riots in the city, in which some of the volunteers were conspicuous, arising from the lax state of discipline in some of the regiments." Henry, *Campaign Sketches*, 124.

20. Skelton, *American Profession of Arms*, 330–31; Haynes, *Polk and the Expansionist Impulse*, 109; Campbell to David Campbell, July 11, 1846, in Campbell, "Mexican War Letters," 137; Johnson, *Gallant Little Army*, 146; Barna Upton to his father, July 29, 1846, Upton Mexican War Letters; Dana, *Monterrey Is Ours*, 85. The Mexican War journals of regular officers are littered with both contempt for the Mexicans and a diehard belief that Americans could exploit and harvest Mexico's resources much more effectively.

21. "I observe you complain of the annoyance of the Volunteers," Taylor wrote a friend, "they [the volunteers' complaints] are trifling to what I have to undergo and submit to, but which I will try and get through in the best way I can and with at least all the good feelings and temper I can command even should they drive me out of my tent." Taylor, *Letters*, 8.

22. Skelton, *American Profession of Arms*, 193, 217; Coffman, *Old Army*, 49. Many West Pointers left the army, frustrated with its broken per-

sonnel system, which did not allow for timely advancement. Private businesses, especially in the transportation industry, eagerly took on these West Pointers, valuing the quality of the scientific curriculum taught at the academy. Skelton, *American Profession of Arms*, 217.

23. Kendall, *Dispatches*, 8–13. McCleod graduated fifty-sixth in his class, which must have been very close to the bottom, considering most classes graduated around fifty students. He started a newspaper in Matamoros called the *Republic of the Rio Grande*, which later changed its name to *The American Flag*. Haile attended West Point from 1836 to 1837. Heitman, *Historical Register*, 1:311. For more information about the advent of the "penny press" and journalists during the Mexican War, see Mitchel Roth, "Journalism and the U.S.–Mexican War," in Francaviglia and Richmond, *Dueling Eagles*, 103–22.

24. Marcy to ZT, June 8, 1846, in U.S. House, *Mexican War Correspondence*, 324–25.

25. ZT to AG, July 2, 1846, ibid., 331.

26. ZT to AG, May 21, 1846, ibid., 300; Grant, *Memoirs*, 104. The general first mentioned Monterrey in official correspondence on May 21, 1846, when he referred to it as the "first city of importance" in the San Juan valley. ZT to AG, May 21, 1846, 300.

27. Duval, *Adventures of Big Foot Wallace*, 178; Stapp, *Prisoners of Perote*, 53, 61. The Mier prisoners referred to Canales as a "cowardly tyrant" and a "brute."

28. Reid, *Scouting Expeditions*, 46–47. The Texans also used sharp tactics to stay alive on long scouts. At night, for example, McCulloch's men would approach a ranch from the same direction as Mexican troops. They usually totally surprised the occupants. Stunned ranchero owners would often provide detailed information about Mexican troops movements to the Texans.

29. Kendall, *Dispatches*, 57.

30. U.S. House, *Mexican War Correspondence*, 306, 553–54. Taylor spent much of his time thinking and writing about steamers. In his mind their absence was the only thing preventing him from moving to Camargo and into Mexico's interior. The general was furious with the Quartermaster Department for not providing the boats sooner. He believed that Thomas Sydney Jesup, head of the department, wanted his campaign to fail.

31. Bliss to Miles, July 5, 1846, Army in Mexico, Letter Book, Records of the Adjutant General's Office (hereafter referred to as AGO), Record Group (hereafter referred to as RG) 94, National Archives (hereafter referred to as NA); Bliss to Miles, July 8, 1846, ibid. Miles's men marched to Reynosa to collect McCulloch's company and the two pieces of Bragg's battery under Lieutenant Thomas. The volunteers, along with three companies of the 7th, marched by land to Camargo. The remainder, including Captain Miles, ascended the river in steamers.

32. Taylor, *Letters*, 24; Reid, *Scouting Expeditions*, 55. Rain poured almost constantly on the Texans, who though accustomed to rough campsites, also had their limits. "Our camp," one Texan remembered, "which was near the river bank, was soon ankle deep in mud; the heavy rain continued to

fall incessantly; we were unable to cook our food, or to sleep with any degree of comfort, for our clothes and blankets were thoroughly saturated with water night and day." Eventually Colonel Wilson agreed that they could move into an abandoned cotton shed just outside of town. Again he was reluctant, concerned about having the Texans too close to the townspeople. Ibid.

33. Reid, *Scouting Expeditions*, 53. While at Reynosa, the Texans one night learned that Canales was at a party not far from the town. They stormed the house and surprised the revelers, but there was no sign of Canales. Rather than revealing the true nature of their mission, the Texans told them that they had heard music and decided to investigate. A volunteer described what happened next: "They [the Mexicans] appeared perfectly satisfied with the explanation, and insisted that we should join the dance and partake of the refreshments. Two or three of the best dancers in our squad laid down their guns, and picking out the prettiest girls for their partners, took their places in the set. . . . [W]e had seen some pretty tall dancing in our time, but we think the feats we witnessed that night, were a little ahead of anything in that line we ever saw before." Ibid., 53, 56–57.

34. "Recollections of the Mexican War," June 15, 1900, 56.

35. Reid, *Scouting Expeditions*, 61. A regular at Reynosa, observing the chaotic scene, recalled, "at dark, hearing a great noise, I looked out in that direction and saw them [the Texans] all on top of it [the cotton shed] dancing a war dance to the infinite amusement of the natives who were collected below." Dilworth, *March to Monterrey*, 37.

36. Meade, *Life and Letters*, 115. He had eight steamboats on hand, with four more on the way.

37. ZT to AG, Aug. 31, 1846, in U.S. House, *Mexican War Correspondence*, 322; Blanchard, Diary and Biography, Louisiana State University Special Collections, Hill Memorial Library, 12–13. Besides Blanchard's men, the discharged Louisianans left behind something else of value: quality, strong-bred American horses. The wiry mustangs of Mexico were unfit for U.S. dragoons or light artillery batteries, so the Louisianans sold their horses to the army for, as one official recorded, a "price [that] has not always been moderate, but in no instance extravagant." Assistant Quartermaster General to Quartermaster General Thomas Jesup, July 28, 1846, in U.S. House, *Mexican War Correspondence*, 674. Blanchard told Major Barbour that his company was the chivalry of Louisiana simmered down and purified of all dross. Barbour commented in his diary: "We will see if they maintain by their deeds their title to this high character." Blanchard had graduated from West Point in 1837 with Joseph Hooker and Braxton Bragg, both of whom were in Mexico with Taylor. Barbour, *Journals*, 99; Cullum, *Biographical Register*, 439.

38. Meade, *Life and Letters*, 117.

4. MATAMOROS TO MONTERREY

1. Meade, *Life and Letters*, 114. Others tried to wade through the marshy stretches. "Imagine to your mind's eye," mused one soldier about the crossings, "three thousand men, feeling their way, wading and swaying here

and there, holding their muskets high over their head to preserve them from the water, while now and then some unlucky fellows would souse into a hole, and tumble over out of sight, until he could scramble up, or be hauled out by his comrades." *Niles Register,* Sept. 26, 1846.

2. Kenly, *Memoir,* 62; Dana, *Monterrey Is Ours,* 98; Henry, *Campaign Sketches,* 136. Marching in darkness had other benefits besides cooler weather. Soldiers later recalled gorgeous clear nights, a beautiful moon, and bright stars that stretched across the sky. Captain Henry remembered that after cresting one hill, he looked behind him and saw his comrades lined up for miles in the moonlight. "None but one entirely devoid of feeling could resist the pleasure derived from so glorious a scene." Henry, *Campaign Sketches,* 143, 151.

3. Kenly, *Memoir,* 63. The army did not possess enough wagons to haul all of the incapacitated soldiers, so most were left by the roadside. Comrades marked the location where these men fell out and returned with a small party as soon as they found water. Sometimes the men were there when they returned, sometimes not. "Very [many men] fell out of our ranks," Lieutenant Dilworth noted. "They would keep up with the guard for a time and then fall out to the side of the road. . . . Having no wagon with me, I was obliged to leave them." Dilworth, *March to Monterrey,* 46.

4. Lander, *Trip to the Wars,* 24; Kenly, *Memoir,* 63.

5. Robertson, *Reminiscences,* 85; Lander, *Trip to the Wars,* 23; Sedgwick, *Correspondence,* 1:9. The soldiers could not believe how much the Rio Grande meandered. "Imagine four of the crookedest things in the world," one soldier wrote, "then imagine four more twice as crooked, and then fancy to yourself a large river three times as crooked as all these put together, and you have a faint idea of the crooked disposition of this almighty crooked river." John Kenly agreed. "The windings of the Rio Grande are remarkable," he wrote. "There is one hacienda on its banks which a boat passes in front of seven times after coming in sight of, and before actually reaching, it." Thorpe, *Anecdotes and Letters,* 45; Kenly, *Memoir,* 49.

6. Robertson, *Reminiscences,* 109; Kendall, *Dispatches,* 69; Madison Mills Diary, Aug. 3, 1846, Filson Historical Society. The river rose about sixty feet over its original water mark, the resulting flood destroying about 800 houses.

7. *New Orleans Picayune,* Aug. 16, 1846.

8. Robertson, *Reminiscences,* 109; *New Orleans Picayune,* Aug. 25, 1846. Ultimately, over a mile of tents, pitched in two rows with each company's colors displayed, lined the San Juan's edge. It was quite a site for steamboat passengers who passed by on their way to Camargo. Scribner, *Camp Life,* 22.

9. Campbell to David Campbell, Aug. 28, 1846, in Campbell, "Mexican War Letters," 140; Robertson, *Reminiscences,* 109; Zenith Matthews Diary, Sept. 7, 1846, Southwestern University, Special Collections. William Campbell, commander of the 1st Tennessee, believed that his regiment lost one man a day to disease. In another example of how many soldiers were ill in Camargo, one volunteer estimated that four to seven men died a day from his regiment. Giddings, *Sketches,* 83; Robertson, *Reminiscences,* 111.

10. Kendall, *Dispatches,* 86. When Taylor learned about Camargo's

sickly condition, he issued a new directive. "There being no accommodations for the sick at Camargo," the order read, "it is directed by the Commanding General that the Volunteer regiments under orders for that place, leave all their serious cases or those not likely to recover in a few days in the General Hospital at Matamoros." Unfortunately the order came too late; most of the sick were already on their way to Camargo when it was issued. Order located in Army of Occupation, Orders, AGO, RG 94, NA.

11. In Camargo a Texan recognized two Mexican spies whom he had detained previously in Matamoros. He searched the men and discovered army commissions and circulars to encourage desertion among Taylor's troops. One was a private and the other an officer in Canales's cavalry unit. "Recollections of the Mexican War," Aug. 15, 1900, 120; Mills Diary, Aug. 3, 1846.

12. Hazlitt to the Commander of the Right Wing of the Army, July 26, 1846, Gillespie's jacket file, Compiled Service Records, Office of the Secretary of War, RG 107, NA; Barton, *Texas Volunteers*, 44.

13. Capt. Dixon Miles, who led the advance into Camargo, had forbidden McCulloch's horsemen to scout outside of that town. Before Taylor arrived, the Texan begged the general to allow him to scout the nearby area. "I could explore the road to Monterrey as far as you may deem proper," he suggested in the letter, "at best we could visit some large ranchos in the country and conciliate the people." McCulloch was concerned, because "I know little about how the people are disposed to us in the country." Taylor thought the idea a good one. "The last named officer [McCulloch] is an excellent partisan," he told Worth, "and may be usefully employed in examining the country in your front so far as deemed prudent." Bliss to Worth, July 19, 1846, Army in Mexico, Letter Book, AGO, RG 94; McCulloch to ZT, July 20, 1846, McCulloch's jacket file, Compiled Service Records, RG 107.

14. ZT to AG, Aug. 10, 1846, in U.S. House, *Mexican War Correspondence*, 408; Reid, *Scouting Expeditions*, 82.

15. Both men turned out to be Mexican infantry.

16. Barna Upton to Friends, Aug. 28, 1846, Barna N. Upton Mexican War Letters, 1842–48, Yale Collection of Western Americana, Beinecke Rare Book and Manuscript Library. *Niles Register*, Sept. 26, 1846. As Kenly observed: "No one can tell from whence they [the rumors] come; the hardiest has not dared to say General Taylor said so and so, but rumor says we are going to Monterrey. And where that is, and how we are going to get there, rumor, as yet, knoweth not." Kenly, *Memoirs*, 65; .

17. Ephraim Kirby Smith to his mother, n.d., in Smith and Judah, *Chronicles of the Gringos*, 76; Barbour, *Journals*, 99.

18. Order 112, Sept. 2, 1846, in U.S. House, *Mexican War Correspondence*, 503; Order 108, Aug. 28, 1846, ibid., 500. The 1st Mississippi was officially named the last regiment to Monterrey on September 2.

19. Gordon, *Jefferson Davis*, 30.

20. Bauer, *Zachary Taylor*, 69–70, 113–14.

21. Giddings, *Sketches*, 99. The volunteers left behind were organized under two temporary brigades commanded by Maj. Gen. Robert Patterson. The brigades included the 2nd Kentucky, 2nd Ohio, 2nd Tennessee, the Geor-

gia and Alabama regiments, and any volunteers excused from the regiments going to Monterrey—in total about 3,500 men. Order 108, Aug. 28, 1846, 500–501.

22. Dana, *Monterrey Is Ours*, 110.

23. Lander, *Trip to the Wars*, 28.

24. Ibid. This account, based on Lander, differs from another written by Johnston's son, who says that 318 voted to disband and 224 to reenlist, much more than the 80 Lander mentions. But Lander was not only in Johnston's regiment but also present at the reenlistment event described. Others corroborated the emotional tone that Johnston undertook when addressing his men. Captain Henry said that the colonel "addressed them in a patriotic strain." Barbour said that Johnston was "disgusted and mortified and did not hesitate to tell his men so to their teeth." Regardless of the details, the result was the same—Johnston had no regiment, and the Texans were sent home. Henry, *Campaign Sketches*, 152; Barbour, *Journals*, 101.

25. ZT to AG, Aug. 31, 1846, in U.S. House, *Mexican War Correspondence*, 322–23. Shivers's new company also contained some of Johnston's original Texas infantrymen. Alexander Lander was one of them.

26. Giddings, *Sketches*, 81.

27. Bauer, *Zachary Taylor*, 27–30.

28. Taylor's orders to Hays emphasized that his mission was to assure the population that the army was there to fight the government, not the people, of Mexico: "The objective of this expedition is to exhibit a respectable force in the neighborhood of San Fernando and to communicate with the alcaldes and civil authorities on certain points. . . . It will be your duty, and the General cannot too much insist upon its importance, to correct these impressions among the people and to restrain the evil influence of the authorities. For this purpose the General directs that you seek interviews with the different alcaldes and represent to them that we have entered the country with no disposition to make war upon the inhabitants." It is amusing to think that Taylor sent a group of "Los Diablos Tejanos" on what amounted to a diplomatic expedition. Bliss to Hays, Aug. 3, 1846, Army in Mexico, Letter Book, AGO, RG 94.

29. Order 109, in U.S. House, *Mexican War Correspondence*, 501–502. Mules are a cross between a male donkey and a female horse. Most outdoorsmen prefer them to horses or donkeys because they are hardy, sure footed, and can carry a heavy load. They also have thick, coarse fur that protects them from inclement weather. Four pack mules were assigned to each regiment's staff. Taylor learned of Grant's success as quartermaster and did not want him reassigned. His adjutant wrote Colonel Garland, "The Commanding General desires that you will retain Lieut. Grant in his position as Quartermaster to the 4th Infantry—his services being represented as very useful by Major Allen." Bliss to Garland, Aug. 29, 1846, Army in Mexico, Letter Book, AGO, RG 94; Lewis, *Captain Sam Grant*, 168.

30. Reid, *Scouting Expeditions*, 104; Grant, *Memoirs*, 106; The arrieros quickly earned the respect of the soldiers. They were tough men who worked hard and were good at what they did. Indeed, as the soldiers observed, packing a mule took skill and patience. The load had to be perfectly balanced

on both sides and bound tightly. Taylor's order emphasizing the use of large animals forced the muleteers to collect wild mules that were less inclined to wear packs than their domesticated brethren. These beasts would roll on the ground to rip the cargo from their body. If they were carrying tent poles, they would run them into a tree so the whole pack would fall off. Most often the ornery creatures would simply "kick and buck" until the pack came off. Many of the marching men carrying their own burdens might have appreciated this behavior. One soldier complained that the straps of his knapsack were so tight that he could hardly breathe. "The pain at time was so excessive that I became bewildered, and all things seemed to swim around me." Scribner, *Camp Life*, 48.

31. Campbell to David Campbell, Aug. 28, 1846, in Campbell, "Mexican War Letters," 141. D. H. Hill believed that Worth was going to march his men to their deaths. The general "has been almost a mad man ever since [he returned to the army] and now publicly declared his intention to sacrifice himself and Brigade if necessary that he may regain his lost reputation." Other soldiers shared these beliefs. Hill, *Fighter from Way Back*, 11.

32. Hill, *Fighter from Way Back*, 11; Henry, *Campaign Sketches*, 179. Colonel Wood's Texans marched with the mules for a while but were replaced by the 4th Artillery—Hill's unit.

33. Giddings, *Sketches*, 114; Robertson, *Reminiscences*, 121. Major Giddings added further: "The first day's march was the most weary and painful of the campaign. No soldier of our regiment will ever forget his sufferings on that unhappy day." Giddings, *Sketches*, 114.

34. Henry, *Campaign Sketches*, 177. Luther Giddings agreed with Henry's poetic assessment: "One enchanting little spot I frequently visited, where the brook danced and sang through banks of flowers, shaded by luxuriant lemon and fig trees, the interlacing branches of which offered a welcome shade and screen to the bather." Giddings, *Sketches*, 118.

35. Taylor, *Letters*, 54. Taylor appreciated the intelligence. "Your communication of yesterday with a copy of 'El monitor' [A Mexican newspaper] and the 'pronuncamiento' [Ampudia's] was received this morning," Taylor's adjutant wrote to Worth. "The Commanding General directs me to thank you for this prompt attention in forwarding important and interesting intelligence. He finds in this news an additional motive for pushing his operations toward Monterrey and is urging everything forward as rapidly as possible." Bliss to Worth, Aug. 28, 1846, Army in Mexico, Letter Book, AGO, RG 94.

36. Prior to the advance's departure on September 4, Taylor sent McCulloch's and Gillespie's companies with Lieutenant Meade to scout the road to Marin. A prisoner indicated that Mexicans under Canales and Lt. Col. José María Carrasco were along the route, but the Texans did not meet any resistance. Worth dispatched 300 men from Child's battalion to support the Texans because he feared the horsemen might get cut off and isolated from the rest of the army . Reid, *Scouting Expeditions*, 118–19.

37. Kenly, *Memoir*, 88. Taylor micromanaged his army's marching dispositions as it entered more hostile country. "Each division," the general specified in Order 115, "will be followed immediately by its baggage train and supply train, with a strong rear guard. The ordnance train, under Captain

Ramsay, will march with the 2d division, between its baggage and supply trains, and will come under the protection of the guards of that division." Order 115, in U.S. House, *Mexican War Correspondence,* 505.

38. Barbour, *Journals,* 104; Kenly, *Memoir,* 90. Kenly declared regarding the landscape, "But in a single word I can say with truth that it exceeds in picturesque beauty my most romantic dreams of nature's loveliest and grandest charms." Ibid.

39. Kenly, *Memoir,* 91–92.

40. "Recollections of the Mexican War," Aug. 15, 1900, 123, 124; Mills Diary, Sept. 16, 1846.

41. Reid, *Scouting Expeditions,* 134; Henry, *Campaign Sketches,* 187.

42. Taylor, *Letters,* 57; Robert Hazlitt to his sister, Sept. 16, 1846, Robert Hazlitt Papers, U.S. Military Academy Library, Special Collections.

43. Henry, *Campaign Sketches,* 186. Ampudia could have posted his men on the steep slopes of the Rinconada Pass and plugged the road with artillery. This is the defensive posture that Taylor took months later at Buena Vista. Lavendar, *Climax at Buena Vista,* 148–50, 155.

44. Mahon, *Second Seminole War,* 226–29. See also Bauer, *Zachary Taylor,* 78–83.

45. Hill, *Fighter from Way Back,* 16; Barbour, *Journals,* 107.

46. Balbontin, *Siege at Monterey,* 335.

47. Henry, *Campaign Sketches,* 190.

48. Ibid., 191; Reid, *Scouting Expeditions,* 141.

49. Cossio, *Historia de Nuevo León,* 247.

50. Reid, *Scouting Expeditions,* 141. Ben McCulloch, who Taylor trusted, might have put in a good word for Gillespie.

51. Giddings, *Sketches,* 144.

52. Ibid.

53. Ibid., 139; Kenly, *Memoir,* 95.

5. TAYLOR'S DIVERSION

1. Zenith Matthews Diary, Sept. 18, 1846, Southwestern University, Special Collections. There were no walnut trees in the grove, despite its name.

2. Meade, *Life and Letters,* 26.

3. Thorpe, *Our Army at Monterrey,* 131–33.

4. Thorpe, *Anecdotes and Letters,* 60.

5. "Recollections of the Mexican War," Aug. 15, 1900, 125.

6. Ibid.

7. Meade, *Life and Letters,* 133.

8. This was the second time that Taylor had asked Duncan to perform a job normally reserved for an engineer. The general probably trusted his talented artillerist to provide a good assessment on whether artillery could successfully navigate the terrain and effectively contribute to an assault on the city from the west.

9. ZT to AG, Oct. 9, 1846, Army in Mexico, Letter Book, AGO, RG 94, NA.

10. Reid, *Scouting Expeditions,* 112.

11. Ibid., 151. Reid suspected something more substantial might have been afoot when he saw orderlies running "to and fro" throughout the camp.

12. "Recollections of the Mexican War," Nov. 15, 1900, 152.

13. Reid, *Scouting Expeditions*, 154, 155.

14. Dilworth, *March to Monterrey*, 67–68.

15. Barbour, *Journals*, 108; Cullum, *Biographical Register*, 1:581–82; *Daily Commonwealth*, Jan. 2, 1847, in Barbour, *Journals*, ix.

16. George Ramsey, an ordnance officer, executed the mortar. Capt. Lucien Webster, an artilleryman, directed the howitzers. George Ramsey to Col. John Mercier, Dec. 8, 1851, author's personal collection.

17. Johnson, *Gallant Little Army*, 21–22; J. Smith, *War with Mexico*, 2:48; Thorpe, *Our Army at Monterrey*, 50.

18. Henry, *Campaign Sketches*, 234.

19. Kendall, *Dispatches*, 116. Lieutenant Pope had asked Garland to support Mansfield's reconnaissance. Reid, *Scouting Expeditions*, 170.

20. Stevens, *Rogue's March*, 58, 91–94, 102–103.

21. Henry, *Campaign Sketches*, 194; Thorpe, *Our Army at Monterrey*, 51.

22. Col. Henry Kinney told Mansfield that entering the city at this point, without knowing the strength or location of the enemy, was dangerous. Mansfield ignored Kinney's warning. See Thorpe, *Our Army at Monterrey*, 50; Mansfield to ZT, Oct. 9, 1846; and Backus, "Brief Sketch," 207.

23. *Niles Register*, Nov. 7, 1846.

24. Henry, *Campaign Sketches*, 194–95. As Garland described in his official report, "We soon found ourselves in narrow streets, where we received a most destructive fire from three directions." Garland to Twiggs, Sept. 29, 1846, Army in Mexico, Letter Book, AGO, RG 94.

25. Henry Wilson to Don Carlos Buell, Sept. 27, 1846, Henry Wilson Papers, Louisiana State University Special Collections, Hill Memorial Library.

26. George Meade to Col. J. J. Abert, Sept. 28, 1846, Records of the Office of the Chief Engineers, RG 77, NA; ZT to AG, Oct. 9, 1846, Army in Mexico, Letter Book, AGO, RG 94.

27. *New Orleans Picayune*, Nov. 4, 1846; Wilson to Buell, Sept. 27, 1846.

28. Backus, "Brief Sketch," 210–11. Garland wrote that Mansfield moved about "seeming to have no care for himself." Garland to Twiggs, Sept. 29, 1846. Engineer John Sanders was another long-serving veteran with Taylor. Both he and Mansfield had graduated second in their respective classes. Sanders's accomplishment is more notable since West Point's curriculum was more mature and difficult when he attended the school in 1830. Heitman, *Historical Register*, vol. 1; Cullum, *Biographical Register*.

29. *Niles Register*, Nov. 7, 1846. When Watson's wife gave birth to a girl in the United States not long after her husband's death, she performed the baby's christening over Watson's corpse and named the girl "Monterey" in memory of the battle. Thorpe, *Anecdotes and Letters*, 21; Henry, *Campaign Sketches*, 195.

30. *Niles Register*, Nov. 7, 1846. One soldier in Watson's battalion wrote: "His loss is deplored by all who knew his generosity of heart and

chivalry of character. His loss to me, individually, is great, but to the battalion it is irreparable." Ibid.

31. John Reynolds to Jane Reynolds, Dec. 6, 1846, John F. Reynolds Papers, Franklin and Marshall College Archives and Special Collections.

32. French, *Two Wars*, 62.

33. Balbontin, *Siege at Monterey*, 338.

34. Peterson, *History of the Wars*, 169–76.

35. Grant, *Memoirs*, 110–11.

36. Thorpe, *Our Army at Monterrey*, 142–44. The soldiers thought that Graham was dead and were stunned to learn after the battle that he was still alive. A surgeon dressed his wounds, and the lieutenant survived until October 12, when his body gave way to illness. Taylor visited Graham repeatedly during his recovery.

37. Robertson, *Reminiscences*, 138; Daniel Russell to Jefferson Davis, Sept. 26, 1846, in *Papers of Jefferson Davis* (hereafter referred to as *POJD*), 3:48.

38. Campbell to David Campbell, Sept. 28, 1846, in Campbell, "Mexican War Letters," 143; Chamberlain to West, Sept. 28, 1846, in S. Smith, *Chile con Carne*, 88.

39. Robertson, *Reminiscences*, 139.

40. Campbell to Quitman, Sept. 27, 1846, Army in Mexico, Letter Book, AGO, RG 94; Robertson, *Reminiscences*, 139; Campbell to David Campbell, Sept. 28, 1846, in Campbell, "Mexican War Letters," 144. The sword was eventually returned to Captain Allen's father by the regiment. One of his soldiers wrote: "Before his death I heard him often remark, that he had assured his father that that sword should never be dishonored in his son's hands; and that pledge has been fulfilled. The sword will again be returned to you, as it has been secured for that purpose." D. Hubbard to Capt Allen's Father, Oct. 5, 1846, in Rowles, *Life and Character of Capt. Wm. B. Allen*, 96.

41. Hubbard to Capt. Allen's Father, Oct. 5, 1846, 96; Davis to John Jenkins, Nov. 16, 1846, in *POJD*, 87; Robertson, *Reminiscences*, 140; Daniel Russell to Davis, Sept. 26, 1846, in *POJD*, 48.

42. Chance, *Davis's Mexican War Regiment*, 45; Reuben Downing to Davis, Sept. 26, 1846, in *POJD*, 44; Russell to Davis, Sept. 26, 1846, 48.

43. Accounts differ as to how close the Mississippians were to the fort, with soldiers believing that they were anywhere from 50 to 150 yards away. The discrepancies probably are a result of the giant arc the regiment formed, so that the distance from each company to the wall varied depending on its location in the formation. Ibid.

44. Balbontin, *Siege at Monterey*, 339.

45. John McManus to Davis, Oct. 18, 1846, in *POJD*, 67; "Sketches of Our Volunteer Officers," 10–12; Chance, *Davis's Mexican War Regiment*, 45.

46. "Sketches of Our Volunteer Officers."

47. John Jenkins to Davis, Nov. 16, 1846, in *POJD*, 87; "Sketches of Our Volunteer Officers," 10. Many of the soldiers referred to this hole as a "sally port," which is a doorway into a fort, while others referred to it as an "open embrasure."

48. Hubbard to Capt Allen's Father, Oct. 5, 1846, 95; Robertson, *Reminiscences*, 140; Quitman to Hamer, Sept. 29, 1846; Cheatham to his sister, Oct. 16, 1846. At the same time, General Quitman ordered the second in command of the Tennessee regiment to storm the fort by bayonet. Campbell did not hear Quitman because he was on the opposite side of the line. Quitman to Hamer, Sept. 29, 1846.

49. Chance, *Davis's Mexican War Regiment*, 47–48.

50. Jefferson Davis, "Memorandum on the Battle of Monterrey," Dec. 31, 1846, in *POJD*, 103; "Sketches of Our Volunteer Officers," 10; Chance, *Davis's Mexican War Regiment*, 47.

51. Campbell to David Campbell, Sept. 28, 1846, in Campbell, "Mexican War Letters," 144; Jenkins to Davis, Nov. 16, 1846, 87–88. After the battle the Mississippians and Tennesseans argued about which regiment entered the fort first. Davis took offense at Campbell's claim that the Tennesseans penetrated the stronghold before the Mississippians. In fact Davis was probably correct since his men benefited from having an opening directly in front of them. Either way, both units entered the garrison with few Mexican soldiers remaining inside.

52. Interestingly, Taylor commended Twiggs in his official report. "Gen. Twiggs, though quite unwell, joined me at this point, and was instrumental in causing the artillery captured from the enemy to be placed in battery." Colonel Campbell thought differently, referring to Twiggs as an "old Granny" who was "unfit for a commander." Campbell to David Campbell, Sept. 28, 1846, in Campbell, "Mexican War Letters," 145; Russell to Davis, Oct. 18, 1846, *POJD*, 70.

53. Butler to ZT, Sept. 30, 1846, Army in Mexico, Letter Book, AGO, RG 94; Hamer to Thomas [Butler], Sept. 25, 1846, ibid.

54. *Niles Register*, Nov. 14, 1846. "We moved rapidly through a labyrinth of lanes and gardens," Maj. Luther Giddings recalled, "without knowing or seeing upon what point of the enemy's line we were about to strike. At every step discharges from the batteries in front became more deadly." Giddings, *Sketches*, 169.

55. Butler to Bliss, Sept. 30, 1846, Army in Mexico, Letter Book, AGO, RG 94.

56. Davis to Quitman, Sept. 26, 1846, in *POJD*, 28.

57. James Taylor to Davis, Sept. 27, 1846, ibid., 51.

58. Russell to Davis, Oct. 18, 1846, ibid., 71; Davis, "Memorandum on the Battle of Monterrey," 104.

59. Thorpe, *Anecdotes and Letters*, 76.

60. ZT to AG, Oct. 9, 1846, Army in Mexico, Letter Book, AGO, RG 94.

61. Giddings, *Sketches*, 172.

62. The next day he and other U.S. soldiers buried the woman "amid showers of grape and roundshot . . . expecting every moment to have another grave to dig for one of ourselves." "Touching Incidents," *Louisville Journal*, Dec. 19,1846 (reprinted in *Niles National Register*, vol. 71), in Smith and Judah, *Chronicles of the Gringos*, 90.

63. Giddings, *Sketches*, 175.

64. Davis, "Memorandum on the Battle of Monterrey," 104.

65. Butler to ZT, Sept. 30, 1846.

66. Henry, *Campaign Sketches*, 197–98; Garland to Twiggs, Sept. 29, 1846.

67. Alcáraz et al., *Apuntes Para La Historia*, 74; *Niles Register*, Dec. 19, 1846. In *Apuntes Para La Historia de La Guerra Entre México Y Los Estados Unidos*, Mexican historians claim that the defending infantry ran out of ammunition and executed a bayonet charge. There is little evidence, however, that such a counterattack took place. A charge may have been contemplated by the Mexicans, but no American at the bridge recorded such a move. More importantly, there was no reason for them to rush the Americans since Mexican musket and cannon fire had prevented them from making any headway across the bridge.

68. Henry, *Campaign Sketches*, 198.

69. Grant, *Memoirs*, 115–16. In the road Captain Henry said the soldiers were "exposed to an incessant fire of bullets, ball, and shells." Henry, *Campaign Sketches*, 200.

70. Russell to Davis, Oct. 18, 1846, in *POJD*, 72.

71. Hooker to William P. Johnston, June 3, 1875, in Johnston, *Life of Albert Sidney Johnston*, 141.

72. Giddings, *Sketches*, 180; *Niles Register*, Nov. 14, 1846; Chance, *Davis's Mexican War Regiment*, 50; Russell to Davis, Oct. 18, 1846, 73.

73. Hooker to Johnston, June 3, 1875, 141; Hamer to Butler, Sept. 25, 1846.

74. Infantry often formed into a square as a defensive maneuver against attacking cavalry, especially when protecting a confined area. This concept was used successfully at Palo Alto to defend a supply train during the battle. Wilcox, *History of the Mexican War*, 57.

75. Barbour, *Journals*, 183–84.

76. Reid, *Scouting Expeditions*, 196.

77. Chamberlain to West, Sept. 28, 1846, in S. Smith, *Chile con Carne*, 90; *Niles Register*, Nov. 14, 1846.

78. "Sketches of Our Volunteer Officers," 10–11. McClung would return to Mississippi and lived until 1855, when he committed suicide.

79. Henry, *Campaign Sketches*, 201.

80. Campbell to David Campbell, Sept. 28, 1846, in Campbell, "Mexican War Letters," 145.

81. Interestingly, Taylor did not recommend a brevet for Garland, despite his bravery and composure under fire. Given his status as the commanding officer of the First Division, this was, as historian Justin Smith states, an "implied censure" against the colonel. Taylor was probably upset that Garland had not been more successful. According to Smith, George Mason Graham, who was with the colonel throughout the fight, later wrote President Polk that Garland's accomplishments were overlooked by the general. Whatever the case, it is strange indeed that Taylor recommended a brevet for David Twiggs, who was supposed to command the First Division but instead had to sleep off the effects of self-dosed medication that day, rather

than the man who replaced the incapacitated general and fought bravely, if not successfully, throughout the day. J. Smith, *War with Mexico*, 1:499–500.

6. WORTH'S HOOK

1. Reid, *Scouting Expeditions*, 14; Chartrand, *Santa Anna's Mexican Army*, 22, 55.

2. Most Texans had at least two Colts since reloading a revolver in the heat of battle was almost impossible. Utley, *Lone Star Justice*, 10.

3. Wilkins, *Highly Irregular Irregulars*, 1–18.

4. Reid, *Scouting Expeditions*, 157–58.

5. Ibid., 158; *New Orleans Picayune*, Oct. 4, 1846.

6. Reid, *Scouting Expeditions*, 158.

7. Mackall, *Son's Recollection*, 97.

8. Reid, *Scouting Expeditions*, 159.

9. Thorpe, *Our Army at Monterrey*, 133–35. Worth afterward described McKavett as an "officer of high merit."

10. Zenith Matthews Diary, Sept. 21, 1846, Southwestern University, Special Collections.

11. McClean, "My Connexion to the Mexican War" (journal), Rosenberg Library, Galveston, Tex., 6–7; Fehrenbach, *Lone Star*, 230, 232.

12. *New Orleans Tropic*, Oct. 21, 1846.

13. The Americans also carried other types of rifles, including the Jenks .64-caliber breechloading flintlock rifle and some Kentucky flintlock rifles. Spurlin, *Texas Volunteers*, 26; Hanson, *Plains Rifle*, 1–2; Wilkins, *Highly Irregular Irregulars*, 10; Dowling, "Infantry Weapons," 228.

14. Reid, *Scouting Expeditions*, 162.

15. Dana, *Monterrey Is Ours*, 132.

16. Chance, *Davis's Mexican War Regiment*, 18.

17. Reid, *Scouting Expeditions*, 163.

18. *New Orleans Picayune*, Nov. 19, 1846.

19. S. D. Allis to his uncle, in *Niles Register*, Nov. 7, 1846; *New Orleans Picayune*, Oct. 4, 1846; Reid, *Scouting Expeditions*, 164.

20. Reid, *Scouting Expeditions*, 165. Woll "reinvaded" Texas in 1842 and briefly seized San Antonio. Before coming to Texas, Gillespie had fought in the Second Seminole War, as had other Texans at Monterrey. A good biography of Gillespie can be found in *Texas Democrat and Register*, Nov. 16, 1846.

21. *New Orleans Picayune*, Oct. 4, 1846; "Recollections of the Mexican War," Nov. 15, 1900, 153.

22. Skelton, *American Profession of Arms*, 197–98; Coffman, *Old Army*, 49, 57.

23. McClean, "My Connexion to the Mexican War," 7–8; Reid, *Scouting Expeditions*, 182.

24. Meade, *Life and Letters*, 128.

25. Duval, *Adventures of Big Foot Wallace*, xiv.

26. Reid, *Scouting Expeditions*, 163. While the attack was taking place, Dixon Miles took three companies of the 7th Infantry down Federation Hill

toward the Bishop's Palace. Worth ordered him to make a diversion while Childs assaulted Independence Hill. The diversion was successful—many of the Mexicans focused their gunfire on Miles's small group rather than on Childs's assault force.

27. "Recollections of the Mexican War," Nov. 15, 1900, 153.

28. Reid, *Scouting Expeditions*, 182; Matthews Diary, Sept. 22, 1846.

29. McClean, "My Connexion to the Mexican War," 8.

30. Ibid.

31. "Diary of Lt. Edmund Bradford," in Smith and Judah, *Chronicles of the Gringos*, 88; Kendall, *Dispatches*, 135; Henshaw, *Recollections*, 83. One of the shots reportedly buried itself in a Mexican soldier and then exploded. An American who witnessed the scene said: "Lieutenant, that man is killed *very* dead. I never saw a man *killed so dead* before in my life." *New Orleans Tropic*, Oct. 5, 1846.

32. "Recollections of the Mexican War," Nov. 15, 1900, 153.

33. Reid, *Scouting Expeditions*, 185.

34. Allis to his Uncle, Nov. 7, 1846.

35. Ibid.; Blanchard, Diary and Biography, Louisiana State University Special Collections, Hill Memorial Library, 18.

36. Apparently the hole was already in the door, but the Mexican soldiers blocked it with some kind of material.

37. Withers to his cousin, Nov. 10, 1846; Mackall, *Son's Recollection*, 98.

38. Reid, *Scouting Expeditions*, 186.

39. Hays to Worth, Sept. 25, 1846. Mexican losses at the palace are unknown, though the Americans buried at least twenty-one soldiers. On Gillespie's grave at the redoubt, one soldier wrote on a smooth board: "Here rest the remains of the gallant Captain Gillespie, of Texas Rangers, who died, fighting bravely at the head of his company, on September 22d, 1846: Here a soldier reclines, from his duties relieved, Who fought 'till life's current was spent, Death envied the laurels the Hero received, And bade him retire to his tent.'" Gillespie's remains were later exhumed and brought to the United States. Marvin, *Battle of Monterey*, 56.

40. Allis to his Uncle, Nov. 7, 1846.

41. *New Orleans Picayune*, Oct. 4, 1846.

42. Hays to Worth, Sept. 25, 1846; Dana, *Monterrey Is Ours*, 135.

43. E. K. Chamberlain to S. C. West, Sept. 28, 1846, in S. Smith, *Chile con Carne*, 97.

7. STREET FIGHT

1. Reid, *Scouting Expeditions*, 190; Hill, *Fighter from Way Back*, 25. Once Worth seized the Saltillo road, he placed men in the pass in case the rumors about Santa Anna coming to Ampudia's rescue were true. He considered the pass to be "Mexico's Thermopylae." Thus far, men posted there had not seen Santa Anna, but they had repulsed a hundred lancers who tried to make their way into the city on September 21.

2. Meade, *Life and Letters*, 130.

3. The absence of orders for Worth became a point of criticism against Taylor after the battle. The future president's supporters claimed that the orders would have taken too long to reach Worth. But in fact the two generals had already established a safe line of communication between Independence Hill and Walnut Springs as evidenced by prior letters successfully passed between them. Taylor himself recalls two messages he received, both of which would have traveled on the same route, in his official report. See ZT to AG, Oct. 9, 1846, Army in Mexico, Letter Book, AGO, RG 94, NA.

4. Vestal, *Bigfoot Wallace*, 98–99, 160–61.

5. Green, *Texian Expedition against Mier*, 82–112 (quote, 90); Duval, *Adventures of Big Foot Wallace*, 167–72; Stapp, *Prisoners of Perote*, 34.

6. Brands, *Lone Star Nation*, 297–307; *Texas Scrapbook*, 37–38; Morton, *Memoir of the Life and Services of Capt. and Brevet Major John Sanders*, 33.

7. Smith to Pemberton [Worth], Sept. 27, 1846, found in "The Second Brigade at Monterrey," *Historical Magazine*, Mar. 1874, 139.

8. Davis to Quitman, Sept. 26, 1846, in *POJD*, 36; Wood to Henderson, Sept. 24, 1846, in Lamar, *Papers*, 136.

9. *POJD*, 66n9.

10. Davis, *Jefferson Davis*, 247; Wilcox, *History of the Mexican War*, 75; Chance, *Davis's Mexican War Regiment*, 18; Dugard, *Training Ground*, 153–54. The percussion, or "cap lock," as it was also known, utilized a small metal cap containing a thin film of fulminate, mercury, or other pressure-sensitive explosive compound placed snugly onto the lock's "nipple" prior to firing. A strike from the lock's hammer detonated the cap, sending a small flame into the rifle's gunpowder charge to fire the weapon. The tight-fitting cap offered far better protection from moisture than the flintlock, which required manually opening the lock's priming pan, filling it with fine-grain priming powder, closing the pan, cocking the hammer, and then firing. Percussion-lock rifles could be reloaded much more quickly and reliably than a flintlock.

11. S. Smith, *Chile con Carne*, 94; Furber, *Twelve Months Volunteer*, 109.

12. Greaves to Davis, Oct. 18, 1846, in *POJD*, 64.

13. French, *Two Wars*, 66; Green, *Texian Expedition against Mier*, 93.

14. French, *Two Wars*, 66.

15. Henry, *Campaign Sketches*, 207–208.

16. Henderson to ZT, Oct. 1, 1846, Army in Mexico, Letter Book, AGO, RG 94.

17. Taylor later wrote that as he was withdrawing his men from eastern Monterrey, he received a message from Worth informing his commander of his intended attack against the western part of the city on the twenty-third. Taylor said that he read the letter with regret and that if he had known Worth was going to attack from the west, he would have kept pressing the Mexicans from the east. Taylor's statement makes little sense since he must have known that Worth was engaged due to all of the smoke and intensity of musketry and artillery fire that emanated from the western part of the city. ZT to AG, Oct. 9, 1846.

18. Reid, *Scouting Expeditions*, 192.

19. Ibid.; Meade, *Life and Letters,* 137. Grant agreed: "He [Worth] resorted to a better expedient for getting to the plaza—the citadel—than we did on the east. Instead of moving by the open streets, he advanced through the houses, cutting passageways from one to another." Grant, *Memoirs,* 117.

20. Green, *Texian Expedition against Mier,* 87–90; Vestal, *Bigfoot Wallace,* 101, 108; Stapp, *Prisoners of Perote,* 33.

21. "Recollections of the Mexican War," Dec. 15, 1900, 169; "Diary of Lt. Edmund Bradford," in Smith and Judah, *Chronicles of the Gringos,* 89.

22. Skelton, *American Profession of Arms,* 175; Morrison, *Best School in the World,* 23; Morton, *Memoir of the Life and Services of Capt. and Brevet Major John Sanders,* 7.

23. Reid, *Scouting Expeditions,* 192; "Recollections of the Mexican War," Dec. 15, 1900, 169.

24. Thorpe, *Anecdotes and Letters,* 117.

25. Doubleday, *My Life in the Old Army,* 92.

26. Ibid., 94.

27. Ibid., 94, 95.

28. "Recollections of the Mexican War," Dec. 15, 1900, 169; Wynkoop, *Anecdotes and Incidents,* 42–43.

29. Mackall, *Son's Recollection,* 98; Reid, *Scouting Expeditions,* 192.

30. Green, *Texian Expedition against Mier,* 87–88; Vestal, *Bigfoot Wallace,* 104; Stapp, *Prisoners of Perote,* 33; "Recollections of the Mexican War," Dec. 15, 1900, 169.

31. Doubleday, *My Life in the Old Army,* 94.

32. Dana, *Monterrey Is Ours,* 137.

33. Ephraim McClean, "My Connexion to the Mexican War" (journal), Rosenberg Library, Galveston, Tex., 9; Duncan to Worth, Sept. 28, 1846.

34. "Recollections of the Mexican War," Dec. 15, 1900, 169; Kendall, *Dispatches,* 139.

35. Alcáraz et al., *Apuntes Para La Historia,* 77.

36. Mackall, *A Son's Recollections,* 101.

37. Zenith Matthews Diary, Sept. 23, 1846, Southwestern University, Special Collections.

38. S. Smith, *Chile con Carne,* 93–95.

39. Ibid.

40. Morton, *Memoir of the Life and Services of Capt. and Brevet Major John Sanders,* 33.

41. "Recollections of the Mexican War," Dec. 15, 1900, 169.

42. Abner Doubleday, *My Life in the Old Army,* 95; Reid, *Scouting Expeditions,* 195. Matthews wrote, "It was a beautiful sight to see the blazing shell flying through the air." Matthews Diary, Sept. 7, 1846.

43. Alcáraz et al., *Apuntes Para La Historia,* 80; Reid, *Scouting Expeditions,* 195; "Recollections of the Mexican War," Dec. 15, 1900, 169.

44. Kendall, *Dispatches,* 138; "Recollections of the Mexican War," Dec. 15, 1900, 169.

45. Vestal, *Bigfoot Wallace,* 161–62; McClean, "My Connexion to the Mexican War." 9.

46. Matthews Diary, Sept. 24, 1846.

47. Reid, *Scouting Expeditions*, 211; "Recollections of the Mexican War," Dec. 15, 1900, 171.

48. *New Orleans Picayune*, Nov. [?], 1846 (article written on September 29); "Recollections of the Mexican War," Dec. 15, 1900, 170; Stevens, *Rogue's March*, 156.

49. *The Mexican War and Its Heroes*, 242.

8. ON TO MEXICO CITY

1. Reid, *Scouting Expeditions*, 224; "Recollections of the Mexican War," Dec. 15, 1900, 171; Wallace, *General William Jenkins Worth*, 105.

2. Quaife, *Diary of James K. Polk*, 2:181. Most of Taylor's men probably agreed with Christopher Haile's view of the ceasefire. "To have taken all of those men prisoners would have been useless. Their arms we did not want; their horses were worthless, with a few exceptions; and it would have been very expensive and troublesome to feed and guard so many men. And moreover, it would have cost many a valuable life to have carried the city at the point of the bayonet." *New Orleans Picayune*, Nov. [?], 1846 (article written on September 29).

3. Marcy to ZT, Oct. 22, 1846, in U.S. House, *Mexican War Correspondence*, 363–64; Jenkins, *History of the War*, 207–208.

4. Marcy to ZT, Oct. 22, 1846, 363–67; ZT to AG, Nov. 12, 1846, in U.S. House, *Mexican War Correspondence*, 374–76; Lavendar, *Climax at Buena Vista*, 134.

5. Bauer, *Mexican War*, 145–65; Lavendar, *Climax at Buena Vista*, 136–37; J. Smith, *War with Mexico*, 1:373.

6. ZT to AG, Oct. 15, 1846, 373.

7. J. Smith, *War with Mexico*, 1:381; Lavendar, *Climax at Buena Vista*, 166–67, 171.

8. Lavendar, *Climax at Buena Vista*, 179; J. Smith, *War with Mexico*, 1:384.

9. Carleton, *Battle of Buena Vista*, 57.

10. Ibid., 85; French, *Two Wars*, 80; Chance, *Davis's Mexican War Regiment*, 95.

11. Lavendar, *Climax at Buena Vista*, 202, 203; J. Smith, *War with Mexico*, 1:391–92; Carleton, *Battle of Buena Vista*, 76–78; Chance, *Davis's Mexican War Regiment*, 98. This maneuver quickly overshadowed Davis's efforts at Monterrey in the popular imagination.

12. Lavendar, *Climax at Buena Vista*, 210; Jenkins, *History of the War*, 235.

13. Lavendar, *Climax at Buena Vista*, 212, 213.

14. Wallace, *General William Jenkins Worth*, 119; Dana, *Monterrey Is Ours*, 193.

15. Scott's decision to have Twiggs lead the army was a curious one. He claimed that every general needed his turn, but such logic makes little sense when the stakes were so high for the American army. Scott would not be reinforced anytime soon, so he could not afford the high number of casualties that could result from a military blunder. The commander may have been

influenced by Ethan Allen Hitchcock, whom he had recently made inspector general of the army. Hitchcock and Worth were bitter enemies, and it was possible that the former was trying to turn Scott against the latter. But Worth also had aggravated Zachary Taylor by questioning his judgment on military matters. Unlike Taylor, though, Scott took such stabs personally, and it was only a matter of time before his temper would erupt against his old friend. Wallace, *General William Jenkins Worth*, 123–25.

16. Henshaw, *Recollections*, 129; Jenkins, *History of the War*, 273.

17. Dana, *Monterrey Is Ours*, 205–206; J. Smith, *War with Mexico*, 2:57–58.

18. Henshaw, *Recollections*, 143; Wallace, *General William Jenkins Worth*, 137–38; Johnson, *Gallant Little Army*, 128; Hitchcock, *Fifty Years in Camp and Field*, 258–59. One example of this leniency is that Worth allowed Mexican citizens who committed crimes against U.S. soldiers to be tried in Mexican courts.

19. Wallace, *General William Jenkins Worth*, 137–39; Hitchcock, *Fifty Years in Camp and Field*, 259; Johnson, *Gallant Little Army*, 120 (quote), 128–29.

20. Wallace, *General William Jenkins Worth*, 147–49.

21. Brooks, *Complete History of the Mexican War*, 370; Henshaw, *Recollections*, 161. Two brigades routed Valencia from the south while Smith flanked the bluff from the north. Johnson, *Gallant Little Army*, 172–76.

22. Semmes, *Service Afloat and Ashore*, 393–95.

23. Bauer, *Mexican War*, 298; Johnson, *Gallant Little Army*, 183; Wilcox, *History of the Mexican War*, 385–87.

24. Ripley, *War with Mexico*, 2:365–66; Thorpe, *Anecdotes and Letters*, 79; Johnson, *Gallant Little Army*, 208.

25. Robert May, *John A. Quitman*, 184, 187–91.

26. Jenkins, *History of the War*, 421.

27. Semmes, *Service Afloat and Ashore*, 458–59; Kendall, *Dispatches*, 383; Grant, *Memoirs*, 157–58.

28. Wallace, *General William Jenkins Worth*, 166–67.

29. Ibid., 173–74, 177–78; Hitchcock, *Fifty Years in Camp and Field*, 320; Wallace, *General William Jenkins Worth*, 179–80, 182. The article about Pillow turned out to be a satirical joke by the newspaper's editors.

EPILOGUE

1. Balbontin, *Siege at Monterey*, 334. Worth received help for his attacks. Taylor's escalating diversion forced Ampudia to keep most of his reserves in eastern Monterrey. Even on the twenty-second, when the Americans did not advance into the city, Taylor maintained troops inside Fort Teneria, which forced Ampudia to keep some soldiers in reserve in case those men sallied forth into the city. It also helped Worth that Ampudia and Conde did not believe that the Americans could climb the western slopes of the hills, constructing weaker redoubts to protect those approaches.

2. Ripley, *War with Mexico*, 1:253–54.

3. Taylor also used his engineers to investigate the placement and strength of Monterrey's fortifications. Some of the general's critics, like George Gordon Meade, believed that he did not understand how the engineers could aid in combat. At Monterrey Taylor used them diligently, and information derived from their reports shaped his assault plan. Meade, *Life and Letters*, 101.

4. Wallace, *General William Jenkins Worth*, 187; *Dallas Morning News*, Oct. 1, 1935.

Bibliography

MANUSCRIPTS AND PERSONAL PAPERS

The Filson Historical Society, Louisville, Ky.

Roger Family Papers
Levi White Papers
Madison Mills Diary

*Franklin and Marshall College Archives and Special Collections,
Lancaster, Pa.*

John F. Reynolds Papers

*Duke University, Rare Book, Manuscript & Special Collections Library,
Durham, N.C.*

Edmund Schriver Papers

Library of Congress, Manuscript Division, Washington, D.C.

John Crittenden Watson Papers
Jefferson Davis Papers

*Louisiana State University Special Collections, Hill Memorial Library,
Baton Rouge*

Henry Wilson Papers
A. G. Blanchard Diary and Biography

Monterrey City Archive (AMMTY), Monterrey, Mexico

U.S. Mexican War Papers, Boxes 1 and 2.

National Archives, Washington, D.C.

Compiled Service Records of Various Texas Volunteers (company and indi-
vidual jacket files)
Office of the Secretary of War, Record Group 107
    Confidential and Unofficial Letters Sent
    Letters Received
    Letters Received, Unregistered Series
    Letters Sent, Military Affairs
    Letters Sent to the President
    Letters to Generals in the Field
    Miscellaneous Letters and Orders, Mexican War
Records of the Adjutant General's Office, Record Group 94
    Army in Mexico, Letter Book
    Army of Occupation, Letter Books
    Army of Occupation, Letters Received
    Army of Occupation, Orders
    Army of Occupation, Special Orders
    Letters to Generals in the Field and to State Governors
    Letters Received
    Letters Sent
    Miscellaneous Letters and Orders, Mexican War
    Papers Captured with General Arista's Baggage
    Department of Matamoros, Orders
Records of the Office of the Chief of Engineers, Record Group 77
    Letters Received by the Topographical Bureau of the War Department
    Letters Sent by the Topographical Bureau
    Unregistered Letters Received

New York Academy of Medicine Library

Mexican War Letters of Nathan Sturges Jarvis

Nuevo Leon State Archive (AGENL), Monterrey, Mexico

Military and Alcaldes, 1845–46

Rosenberg Library, Galveston, Tex.

Ephraim McClean, "My Connexion to the Mexican War" (journal)

Southwestern University, Special Collections, Georgetown, Tex.

Zenith Matthews Diary

United States Military Academy Library, Special Collections,
West Point, N.Y.

James Duncan Papers
Robert Hazlitt Papers
Joseph Mansfield Letters

University of North Carolina at Chapel Hill, Southern Historical
Collection, Chapel Hill

Benjamin Cheatham Papers

University of Texas at Arlington Libraries, Special Collections Division,
Arlington

Albert Sidney Johnston Papers

University of Texas at Austin, Justin Smith Papers, Benson Latin American
Collection, Austin

James Mullan Jr. Diary
Colonel Wood's Report

Yale Collection of Western Americana, Beinecke Rare Book and
Manuscript Library, Hew Haven. Conn.

Barna N. Upton Mexican War Letters, 1842–48
William T. Withers Letters

GOVERNMENT DOCUMENTS

U.S. House of Representatives. *Correspondence with General Taylor.* 30th
Cong., 1st sess. H. Exec. Doc. 17, 1848.
U.S. House of Representatives. *Dispatches from General Taylor.* 29th Cong.,
1st sess. H. Exec. Doc. 197, 1845.
U.S. House of Representatives. *Mexican War Correspondence.* 30th Cong.,
1st sess. H. Exec. Doc. 60, 1848.
U.S. House of Representatives. *Official Dispatches from General Taylor.*
29th Cong., 1st sess. H. Exec. Doc. 207, 1845.
U.S. House of Representatives. *Regulars and Volunteers Engaged in the Mex-*
ican War. 30th Cong., 1st sess. H. Exec. Doc. 62, 1848.
U.S. House of Representatives. *Report of the Secretary of War Concerning the*
Call-up of Volunteers. 29th Cong., 1st sess. H. Exec. Doc. 402. 1845.
U.S. House of Representatives. *Reports from General Taylor.* 29th Cong., 1st
sess. H. Exec. Doc. 209, 1845.
U.S. House of Representatives. *Volunteers Received into the Service of the*
United States. 29th Cong., 2nd sess. H. Doc. 42, 1845.

U.S. House of Representatives. *Volunteers Terms of Service.* 29th Cong., 2nd sess. H. Exec. Doc. 48, 1845.

U.S. Senate. *Message from the President Concerning General Gaines's Illegal Call Up of Volunteers.* 29th Cong., 1st sess. S. Doc. 387, 1845.

U.S. Senate. *Message from the President Concerning Illegal Call-up of Volunteers.* 29th Cong., 1st sess. S. Doc. 378, 1845.

NEWSPAPERS

American Flag (Matamoros, Mex.)
El Diario (del Gobierno) (Mexico City)
El Monitor Republicano (Mexico City)
New Orleans Daily Tropic
New Orleans Delta
New Orleans Picayune
Niles Register
Seminario Político del Gobierno de Nuevo León
Boletin Oficial (special editions published in the days before the battle)
Tampico Esperanza
(Austin) Texas Democrat and Register
Republic of the Rio Grande (Matamoros, Mex.)

PUBLISHED MEMOIRS AND OTHER ACCOUNTS

Ampudia, Pedro de. *El Ciudadano, General Pedro De Ampudia Ante El Tribunal Respetable de la Opinión Pùblica.* San Luis Potosí, 1846.

———. *Vindicación del Ciudadano Pedro de Ampudia.* San Juan Bautista, 1845.

Backus, Electus. "A Brief Sketch of the Battle of Monterrey." *The Historical Magazine* 10 (July 1866).

Balbontin, Manuel. *La Invasión Americana, 1846 a 1848.* México, D.F.: Tip. De Gonzalo A. Esteva, 1883.

———. "The Siege at Monterrey." *Journal of the Military Service Institution of the United States* 8 (1888).

Barbour, Philip. *The Journals of the Late Major Philip Norbourne Barbour and His Wife Martha Isabella Hopkins Barbour.* Edited by Rhoda Van Bibber Tanner Doubleday. New York: G. P. Putnam's Sons, 1901.

Campaña Contra Los Americanos del Norte, Primera Parte, Relación Histórica de los Cuarenta Días. Linares, Mex.: Ignacio Cumplido, 1846.

Campbell, William Bowen. "Mexican War Letters of Col Williams Bowen Campbell, of Tennessee, Written to Governor David Campbell, of Virginia." *Tennessee Historical Magazine,* June 1915.

Carleton, James. *The Battle of Buena Vista.* New York: Harper & Brothers, 1848.

Carpenter, William. *Travels and Adventures in Mexico.* New York: Harper & Brothers, 1851.

Chamberlain, Samuel. *My Confession.* New York: Harper & Brothers, 1956.

Claiborne, J. F. H. *Life and Correspondence of John A. Quitman.* Volume 1. New York: Harper & Brothers, 1860.

Curtis, Samuel Ryan. *Being the Diary of Samuel Ryan Curtis 3rd Ohio Volunteer Regiment*. Edited and annotated by Joseph Chance. Fort Worth: Texas Christian University, 1994.

Dana, Napoleon Jackson Tecumseh. *Monterrey Is Ours: The Mexican War Letters of Lieutenant Dana, 1845–1847*. Edited by Robert H. Ferrell. Lexington: University Press of Kentucky, 1990.

Davis, Jefferson. *The Papers of Jefferson Davis*. Vol. 3, *July 1846–December 1848*. Edited by James T. McIntosh. Baton Rouge: Louisiana State University Press, 1971.

Davis, Varina. *Jefferson Davis: Ex-President of the Confederate States of America; A Memoir by his Wife*. Volume 1. New York: Belford, 1890.

Deas, Edward. "Reminiscences of the Campaign on the Rio Grande." *Historical Magazine*, January 1870.

Dilworth, Rankin. *The March to Monterrey: The Diary of Lt. Rankin Dilworth*. Edited and annotated by Joseph Chance and Lawrence Clayton. El Paso: Texas Western Press, 1996.

Doubleday, Abner. *My Life in the Old Army*. Edited by Joseph Chance. Fort Worth: Texans Christian University Press, 1998.

Duval, John. *The Adventures of Big Foot Wallace*. Macon: J. W. Burke, 1870.

Furber, George. *The Twelve Months Volunteer*. Cincinnati: J. A. & U. P. James, 1857.

Giddings, Luther. *Sketches of the Campaign in Northern Mexico by an Officer of the First Ohio Volunteers*. New York: Putnam, 1853.

Grant, U. S. *Personal Memoirs*. Volume 1. London: Searle and Rivington, 1886.

Green, Thomas. *Journal of the Texian Expedition against Mier*. New York: Harper & Brothers, 1845.

Gregg, Josiah. *Diary & Letters of Josiah Gregg*. Edited by Maurice Garland Fulton. Norman: University of Oklahoma Press, 1941.

Hamilton, Holman. *Zachary Taylor*. 2 vols. Indianapolis: Bobbs-Merrill, 1941.

Hays, Jack. "The Texan Rangers at Monterrey." *Historical Magazine*, January 1873.

Henry, William Seaton. *Campaign Sketches of the War with Mexico*. New York: Arno, 1847.

Henshaw, John Corey. *Recollections of the War with Mexico*. Edited by Gary F. Kurutz. Columbia: University of Missouri Press, 2008.

Hill, Daniel Harvey Hill. *A Fighter from Way Back: The Mexican War Diary of Lt. Daniel Harvey Hill, 4th Artillery, USA*. Edited by Nathaniel Cheairs Hughes and Timothy Johnson. Kent, Ohio: Kent State University Press, 2002.

Hitchcock, Ethan Allen. *Fifty Years in Camp and Field: Diary of Major General Ethan Allen Hitchcock, U.S.A.* Edited by W. A. Croffut. New York: G. P. Putnam's Sons, 1909.

Holland, James. "Diary of a Texan Volunteer in the Mexican War." *Southwestern Historical Quarterly* 30, no. 1 (July 1926).

Jarvis, N. S. "An Army's Surgeons Notes of Frontier Service—Mexican War, Captain N. S. Jarvis." *Journal of the Military Service Institution of the United States* 60 (1907).

Johnston, William Preston. *The Life of Albert Sidney Johnston*. New York: D. Appleton, 1879.

Kendall, George Wilkins. *Dispatches from the Mexican War.* Edited by Lawrence Delbert Cress. Norman: University of Oklahoma Press, 1999.

Kenly, John. *Memoir of a Maryland Volunteer.* Philadelphia: J. B. Lippincott, 1873.

French, Samuel. *Two Wars: An Autobiography of General Samuel G. French.* Nashville: *Confederate Veteran*, 1901.

Lamar, Mirabeau. *The Papers of Mirabeau Lamar.* Volume 4, pt. 1. Edited by Charles Adams Gulick and Winnie Allen. Austin: Von Boeckmann-Jones, 1924.

Lander, Alexander. *Trip to the Wars, Comprising the History of the Galveston Riflemen.* Monmouth, N.J.: Atlas Office, 1847.

Mackall, William. *A Son's Recollection of His Father.* New York: E. P. Dutton, 1930.

McClellan, George. *The Mexican War Diary of George McClellan.* Edited by William Starr Myers. Princeton: Princeton University Press, 1917.

Meade, George Gordon. *The Life and Letters of George Gordon Meade.* Volume 1. New York: Charles Scribner's Sons, 1913.

Polk, James K. *The Diary of James K. Polk.* Edited and Annotated by Milo Milton Quaife. Chicago: A. C. McClung, 1910.

"Recollections of the Mexican War." *The Pioneer,* April 15, June 15, August 15, November 15, December 15, 1900.

Reid, Samuel. *The Scouting Expeditions of McCulloch's Texas Rangers.* Philadelphia: G. B. Zieber, 1847.

Ripley, R. S. *The War with Mexico.* 2 vols. New York: Harper & Brothers, 1849.

Robertson, John. *Reminiscences of a Campaign in Mexico by a Member of the Bloody First.* Nashville: J. York, 1849.

Rogers, William P. "The Diary and Letters of William P. Rogers." Edited by Eleanor Damon Pace. *Southwestern Historical Quarterly* 32, no. 4 (April 1929).

Rowles, W. P. *The Life and Character of Wm. B. Allen.* Columbia, Mo.: *Democratic Herald* Book Office, 1853.

Scribner, B. F. *Camp Life of a Volunteer: A Campaign in Mexico, or a Glimpse at Life in Camp, By One Who Has Seen the Elephant.* Philadelphia: Grigg, Elliot, 1847.

Sedgwick, John. *Correspondence of John Sedgwick, Major-General.* 2 vols. New York: De Vinne, 1902–1903.

Semmes, Raphael. *Service Afloat and Ashore during the Mexican War.* Cincinnati: Wm. H. Moore, 1851.

Stapp, William Preston. *The Prisoners of Perote.* 1845. Reprint, Austin: University of Texas Press, 1977.

Smith, Ephraim Kirby. *To Mexico with Scott.* Cambridge: Harvard University Press, 1917.

Smith, Franklin. *The Mexican War Journal of Captain Franklin Smith.* Edited by Joseph Chance. Jackson: University Press of Mississippi, 1991.

Smith, George Winston, and Charles Judah. *Chronicles of the Gringos: The U.S. Army in the Mexican War.* Albuquerque: University of New Mexico Press, 1968.

Smith, Persifor. "The Second Brigade at Monterrey." *Historical Magazine,* March 1874.

Smith, S. Compton. *Chile Con Carne.* Milwaukee: Ford and Fairbanks, 1857.

Stevens, Isaac. *Campaigns of the Rio Grande and of Mexico.* New York, Appleton, 1851.

Taylor, Zachary. *Letters of Zachary Taylor from the Battlefields of the Mexican War.* Edited by William Samson. Rochester: Genesee, 1908.

Thorpe, Thomas Bangs. *Anecdotes and Letters of Zachary Taylor.* New York: Appleton, 1848.

Wilcox, Cadmus. *History of the Mexican War.* Washington, D.C.: Church News, 1892.

Wynkoop, J. M. *Anecdotes and Incidents: Comprising Daring Exploits.* Pittsburgh: N.p., 1848.

BOOKS AND ARTICLES

Alcáraz, Ramón, et al. *Apuntes Para La Historia de La Guerra Entre México y Los Estado Unidos.* México, D.F.: Tip. de M. Payno, 1848. Translated into English with notes by Albert Ramsey. *The Other Side or Notes for the History of the War between Mexico and the United States.* New York: Burt Franklin, 1850.

Barcena, Roa. *Recuerdos de la Invasión Norte-Americana.* México, D.F.: J. Buxó, 1883.

Barton, Henry. *Texas Volunteers in the Mexican War.* Waco, Tex.: Texian, 1970.

"Battles of the Rio Grande." *Southern Quarterly Review,* November 1850.

Bauer, K Jack. *The Mexican War, 1846–1848.* New York: Macmillan, 1974.

——. *Zachary Taylor, Soldier, Planter, Statesman of the Old Southwest.* Baton Rouge: Louisiana State University Press, 1985.

Benavides, Bertha Villarreal de. "Eran la élite la aristocracia del Ejército Americano." *Actas: Revista de Historia de la Universidad Autónoma de Nuevo León* 4 (July–December 2003).

Borneman, Walter. *The Man Who Transformed the Presidency.* New York: Random House, 2008.

Brands, H. W. *Lone Star Nation.* New York: Doubleday, 2004.

Brooks, Nathan Covington. *A Complete History of the Mexican War: Its Causes, Conduct, and Consequences.* Philadelphia: Grigg, Elliot, 1851.

Cárdenas, Leticia Martínez, César Morado Macías, and J. Jesús Ávila. *La Guerra México–Estados Unidos: Su Impacto en Nuevo León, 1835–1848.* México, D.F.: January 2003.

Chance, Joseph. *Jefferson Davis's Mexican War Regiment.* Jackson: University Press of Mississippi, 1991.

Chartrand, Rene. *Santa Anna's Mexican Army, 1821–48.* London: Osprey, 2004.

Coffman, Edward M. *The Old Army: A Portrait of the American Army in Peacetime, 1784–1898.* New York: Oxford University Press, 1986.

Cossio, David. *Historia de Nuevo León.* Monterrey, N.L.: J. Cantú Leal, 1925.

Cullum, George W. *Register of the Officers and Graduates of the U.S. Military Academy, at West Point, N.Y., from March 16, 1802, to January 1, 1850, Volume I.* New York: J. F. Trow, 1850.

Dillon, Lester. *American Artillery in the Mexican War, 1846–1848.* Austin: Presidial, 1975.

Dowling, R. L. "Infantry Weapons of the Mexican War." *Antiques,* November 1940.

Dufour, Charles. *The Mexican War: A Compact History.* New York: Hawthorn, 1968.

Dugard, Martin. *The Training Ground: Grant, Lee, Sherman, and Davis in the Mexican War.* New York: Little, Brown, 2008.

Eisenhower, John. *So Far from God.* Norman: University of Oklahoma Press, 1989.

Fehrenbach, T. R. *Fire and Blood.* New York: Bonanza, 1985.

———. *Lone Star: A History of Texas and the Texans.* New York: Macmillan, 1968.

Forman, Sidney. *West Point.* Garden City, N.J.: Doubleday, 1965.

Francaviglia, Richard, and Douglas Richmond, eds. *Dueling Eagles: Reinterpreting the U.S.–Mexican War, 1846–1848.* Fort Worth: Texas Christian University Press, 2000.

Frost, John. *History of Mexico and Its Wars.* New Orleans: Armand Hawkins, 1882.

———. *The Mexican War and Its Warriors.* New Haven, Conn.: H. Mansfield, 1850.

Ganoe, William. *History of the United States Army.* New York: D. Appleton, 1924.

Garza, Israel Cavazos. *Breve Historia de Nuevo León.* México, D.F.: Colegio de México, Fideicomiso Historia de las Américas : Fondo de Cultura Económica, 1994.

González-Quiroga, Miguel Ángel. "Nuevo León Ante La Invasión Norteamericana," *Nuevo León Ocupado: Aspectos de la Guerra México–Estados Unidos.* Monterrey, N.L.: Fondo Editorial Nuevo León, 2006.

González-Quiroga, Miguel Ángel, and César Morado Macías. *Nuevo León Ocupado: Aspectos de la Guerra México–Estados Unidos.* Monterrey, N.L.: Fondo Editorial Nuevo León, 2006.

Gordon, Armistead. *Jefferson Davis.* New York: C. Scribner's Sons, 1918.

Hanson, Charles. *Plains Rifle.* Harrisburg, Pa.: Stackpole 1960.

Haynes, Sam W. *James K. Polk and the Expansionist Impulse.* New York: Longman, 2002.

Heitman, Francis Bernhard. *Historical Register and Dictionary of the United States Army, Volume I.* Washington, D.C.: GPO, 1903.

Henderson, Harry McCorry. *Colonel Jack Hays.* San Antonio: Naylor, 1954.

Jenkins, John. *History of the War between the United States and Mexico, from the Commencement of Hostilities to the Ratification of the Treaty of Peace.* Auburn, Ala.: Derby, Miller, 1849.

Johnson, Timothy. *A Gallant Little Army: The Mexico City Campaign.* Lawrence: University Press of Kansas, 2007.

Kluger, Richard. *Seizing Destiny.* New York: A. A. Knopf, 2007.

Krauze, Enrique. *Mexico: Biography of Power: A History of Modern Mexico.* New York: Harper Collins, 1997.

Lavendar, David. *Climax at Buena Vista.* Philadelphia: J. B. Lippincott, 1966.

Lewis, Lloyd. *Captain Sam Grant.* Boston: Little, Brown, 1950.

Macías, César Morado."Aspectos Militares: Tres Guerras Ensambladas." *La Guerra México-Estados Unidos: Su Impacto en Nuevo León.* México, D.F.: Senado de la República, 2003.

Mahon, John. *History of the Second Seminole War.* Gainesville: University Press of Florida, 1967.

Mansfield, Edward. *The Mexican War: A History of Its Origin.* New York: A. S. Barnes 1848.

Marvin, William. *The Battle of Monterey and Other Poems.* Danville, Va: A. S. M'Grorty, 1851.

May, Robert. *John A. Quitman.* Baton Rouge: Louisiana State University Press, 1985.

——. *The Mexican War and Its Heroes, Being a Complete History of the Mexican War.* Philadelphia: Grigg, Elliot, 1849.

Merk, Fredrick. *Manifest Destiny and Mission in American History.* Cambridge: Harvard University Press, 1963.

Morrison, James. *The Best School in the World.* Kent, Ohio: Kent State University Press, 1986.

Morton, James St. Clair. *Memoir of the Life and Services of Capt. and Brevet Major John Sanders, of the Corps of Engineers, U.S. Army.* Pittsburgh: W. S. Haven, 1861.

Nichols, Edward. *Zach Taylor's Little Army.* New York: Doubleday, 1963.

Paz, Eduardo. *La Invasión Norte Americana.* Mexico, D.F.: C. Paz, 1889.

Peterson, Charles. *A History of the Wars of the United States.* Philadelphia, Jas. B. Smith, 1859.

Powell, C. Frank. *Life of Major General Zachary Taylor.* New York: D. Appleton, 1846.

Rives, George Lockhart. *The United States and Mexico, Volume II.* New York: Charles Scribner's Sons, 1913.

Robles, Guillermo Vigil Y. *La Invasión de México Por Los Estado Unidos.* México, D.F.: 1923.

Robinson, Fay. *Mexico and Her Military Chieftains.* Philadelphia: E. H. Butler, 1847.

Roland, Charles. *Albert Sidney Johnston, Soldier of Three Republics.* Lexington: University Press of Kentucky, 2001.

Salazar, Raúl Martínez. "Sangre y fuego en las calles de Monterrey." *Actas: Revista de Historia de la Universidad Autónoma de Nuevo León* 4 (July–December 2003).

Seitz, Don. *Braxton Bragg, General of the Confederacy.* Columbia, Mo.: State Company, 1924.

Skelton, William B. *An American Profession of Arms: The Army Officer Corps, 1784–1861.* Lawrence: University Press of Kansas, 1992.

"Sketches of Our Volunteer Officers: Alexander Keith McClung." *Southern Literary Messenger*, January 1855.

Smith, Justin Harvey. *The War with Mexico*. 2 vols. New York: Macmillan, 1919.

Spurlin, Charles. *Texas Volunteers in the Mexican War*. Austin: Eaken, 1998.

Stevens, Peter. *The Rogue's March: John Riley and the St. Patrick's Battalion*. Washington, D.C.: Brassey's 1999.

Sullivan, M. Dix. *The Field of Monterey*. N.p., 1846.

——. *A Texas Scrapbook, Compiled by D. W. C. Baker*. New Orleans: A. S. Barnes, 1875.

Thorpe, Thomas Bangs. *Our Army at Monterey*. Philadelphia: Carey and Hart, 1847.

——. *Our Army on the Rio Grande*. Philadelphia: Carey and Hart, 1846.

Traas, Adrian George. *From the Golden Gate to Mexico City: The U.S. Army Topographical Engineers in the Mexican War*. Washington, D.C.: Office of History, Corps of Engineers, 1993.

Tyler, Ronnie. *The Mexican War: A Lithographic Record*. Austin: Texas State Historical Association, 1973.

Utley, Robert. *Lone Star Justice: The First Century of the Texas Rangers*. New York: Berkley, 2003.

Valades, Jose. *Breve Historia de la Guerra con los Estados Unidos*. Mexico, D.F.: Editorial Patria, 1947.

Valtier, Ahmed. "Fatídica Orden: Asalto Yanqui Sobre Monterrey." *Atisbo*, Year 1, vol. 4 (September 2006).

——. "Mapas y Planos: El teniente Adolphus Heiman y su plano de Monterrey." *Actas: Revista de Historia de la Universidad Autónoma de Nuevo León* 4 (July–December 2003).

Valtier, Ahmed, and Pablo Ramos. "Josefa Zozoya, La Heroina de Monterrey." *Atisbo*, Year 2, vol. 10 (September 2007).

Vestal, Stanley. *Bigfoot Wallace*. Boston: Houghton Mifflin, 1942.

Wallace, Edward. *General William Jenkins Worth, Monterey's Forgotten Hero*. Dallas: Southern Methodist University Press, 1953.

Webb, Walter Prescott. *The Texas Rangers: A Century of Frontier Defense*. Austin: University of Texas Press, 1935.

Weems, John Edward. *To Conquer a Peace: The War between the United States and Mexico*. Garden City, N.J.: Doubleday, 1974.

Weigley, Russell. *History of the United States Army*. New York: Macmillan, 1967.

Wilkins, Frederick. *The Highly Irregular Irregulars: Texas Rangers in the Mexican War*. Austin: Eakin, 1990.

Wilson, James. *Address on the Occasion of Removing the Remains of Captains Walker*. N.p.: Office of the Inn San Antonio Lodge, 1856.

Winders, Richard Bruce. *Mr. Polk's Army: The American Military Experience in the Mexican War*. College Station: Texas A&M University Press, 1997.

Wheelan, Joseph. *Invading Mexico*. New York: Carroll & Graf, 2007.

Index

References to illustrations appear in italics.

Printed in the USA
CPSIA information can be obtained
at www.ICGtesting.com
LVHW041159260923
759109LV00010B/244/J